Cambridge IGCSE™ and O Level

Economics

Third Edition

Paul Hoang

Margaret Ducie

Cambridge International Education material in this publication is reproduced under licence and remains the intellectual property of Cambridge University Press & Assessment.

Third-party websites and resources referred to in this publication are not endorsed.

All questions have been written by the authors.

Although every effort has been made to ensure that website addresses are correct at time of going to press, Hachette Learning cannot be held responsible for the content of any website mentioned in this book. It is sometimes possible to find a relocated web page by typing in the address of the home page for a website in the URL window of your browser.

Hachette UK's policy is to use papers that are natural, renewable and recyclable products and made from wood grown in well-managed forests and other controlled sources. The logging and manufacturing processes are expected to conform to the environmental regulations of the country of origin.

To order, please visit www.HachetteLearning.com or contact Customer Service at education@hachette.co.uk/ +44 (0)1235 827827.

ISBN: 978 1 0360 1073 7

© Paul Hoang and Margaret Ducie 2025

First published in 2013
Second edition published in 2018
This edition published in 2025 by
Hachette Learning,
An Hachette UK Company
Carmelite House
50 Victoria Embankment
London EC4Y 0DZ

www.HachetteLearning.com

The authorised representative in the EEA is Hachette Ireland, 8 Castlecourt Centre, Dublin 15, D15 XTP3, Ireland (email: info@hbgi.ie)

Impression number   10 9 8 7 6 5 4 3 2 1

Year   2029 2028 2027 2026 2025

Cover photo © Rawpixel.com – stock.adobe.com

Illustrations by Aptara Inc.

Typeset in India by Aptara Inc.

Printed in Great Britain by Bell and Bain Ltd, Glasgow

A catalogue record for this title is available from the British Library.

MIX
Paper | Supporting
responsible forestry
FSC™ C104740

Contents

Introduction

This book has been written for all students of Cambridge IGCSE™, IGCSE (9–1) and O Level Economics (0455/0987/2281), and supports the syllabuses for examination from 2027. It provides the detail and guidance that are needed to support you throughout the course and help you prepare for your examinations. It will also be of great use to anyone who wants to learn more about the key concepts of economics.

This book will be valuable to students of economics whether you are:

» studying the subject for the first time at school or college and need a comprehensive and clearly written textbook
» revising the subject before your examinations and need a study guide to help you with key definitions, techniques and examination advice
» studying the subject on your own through distance or open learning and need a complete programme of supportive questions and activities with suggested answers.

Building on the successful formula of the previous edition, this third edition updates all existing chapters. Material that is no longer covered by the new syllabus has been removed and new subject material has been added.

This book has been written with the international student in mind. It explains economic theory using real-life examples and case studies from around the world.

How to use this book

To make your study of economics as rewarding and successful as possible, this textbook, which is endorsed for the Cambridge Pathway, offers the following important features:

Chapter overview

Each chapter starts with an outline of the subject material to be covered.

Organisation

The content is in the same order as the syllabus: chapter titles and chapter section headings match those of the syllabus.

Approach

The subject material is written in an informative yet lively way that allows complete understanding of each topic to be gained.

Practice questions

These questions are designed to show you the different types of questions relevant to the syllabus and to prepare you for assessment. Note that the questions within the chapters are only part questions, as they are intended to consolidate understanding of the specific chapter being reviewed.

Revision checklist

This checklist lists the key concepts and topics you have covered in the chapter and the key points you need to know.

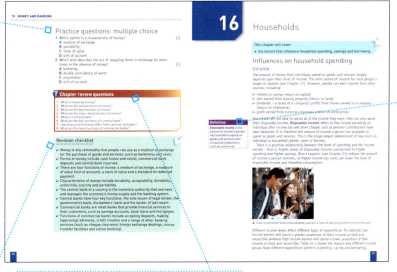

Chapter review questions

These questions, which correspond with the chronological order of the text, encourage you to read, reflect and write your own answers.

Definitions

Definitions of key terms help you develop your use of economics terminology.

Study tips

Study tips encourage critical thinking and emphasise that you need to be able to present and justify an opinion, underpinned by economic principles and theories.

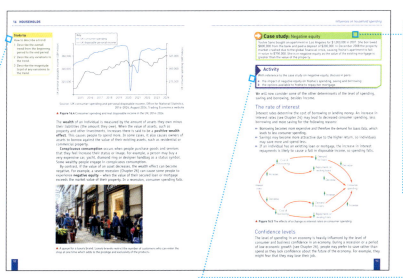

Activities

Activities appear throughout the book and encourage you to investigate real-life applications of economics as a dynamic subject in your local environment as well as globally.

Case study

Case studies based on a range of international examples put economics concepts into a real-world context to help you understand and think about how they work in practice.

Answers

Answers to the practice questions and chapter review questions are available in the accompanying online Teacher Guide and online at www.hachettelearning.com/answers-and-extras.

Exam preparation and technique

Revision

You should be able to perform to the best of your ability if you:

» ensure that you have worked through all the activities and practice questions in this book
» revise thoroughly before your examinations – allow plenty of time for this and avoid leaving it until the last minute.

You can also help yourself greatly if you take the following steps.

» Obtain a copy of the syllabus. You should also be able to obtain past examination papers and mark schemes from your teachers. It is important that you check the progress of your learning and revision by ticking each topic against the syllabus content.
» The style and nature of questions differ between papers, so you must be clear about the types of questions that will feature in the papers you will take.
» Make sure you check the instructions on the question paper, the length of the paper and the number of questions you have to answer.
» Allocate your time sensibly between each question. Every year, students waste time by spending too long on some questions, which leaves them with too little time (or no time at all) for others. You should spend longer writing an answer to a question worth 8 marks than you would when writing an answer worth 4 marks.

Examination papers and key command words

The information in this section is taken from the Cambridge International Education syllabus. You should always refer to the appropriate syllabus document for the year of examination to confirm the details and for more information. The syllabus document is available on this website: www.cambridgeinternational.org

For Cambridge IGCSE™, IGCSE (9–1) and O Level Economics for examination from 2027, the externally assessed examination papers are:

	Length	Type of paper	Type of questions
Paper 1 (30%)	1 hour	Multiple-choice questions	40 multiple-choice questions (students answer all 40 multiple-choice questions)
Paper 2 (70%)	2 hours	Structured questions	Students answer **one** compulsory question with six parts in Section A, and **three** questions from a choice of four in Section B

Remember to learn the meanings of different command words used in questions. The following table should help you.

Command word	Meaning
Analyse	Examine in detail to show meaning, identify elements and the relationship between them.
Calculate	Work out from given facts, figures or information.
Define	Give precise meaning.
Describe	State the points of a topic/give characteristics and main features.
Discuss	Write about issue(s) or topic(s) in depth in a structured way.
Explain	Set out purposes or reasons/make the relationships between things evident/provide why and/or how and support with relevant evidence.
Give	Produce an answer from a given source or recall/memory.
Identify	Name/select/recognise.
State	Express in clear terms.

Finally ...

Economics can help to explain real-world events, issues and problems, such as why:

» the most expensive can of Coca-Cola, made for astronauts, is $1250 per can
» one of the world's fastest cars, the Koenigsegg Jesko Absolut, is priced at a cool $3 million (before taxes)
» the price of a bus fare is relatively low
» the average doctor, lawyer, pilot and dentist have high earnings
» private sector firms do not supply street lighting and public roads
» diamonds (a non-essential product) are expensive, whereas water (a vital good) is not
» the average farm worker (who harvests products essential for life) is paid a low wage whereas the average investment banker (who produces nothing of real substance) is paid a high salary.

▲ Why is the Koenigsegg Jesko Absolut so expensive?

Economics helps to explain everyday issues that occur in a constantly changing global environment. It is a 'live' subject and you are encouraged to watch the news and read newspapers to refresh the case studies you learn in class.

Enjoy the course and using this book!

Paul Hoang and Margaret Ducie

Endorsement statement

Endorsement indicates that a resource has passed Cambridge International Education's rigorous quality-assurance process and is suitable to support the delivery of their syllabus. However, endorsed resources are not the only suitable materials available to support teaching and learning, and are not essential to achieve the qualification. For the full list of endorsed resources to support this syllabus, visit www.cambridgeinternational.org/endorsedresources

Any example answers to questions taken from past question papers, practice questions, accompanying marks and mark schemes included in this resource have been written by the authors and are for guidance only. They do not replicate examination papers. In examinations the way marks are awarded may be different. Any references to assessment and/or assessment preparation are the publisher's interpretation of the syllabus requirements. Examiners will not use endorsed resources as a source of material for any assessment set by Cambridge International Education.

While the publishers have made every attempt to ensure that advice on the qualification and its assessment is accurate, the official syllabus, specimen assessment materials and any associated assessment guidance materials produced by the awarding body are the only authoritative source of information and should always be referred to for definitive guidance.

Our approach is to provide teachers with access to a wide range of high-quality resources that suit different styles and types of teaching and learning.

For more information about the endorsement process, please visit www.cambridgeinternational.org/endorsed-resources

Acknowledgements

Photos reproduced by permission of: **p.vii** Artur Nyk/stock.adobe.com; **p.1** incamerastock/Alamy Stock Photo; **p.4** littleny/Fotolia; **p.6** *tl* Paulo Nabas/stock.adobe.com, *tr* Inzyx/Fotolia, *bl* kustov – Fotolia, *br* Kadmy/Fotolia; **p.7** Ian Shaw/Alamy Stock Photo; **p.17** David Wall/Alamy Stock Photo; **p.18** Ruben/stock.adobe.com; **p.19** Georgii/stock.adobe.com; **p.22** Helix/Fotolia; **p.24** jetcityimage/stock.adobe.com; **p.28** bongkarn/stock.adobe.com; **p.38** Monkey Business/stock.adobe.com; **p.41** ABCDstock/Shutterstock.com; **p.42** elxeneize/Shutterstock.com; **p.43** So-Shan Au; **p.46** *t* Blue Jean Images/Alamy Stock Photo, *b* 8th/stock.adobe.com; **p.49** Pixavril/stock.adobe.com; **p.54** Urbanmyth/Alamy Stock Photo; **p.56** asab974/stock.adobe.com; **p.58** Monkey Business/stock.adobe.com; **p.61** Jim Holden/Alamy Stock Photo; **p.62** Anton Ivanov Photo/stock.adobe.com; **p.65** Kadmy/stock.adobe.com; **p.72** Ruben Pinto/Fotolia; **p.75** NGCHIYUI/Shutterstock.com; **p.76** Paul Hoang; **p.77** dmitriizotov/stock.adobe.com; **p.79** Craig McAteer/Alamy Stock Photo; **p.81** *t* So-Shan Au; *b* Imaginechina Limited/Alamy Stock Photo; **p.82** Lou-Foto/Alamy Stock Photo; **p.83** Chronicle/Alamy Stock Photo; **p.87** Elena Butinova/stock.adobe.com; **p.89** twinsterphoto/stock.adobe.com; **p.92** Leo Zank/Shutterstock.com; **p.94** Dmytro/stock.adobe.com; **p.95** Christian/stock.adobe.com; **p.97** *t* Vesna Cvorovic/Fotolia, *b* Justin Kase z12z/Alamy Stock Photo; **p.101** burnstuff2003/stock.adobe.com; **p.103** Ben Chams/Fotolia; **p.110** *l* CandyRetriever/stock.adobe.com, *r* Sergio Azenha/Alamy Stock Photo; **p.111** Ruan Jordaan/peopleimages.com/stock.adobe.com; **p.116** Mar Photographics/Alamy Stock Photo; **p.119** Filipiakf/stock.adobe.com; **p.121** *t* antpkr/stock.adobe.com, *b* rblfmr/Shutterstock.com; **p.122** *l* Dario Pignatelli/Bloomberg via Getty Images, *r* imageBROKER.com GmbH & Co. KG / Alamy Stock Photo; **p.123** Hein van Tonder/stock.adobe.com; **p.124** Paulo/stock.adobe.com; **p.130** Emma Wood/Alamy Stock Photo; **p.131** *t* Paul Hoang, *bl* Ringo Chiu/Shutterstock.com, *br* Stefan Constantin 22/Shutterstock.com; **p.132** Connect Images – Curated/Shutterstock.com; **p.136** Feroze Edassery/Shutterstock.com; **p.141** Hussain Warraich/Shutterstock.com; **p.142** Rawpixel.com/Shutterstock.com; **p.146** ndk100/stock.adobe.com; **p.148** makistock/stock.adobe.com; **p.149** Postmodern Studio/stock.adobe.com; **p.150** LiliyaDzyba/stock.adobe.com; **p.155** Neil Juggins/Alamy Stock Photo; **p.157** Radharc Images/Alamy Stock Photo; **p.163** ma8/stock.adobe.com; **p.164** Almas/Fotolia; **p.171** kanvag/Fotolia; **p.172** Alexander/stock.adobe.com; **p.175** Irina Shats/stock.adobe.com; **p.176** Marius Karp/stock.adobe.com; **p.180** Adrian Sherratt/Alamy Stock Photo; **p.182** Gorodenkoff/stock.adobe.com; **p.190** Christopher Furlong/Getty Images; **p.192** kamilpetran/stock.adobe.com; **p.197** Imaginechina Limited/Alamy Stock Photo; **p.210** Cathy Yeulet/123RF; **p.213** Oksana Perkins/stock.adobe.com; **p.217** Simon Lowthian/Alamy Stock Photo; **p.225** © United Nations, https://www.un.org/sustainabledevelopment/. The content of this publication has not been approved by the United Nations and does not reflect the views of the United Nations or its officials or Member States; **p.232** 2007 Digital Vision/photolibrary.com; **p.234** YOSHIKAZU TSUNO/AFP/Getty Images; **p.236** lulu/Fotolia; **p.247** Tim/stock.adobe.com; **p.249** Megapress/Alamy Stock Photo; **p.250** Hero Images Inc./Alamy Stock Photo; **p.251** vivien/Fotolia; **p.253** Chris Chambers/stock.adobe.com; **p.256** ALBERT GEA/AFP/Getty Images; **p.260** c.dellwo/stock.adobe.com; **p.262** Brent Lewin/Getty Images; **p.265** August First Film Studio/Album/Alamy Stock Photo; **p.267** Nikolai Sorokin/Fotolia; **p.272** Richard Wood/Alamy Stock Photo; **p.273** AFP/Getty Images; **p.277** Tomohiro Ohsumi/Bloomberg via Getty Images; **p.283** Barry Iverson/Alamy Stock Photo.

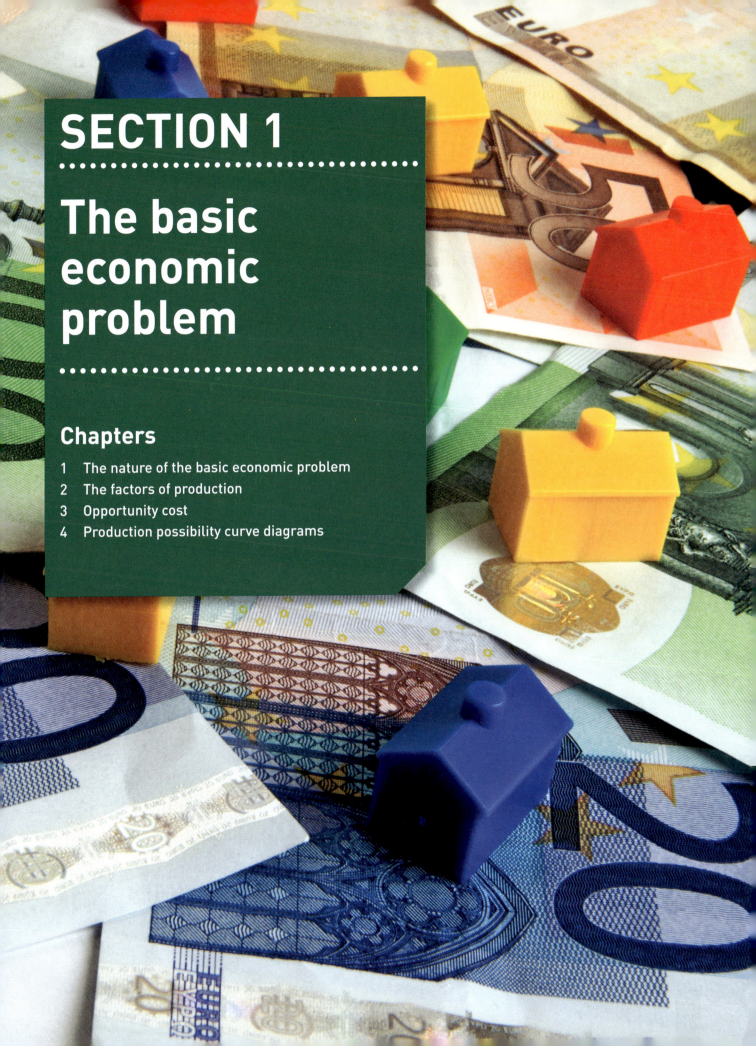

SECTION 1

The basic economic problem

Chapters

1

The nature of the basic economic problem

★ a definition of the basic economic problem
★ the concept of scarcity
★ examples of the basic economic problem in the context of consumers, workers, producers/firms and governments
★ the three basic economic questions which determine resource allocation
★ the differences between economic goods and free goods.

The basic economic problem: finite resources and unlimited wants

In every country, resources are limited. Governments, firms (businesses) and individuals have to make decisions about how to allocate scarce resources to satisfy their unlimited needs and wants. This is known as the **basic economic problem**, which exists in every economy: how best to allocate scarce resources to satisfy people's unlimited needs and wants. Essentially, economics is the study of how scarce resources (see Chapter 2) are allocated to satisfy the unlimited needs and wants of individuals, governments and firms in an economy.

▲ **Figure 1.1** The cause of the basic economic problem

The three main **economic agents** (or decision-makers) in an economy are:

➤➤ consumers (individuals or households)
➤➤ firms (businesses which operate in the **private sector** of the economy)
➤➤ the government.

Firms and individuals produce goods and services in the private sector of the economy and the government produces goods and services in the **public sector**. For example, the government might provide education and healthcare services for the general public. All economic agents (governments, firms and individuals) produce and consume goods and services.

Workers are affected by the number of available jobs in the economy, which may be limited compared to the number of people seeking employment. This scarcity of job opportunities forces workers to make choices about accepting lower-paying jobs, relocating to other areas, or investing in further education to improve their employment prospects. (See Chapter 17 for more on workers.)

Definitions

The **basic economic problem** is concerned with how best to allocate scarce resources in order to satisfy people's unlimited needs and wants.

Economic agents are households (private individuals in society), firms that operate in the private sector of an economy and the government (the public sector of an economy).

Private sector refers to the economic activity of private individuals and firms. The private sector's main aim is to earn profit for its owners.

Public sector refers to economic activity directly involving the government, such as the provision of state education and healthcare services. The public sector's main aim is to provide a service.

Resource allocation and the three basic economic questions

The three basic economic questions addressed by economic agents are:

1 What to produce?
2 How to produce it?
3 For whom to produce it?

Economic agents respond to these questions based on the needs and wants of a particular society.

> ### Activity
> Discuss how a private firm producing running shoes would answer the three basic economic questions.

Goods are physical items that can be produced, bought and sold. Examples are furniture, clothing, toothpaste and pencils. **Services** are non-physical items that firms provide and customers pay for. Examples are haircuts, bus journeys, education, concerts, telephone calls and internet access.

> ### Activities
> **1** Make a list of the goods and services provided by the public sector of your economy.
> **2** Identify the goods and services which are free to individuals and those for which you have to pay.
> **3** List which goods/services could be provided by a private firm as well as by the public (government) sector.
> **4** Compare and contrast the aims and objectives of a government-funded swimming pool and a private health and leisure club.

Needs are the essential goods and services that humans need for survival. These include nutritional food, clean water, shelter, protection, clothing and access to healthcare and education. All individuals have a right to have these needs met. This is stated in Articles 25 and 26 of the United Nations Universal Declaration of Human Rights, drafted in December 1948.

Article 25 states:
Everyone has the right to a standard of living adequate for the health and well-being of himself and of his family, including food, clothing, housing and medical care and necessary social services, and the right to security in the event of unemployment, sickness, disability, widowhood, old age or other lack of livelihood in circumstances beyond his control.

Article 26 states:
Everyone has the right to education. Education shall be free, at least in the elementary and fundamental stages. Elementary education shall be compulsory. Technical and professional education shall be made generally available and higher education shall be equally accessible to all on the basis of merit.

Wants are goods and services that are not necessary for survival but are human desires – that is, things we would like to have. Wants are unlimited, as most people are rarely satisfied with what they have and are always striving for more. Wants are a matter of personal choice and are a part of human nature.

Definitions

Goods are physical items such as tables, cars, toothpaste and pencils.
Services are non-physical items such as haircuts, bus journeys, telephone calls and internet access.
Needs are goods and services that are essential for survival.
Wants are goods and services that are not necessary for survival but are demanded by economic agents to fulfil their desires.

According to the World Bank, in 2022, 648 million of the world's people were living on less than $2.15 per day.

Source: 'Half of the global population lives on less than US$6.85 per person per day' by Marta Schoch, Samuel Kofi Tetteh Baah, Christoph Lakner, Jed Friedman, 8 December 2022, World Bank Blogs website: worldbank.org.

A handful of the richest people on the planet have as much wealth as the poorest half of the world's population. The study of economics can help to explain why this happens and offer possible solutions to the basic economic problem.

> **Activities**
>
> 1 Make a list of your top 10 wants and needs.
> 2 Is there anything in your list of needs that you could actually survive without?
> 3 Is there anything in your list of wants that might be considered as a need?
> 4 Identify a shortage of any good or service in your economy. Explain why the shortage has occurred.

Definitions

Economic goods are those which are limited in supply.
Free goods are goods which are unlimited in supply. Hence, there is no opportunity cost in terms of their output.
Opportunity cost is the cost of the next best opportunity forgone when making a decision.

Economic goods and free goods

An **economic good** is one which is limited in supply, such as oil, wheat, cotton, housing and cars. It is scarce in relation to the demand for the product, so human effort is required to obtain an economic good.

Free goods are unlimited in supply, such as the air, seawater, rainwater, sunlight and (to some extent) public domain web pages. There is no **opportunity cost** in the production or consumption of free goods.

A free good is not the same as a good that one can obtain without having to pay (such as education or healthcare services provided by the government). For education and healthcare services, and similar, there is an opportunity cost (the money could have been spent on the provision of other goods and services) and such services are funded by taxpayers' money.

> **Activity**
>
> Make a list of 10 goods which are limited in supply (economic goods) and a second list of goods which are unlimited in supply (free goods). How many goods did your class think of that are unlimited in supply?

▲ **Figure 1.2** Examples of free goods (seawater and air)

Practice questions: multiple choice

1 What is the basic economic problem faced by all societies?   [1]
   A achieving happiness
   B an inefficient economic system
   C rewarding factors of production
   D scarcity of resources

2 Which product is **most** likely to be classified as a free good?   [1]
   A birthday presents
   B public transportation
   C seawater
   D state (government-funded) education

? Chapter review questions

1 What is economics the study of?
2 What is the difference between a need and a want?
3 What is meant by the basic economic problem?
4 What is meant by economic agents?
5 What are the three fundamental questions that all economies face?
6 What is the difference between goods and services?
7 How do economic goods differ from free goods?

Revision checklist

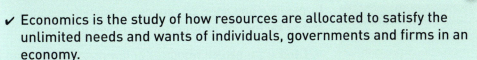

✔ Economics is the study of how resources are allocated to satisfy the unlimited needs and wants of individuals, governments and firms in an economy.
✔ The basic economic problem is concerned with how best to allocate scarce resources in order to satisfy people's unlimited needs and wants.
✔ Three fundamental questions arise from the basic economic problem: what to produce, how to produce it and for whom to produce it.
✔ Economic agents comprise consumers (individuals and households), businesses (firms) and the government.
✔ Firms and individuals produce goods and services in the private sector, whereas the government operates in the public sector.
✔ Goods are physical items that can be produced, bought and sold. Services are non-physical items that can be provided by firms and governments and are usually paid for by customers.
✔ Needs are the essential goods and services required for human survival.
✔ Wants are goods and services that are not necessary for survival but are human desires. These are infinite due to human nature.
✔ Economic goods are limited in supply, whereas free goods are unlimited in supply and so have no opportunity cost in terms of output and consumption.

2 The factors of production

This chapter will cover:

★ a definition and examples of factors of production
★ the rewards for factors of production
★ the causes of changes in the quantity and quality of factors of production.

Defining factors of production

To produce any good or service, one needs resources. These resources are known as the **factors of production** and they are divided into four categories:

» **Land** – the natural resources or raw materials required in the production process, such as oil, coal, water, wood, metal ores and agricultural products.
» **Labour** – the human resources required in the production process, including skilled and unskilled labour.
» **Capital** – the manufactured resources required in the production process, such as machinery, tools, equipment and motor vehicles.
» **Enterprise** – the skills a businessperson requires to combine and manage successfully the other three factors of production.

▲ Factors of production: land, labour, capital and enterprise

For example, the factors of production required to produce cans of Coca-Cola are as follows:

» **Capital** – factory buildings, machinery, computers, tools and delivery trucks to transport the drinks to warehouses and retailers.

» **Enterprise** – the risk-taking and business skills necessary to organise the production process successfully, and to motivate workers so they work to the best of their ability, in the pursuit of profit for the company.

» **Labour** – people to work on the production line, perform administrative tasks, promote the drinks effectively to customers and manage the company.

» **Land** – the natural resources required to make Coca-Cola, such as sugar, water and caffeine (from cacao beans).

> ### Activities
>
> 1 Consider the resources (factors of production) required to deliver an International GCSE Economics lesson.
>
>
>
> ▲ What resources are used to deliver a lesson?
>
> 2 Discuss whether it is possible to know which of the four factors of production is the most important for economic activity.

> ### Activity
>
> In class, discuss why all four factors of production are required in the following cases:
>
> a For the construction of roads.
> b To provide haircuts to clients.

Factors of production and their rewards

As the factors of production are productive resources, each has a reward for its use in the production process:

» The reward for land is called **rent**. Rental income comes from the ownership of property, such as physical and related assets, and is paid by the tenants of the land resources.

» The reward for labour is called **wages and salaries**. Wages are paid to workers on an hourly basis, such as those who earn a national minimum wage (see Chapter 17). Salaried staff are paid a fixed amount per month.

» The reward for capital is called **interest**. If the interest rate (see Chapter 24) is high, it becomes less worthwhile for businesses and households to borrow money for production purposes because the cost of borrowing is high, and vice versa.

» The reward for enterprise is called **profit**. This is the return for the entrepreneur's good business ideas and for taking the risks in starting up and running the organisation. Profit is what remains after all business costs are paid, including payment to the other factors of production.

Collectively, the four rewards for the factors of production are known as **income**.

Causes of changes in the quantity and quality of factors of production

The quantity and quality of factors of production will change if there is a change in the demand for and/or supply of land, labour, capital or enterprise. Possible changes include the following:

» Changes in the **costs of factors of production** – for example, if labour costs increase because of an increase in the national minimum wage (see Chapter 17), this would tend to reduce the demand for labour.

» Government policies can affect the **costs of production**, such as through taxes and subsidies (see Chapter 14). For example, lower income taxes can help to create incentives for people to work, thus increasing the quantity of labour resources. If a business has to comply with regulations, this will tend to increase costs of production. By contrast, subsidies help to reduce production costs, thereby increasing output of goods and services.

» **New technologies**, such as automation or artificial intelligence (AI), allow firms to increase output. Higher productivity also enables firms to cut their average costs of production (see Chapter 19).

» **Net migration of labour** (see Chapter 17) will affect the quantity of labour in the economy. If there are more people migrating to a country than there are people emigrating from that country, the quantity of labour in that country will increase, **ceteris paribus** (Latin for 'all other things remaining equal').

» **Improvements in education, training and healthcare** will improve the quality of labour as workers become more valuable to firms. This helps to boost production.

» **Unfavourable weather conditions** (such as severe droughts or flooding) will reduce the supply of agricultural products. Conversely, good weather conditions will increase supply, thus increasing agricultural output.

> ### Activity
> Use the internet to investigate global employment opportunities in selected countries around the world.

Practice questions: multiple choice

1 Which option is **not** an example of capital as a resource?　　[1]
　A computers
　B factory
　C machinery
　D natural resources

2 Which event is **most** likely to cause an increase in the average cost
　of labour?　　[1]
　A a decrease in the national minimum wage
　B an increase in the national minimum wage
　C government tax policies
　D net migration of labour into the country

? Chapter review questions

1　What is meant by factors of production?
2　What are the four factors of production?
3　What are the various rewards for factors of production?
4　What is the collective name for the four returns on the factors of production?
5　What are the various causes of changes in the quantity and quality of factors of
　　production?

Revision checklist

✔ Factors of production are the resources required to produce a good or
　service, namely land, labour, capital and enterprise.
✔ The return on the four factors of production are rent (land), wages and
　salaries (labour), interest (capital) and profit (enterprise). Collectively,
　the rewards are called income.
✔ The quantity and quality of factors of production will change if there
　is a change in the demand for and/or supply of land, labour, capital
　or enterprise. This could be due to changes in the costs of factors of
　production, government policies, new technologies, migration of labour,
　changes in educational levels of the labour force and even climatic
　conditions.

3 Opportunity cost

This chapter will cover:

★ a definition of opportunity cost, with examples
★ the influence of opportunity cost on decisions made by consumers, workers, producers/firms and governments.

Defining opportunity cost

Opportunity cost is the cost of the next best opportunity forgone (given up) when making economic decisions. Every choice made has an opportunity cost because in most cases there is an alternative.

Some examples of opportunity cost are as follows:

»» The opportunity cost of choosing to study International GCSE Economics is another International GCSE subject you could be studying instead.
»» The opportunity cost of visiting the cinema on Saturday night could be the money you would have earned from doing casual work instead of going to the cinema.
»» The opportunity cost of building an additional airport terminal could be using the same government funds to build public housing for low-income families.
»» The opportunity cost of a school purchasing 100 laptops for use in classrooms might be the science equipment that the school could not buy as a result.
»» The opportunity cost of going to university to study for a degree is the loss in income that would have been earned if the undergraduate student had chosen to work instead during that time.

▶ Case study: US federal government spending

According to the Federal Ministry of Finance, the US federal government announced spending of over $6.75 trillion in 2024 on the following:

• 21% on social security
• 14% on healthcare services
• 13% on Medicare (federal health insurance program)
• 13% on national defence
• 13% on federal debts (interest repayments)
• 10% on income security
• 5% on veterans' benefits and services
• 5% on education, training, employment and social services
• 2% on transportation
• 1% on community and regional development
• 3% on other items of expenditure.

Source: 'How much has the US government spent this year?'
US Treasury, 2024, US Fiscal data website

The government raises a finite amount of taxation revenue and must decide how much of the budget to allocate to each area of public spending. There is an opportunity cost attached to the decisions made, as increased spending in one area may lead to decreased spending in another.

> **Activity**
>
> Investigate the major components of government spending in your country or a country of your choice. Be prepared to share your findings with others in the class.

The influence of opportunity cost on decision-making

Opportunity cost directly influences the decisions made by consumers, workers, producers (firms) and governments. Referring to the basic economic problem (see Chapter 1), there are competing uses for an economy's scarce resources. Thus, there is an opportunity cost when the aforementioned economic agents allocate scarce resources.

» **Consumers** have limited incomes, so whenever they purchase a particular good or service, they give up the benefits of purchasing another product.
» **Workers** tend to specialise (see Chapter 17) – for example, as secondary school teachers, accountants, doctors and lawyers. By choosing to specialise in a particular profession, workers give up the opportunity to pursue other jobs and careers.
» **Producers** (firms) need to choose between competing business opportunities. For example, Toyota has to decide how best to allocate its research and development expenditure in terms of developing either its hybrid cars or its electric vehicles.
» **Governments** constantly face decisions that involve opportunity cost. If a government chooses to spend more money on improving the economy's infrastructure (such as improving its transportation and communications networks), it has less money available for other uses (such as funding education and healthcare).

In general, decision-makers will choose the option that gives them the greatest economic return. For example, a government might prioritise welfare benefits in order to improve economic well-being.

> **Activities**
>
> 1 Discuss whether quantitative or qualitative factors play a bigger role in economic decision-making.
> 2 To what extent does the concept of opportunity cost apply to your own decisions about post-16 and university education?

Practice question: structured question

The opportunity costs for a farmer in terms of corn and wheat production are shown in the following table.

Corn production (units)		Wheat production (units)
65	plus	30
55	plus	35

Calculate the opportunity cost for the farmer of producing 1 unit of wheat. [2]

Practice questions: multiple choice

1 Juke bought a new games console for $295 but has never used it. The second-hand value of his console is $195. What is the opportunity cost of Juke owning the games console?   [1]

   A $0

   B $100

   C $195

   D $295

2 What is the opportunity cost to the economy if the government decides to build a new motorway (highway)?   [1]

   A the cost of relocating and compensating residents in order to build the motorway

   B the money spent on building the motorway

   C the other projects that could have been undertaken had the motorway not been built

   D the overall cost to taxpayers of financing the motorway project

> ### Activity
>
> Discuss the costs and benefits of the government building a new airport. What are the key opportunity costs of such a decision?

❓ Chapter review questions

1 How is opportunity cost defined?

2 What might be the opportunity cost of a student studying International GCSE Economics?

3 Why do consumers face opportunity costs in decision-making?

4 Why do workers face opportunity costs in decision-making?

5 Using an example, explain why producers (firms) face opportunity costs in decision-making.

6 Using an example, explain why governments face opportunity costs in decision-making.

Revision checklist

✔ Opportunity cost is a very important concept in the study of economics, as it affects the decision-making of consumers, workers, producers (firms) and governments.

✔ Opportunity cost is the cost of the next best opportunity forgone when making a decision.

✔ Opportunity cost arises because economic agents have to make competing choices regarding what to do with their finite resources. Thus, there is an opportunity cost when economic agents allocate scarce resources.

4

Production possibility curve diagrams

This chapter will cover:

★ a definition of production possibility curves (PPC)
★ how to draw and interpret appropriate PPC diagrams
★ the significance of the location of production points on PPC diagrams
★ the causes and consequences of movements along a PPC and shifts of a PPC.

Defining production possibility curve

A **production possibility curve (PPC)** shows the maximum combination of any two categories of goods and services that can be produced in an economy, at any point in time. Essentially, it shows the productive capacity of the economy.

Interpreting PPC diagrams

Assume a country can only produce two types of goods: wooden furniture and olive oil. It has a limited amount of land, labour and capital. In Figure 4.1, if producers wish to increase production of olive oil from O_1 to O_2, then the amount of wooden furniture manufactured will have to decrease from W_1 to W_2. The opportunity cost of producing the extra O_1 to O_2 litres of olive oil is therefore W_1 to W_2 tonnes of wooden furniture.

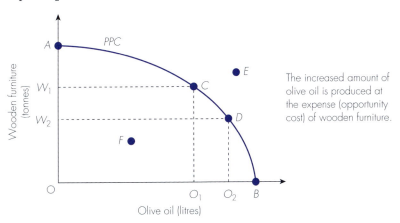

The increased amount of olive oil is produced at the expense (opportunity cost) of wooden furniture.

▲ **Figure 4.1** A PPC diagram

The production points in Figure 4.1 are as follows:

» Point A – all resources are dedicated to the production of wooden furniture.
» Point B – all resources are dedicated to the production of olive oil.
» Point C – W_1 tonnes of wooden furniture are produced along with O_1 litres of olive oil.
» Point D – W_2 tonnes of wooden furniture and O_2 litres of olive oil are produced.
» Point E – this point is beyond the production possibility curve. It lies outside the productive capacity of the economy, so it is currently unattainable.

» Point *F* – this point is within the productive capacity of the economy. This means that the production of both olive oil and wooden furniture can increase without any opportunity cost, as some factors of production are currently not being used.

Practice questions: multiple choice

Study the diagram below, which shows the PPC for Country Y. It produces only two products: wheat and barley.

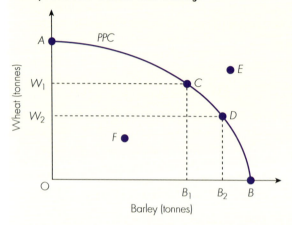

1 If Country Y wishes to increase the production of wheat from W_2 to W_1, what is the opportunity cost?   [1]
   A a reduction in barley production from B_2 to B_1
   B an increase in barley production from B_1 to B_2
   C an outward shift of the PPC towards point *E*
   D *C* to *D*

2 At which point is there spare capacity in the economy?   [1]
   A point *C*
   B point *D*
   C point *E*
   D point *F*

Causes and consequences of shifts and movements of the PPC

Movements along a PPC and opportunity cost

For a country to be on its PPC, two conditions have to be met:

» All resources are used – there is no unemployment of factors of production.
» There is efficiency in the use of resources – factors of production are allocated to their best use/purpose.

A movement along a PPC results in an opportunity cost. This means that if a country wants to produce more of one product, it has to produce less of another product. In Figure 4.2, a movement along the PPC from point *X* to point *Y* means more consumer goods are produced (from *A* to *B*). However, this comes at the expense of producer goods, as fewer producer goods are produced (from *C* to *D*).

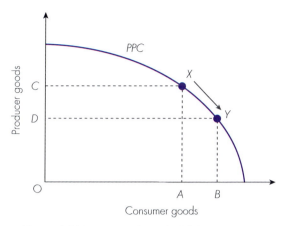

▲ **Figure 4.2** Movement along the PPC

Shifts of the PPC in terms of an economy's growth

For a country to shift its PPC outwards, as shown in Figure 4.3, there must be economic growth (see Chapter 26). This can come about in the following ways:

» An increase in the **quality** of factors of production (see Chapter 2), such as more highly skilled labour achieved through investments in education, research and training. Technological advances and improved production techniques can also lead to increased productivity.
» An increase in the **quantity** of factors of production, such as the discovery of new resources, the reclamation of land or net migration of labour into a country.

In Figure 4.3, economic growth causes an outward shift of the PPC from PPC_1 to PPC_2. This means the economy can produce more goods and services, without necessarily incurring an opportunity cost.

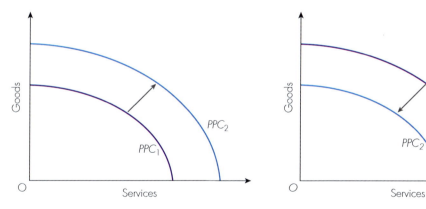

▲ **Figure 4.3** An outward shift of the PPC   ▲ **Figure 4.4** An inward shift of the PPC

Economies strive to increase their productive capacity. For example, advances in technology will result in higher productivity and output for an economy. This means that even with the same amount of factors of production, more goods and services can be produced, resulting in an outward shift of the PPC.

By contrast, detrimental changes can cause the PPC to shift inwards. These changes might include a major natural disaster, the outbreak of a pandemic, or a war that destroys a large proportion of the economy's farmland, factories and infrastructure. In Figure 4.4, the PPC shifts inwards from PPC_1 to PPC_2. This represents a decrease in the productive capacity of the economy.

Activity

Low-lying areas of Bangladesh are prone to flooding each year. Crops are lost and thousands of people lose their homes. During times of severe flooding, roads and railways are damaged and farmers find it impossible to get their dwindled crops to market.

a Draw a PPC diagram and explain the impact of flooding on the productive capacity of Bangladesh.

b On the diagram, draw and label a point where some of the factors of production will be idle.

c On the diagram, draw and label a point that is unattainable.

Practice questions: multiple choice

1 Which is **most** likely to cause an inwards shift of a country's production possibility curve (PPC)?   [1]

   A a natural disaster in the economy

   B an increase in the quantity of factors of production

   C better quality factors of production

   D higher opportunity costs of production

2 Which best describes a movement along an economy's PPC?   [1]

   A a decrease in the labour force due to a major natural disaster

   B a shift from producing more of Good A to producing more of Good B

   C a technological improvement in the production of both goods and services

   D an increase in the resources available to the economy

Practice question: structured question

Country Y has decided to reallocate resources from the production of capital goods to consumer goods.

a Draw a PPC diagram for Country Y before and after the reallocation of resources.   [2]

b Explain how the reallocation of resources affects the position on the PPC for Country Y.   [2]

c Explain the potential long-term impact of this decision on economic growth in Country Y.   [2]

Activity

Using real-world examples, discuss why an outwards shift of the PPC is not always good for the economy.

Chapter review questions

1 What is meant by the productive capacity of an economy?

2 What does a PPC diagram show?

3 How is the concept of opportunity cost shown on a PPC diagram?

4 Which two conditions must hold for an economy to be operating on its PPC?

5 What does a movement along a PPC mean?

6 What are the causes of an outward shift of a PPC?

Revision checklist

✔ A PPC shows the maximum combination of any two categories of goods and services that can be produced in an economy. It shows the productive capacity of the economy.

✔ A PPC diagram is a graphical representation of the maximum combinations of two products that can be produced in an economy, when all resources are used efficiently.

✔ For a country to be on its PPC, two conditions have to be met: full use of all factors of production (there are no unemployed resources) and efficient use of all resources (all factor inputs are put to their best use).

✔ Movements along a PPC incur an opportunity cost.

✔ Economies strive to increase their productivity capacity, as shown by an outward shift of the PPC.

✔ Detrimental changes, such as natural disasters or war, can cause the PPC to shift inwards.

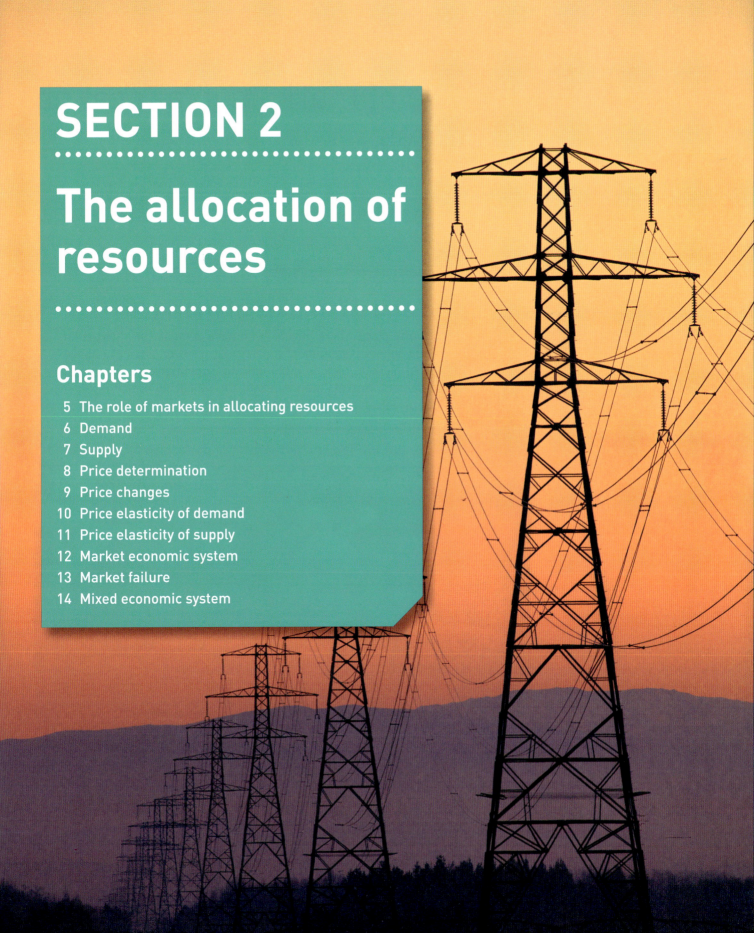

SECTION 2

The allocation of resources

Chapters

The role of markets in allocating resources

By the end of this chapter, students should be able to:

★ define a market
★ provide examples of markets
★ explain the role of buyers and sellers.

Definition and examples of markets

Definitions

A **market** refers to any place where buyers and sellers engage in trade. Examples of markets include retail outlets, supermarkets and stock markets.
The **market system** refers to the method of allocating scarce resources through the market forces of demand and supply.

A **market** refers to any place where buyers (who have demand for a particular good or service) and sellers (suppliers of a particular good or service) engage in trade. Examples of markets include retail outlets, supermarkets, restaurants, hotels and stock markets. Markets are important for allocating scarce resources through the forces of demand (see Chapter 6) and supply (see Chapter 7).

▲ A market is a place where buyers and sellers engage in trade

The market system

The **market system**, also known as the **price mechanism**, establishes market equilibrium. This is the point where the demand for a product equals the supply at a given price (see Chapter 8). When a market is able to reach equilibrium, this means there are no shortages or surpluses. Shortages exist in a market when the demand for a product exceeds the supply at a given price. In contrast, surpluses exist in a market when the supply exceeds the demand at a given price. Therefore, the market system refers to the method of allocating scarce resources through the market forces of demand (buyers) and supply (sellers).

The demand curve for a product (see Chapter 6) shows that consumers in the market will tend to buy more as the market price falls. The supply curve of a product (see Chapter 7) shows that firms in the market will tend to produce or supply more as the market price rises. When the opposing market forces of demand and supply are in balance, an equilibrium price and quantity are established, where all products offered for sale at that price are bought by consumers.

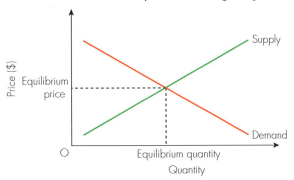

▲ **Figure 5.1** Market equilibrium

Market disequilibrium occurs when the market price is either above or below the equilibrium price (where demand equals supply). If the price of a product is above the equilibrium price, consumers will consider the product too expensive. The quantity supplied will therefore exceed the quantity demanded. To sell off this excess supply in the market, the price must be reduced.

By contrast, if the price of a product is below the equilibrium price, the product will be seen as too cheap to attract sufficient supply. The quantity demanded will therefore exceed the quantity supplied. To create an incentive for new firms to enter the market or for existing firms to supply more, the price must be raised. Hence, the market system will tend to get rid of market disequilibrium in the long run.

Case study: Record coffee prices

In 2024, the export price of coffee beans rose to a 47-year record high, driven by severe droughts and climate issues in Brazil and Vietnam, the world's two largest suppliers of coffee beans. Higher disposable income across Asia and emerging markets also caused a significant increase in the demand for coffee.

Activity

Discuss how the significant increase in the price of coffee is likely to affect the Vietnamese and Brazilian economies. Which stakeholder groups win or lose from this?

The role of buyers and sellers

All economies face the basic economic problem of scarcity of resources. All economic systems (see also Chapters 12 and 14) must address three key economic questions about determining resource allocation:

1 **What production should take place?** This question is about deciding which goods and services should be provided in the economy. For example, is it better for the economy to have more roads and airports or to have more schools and hospitals? As resources are limited in supply, decision-makers realise there is an opportunity cost (see Chapter 3) in answering this question. In a market economy, consumers (buyers) decide what goods and services need to be produced or provided by suppliers (sellers). For example, the increased demand for electric vehicles means more suppliers will produce these.

2 **How should production take place?** This question is about the methods and processes used to produce the desired goods and services. For example, sellers will have to decide which combination of factors of production (land, labour, capital and enterprise) to use in the production process.

3 **For whom should production take place?** This question is about which consumers receive goods and services. For example, should any goods and services be provided free to everyone in the economy, irrespective of their willingness and ability to pay for them? Or should goods and services only be produced for those who can pay?

In a market system, the decision about what, how, and for whom production should take place is determined by the forces of demand (buyers) and supply (sellers). See Chapter 12 for more details on this.

Practice question: multiple choice

Which option is **not** a key economic question that is addressed by
the market economy?   [1]
A For whom should production take place?
B How should production take place?
C What production should take place?
D Why should production take place?

Practice question: structured question

Explain, with a relevant example, how prices are determined in a market
system.   [4]

Table 5.1 A summary of the role of buyers and sellers

Buyers (consumers, firms, governments)	Sellers (producers and suppliers of goods and services)
Create demand for a good or service	Create supply of a good or service
Tend to buy more when the market price falls, and vice versa	Tend to supply more when the market price increases, and vice versa

Collectively they determine what, how and for whom production should take place.

❓ Chapter review questions

1 What is a market?
2 What is meant by the market system?
3 What is meant by market equilibrium?
4 How does market disequilibrium occur?
5 What are the three key economic questions that all economies must address?
6 What is the role of buyers and sellers in a market?

Revision checklist

✔ A market is any place where buyers and sellers can engage in trade and exchange. Examples of markets include retail outlets, supermarkets, hotels, e-commerce and the stock market.

✔ The market system refers to the method of allocating scarce resources through the market forces of demand (buyers) and supply (sellers).

✔ Market equilibrium is established where the market demand for a product is equal to the market supply of the product.

✔ Market disequilibrium occurs when the market price is either above (creating surpluses) or below (creating shortages) the equilibrium price.

✔ All economies must address three key economic questions about determining resource allocation: what, how and for whom should production take place? Buyers and sellers play a vital role in this process.

Demand

Defining demand

Definitions

Demand refers to the quantity of a good or service that consumers are both willing and able to buy at various prices, over a given period of time.

The **law of demand** states that quantity demanded falls as price rises, while the quantity demanded rises at lower prices.

Demand refers to the quantity of a good or service that consumers are both **willing** and **able** to buy at various prices, over a given period of time. The higher the price of a product, the lower its demand tends to be. This is sometimes referred to as **effective demand** to distinguish genuine demand from a desire to buy something.

The amount of a good or service demanded at each price level is called the **quantity demanded**. (Note that quantity demanded is not the same as demand. This will be explained later in this chapter.) In general, the quantity demanded falls as price rises, while the quantity demanded rises at lower prices. Hence, there is an inverse relationship between the price of a good or service and the quantity demanded. This rule is known as the **law of demand**. There are two reasons for this relationship:

» As the price of a good or service falls, the customer's real income rises – that is, with the same amount of income, the customer is able to buy more of the product at lower prices.

» As the price of a good or service falls, a larger number of customers are able to pay, so they are more likely to buy the product.

Study tip

Some of the non-price determinants of demand can be remembered by the acronym MISC: **m**arketing, **i**ncome, **s**ubstitutes and **c**omplements.

> **Activity**
>
> Choose an item that you can buy in your country.
>
> **a** What are the factors that affect the demand for this product?
> **b** Which factor is the most important? Why?
>
> Produce your findings in an A3 poster format for displaying in the classroom.

Determinants of demand

Although price is regarded as the key determinant of the level of demand for a good or service, it is not the only factor that affects the quantity demanded. Other determinants of demand can be remembered by the acronym HIS AGE:

» **Habits, fashions and tastes** – changes in habits, fashions and tastes can affect the demand for all types of goods and services. When products become fashionable (such as the latest smartphones) this leads to an increase in demand for them. Products that become unfashionable (such as last season's clothes) have a reduced level of demand.

▲ Fashionable products experience an increase in demand

>> **Income** – higher levels of income mean that customers are able and willing to buy more goods and services. For example, the average person in the USA will have a higher level of demand for goods and services than the average person in Vietnam or Pakistan.

>> **Substitutes and complements** – **substitutes** are goods or services that people can use instead of each other, such as Coca-Cola or Pepsi and tea or coffee. If the price of one product falls, then it is likely the demand for its substitute will also fall. **Complements** are products that people demand jointly, such as tennis balls and tennis racquets or cinema movies and popcorn. If the price of one product increases, then the demand for its complement is likely to fall.

>> **Advertising** – firms use marketing messages to inform, remind and persuade customers to buy their products. Companies such as McDonald's, Apple and Samsung spend hundreds of millions of dollars each year on their advertising budgets in an attempt to increase the demand for their products.

>> **Government policies** – rules and regulations and taxes on products, such as tobacco and alcohol, will affect the demand for certain goods and services. Sales taxes cause prices to increase, thereby reducing the quantity of demand. By contrast, government subsidies for educational establishments and energy-efficient car makers, for example, help to encourage more demand for education and environmentally friendly cars due to their relatively lower prices.

>> **Economy** – the state of the economy (whether it is in an economic boom or a recession) has a huge impact on the spending patterns of the population. The COVID-19 pandemic, for example, caused the demand for most goods and services around the world to decline. This was due to national lockdowns and households' and businesses' lack of confidence in the economy.

There are other factors that can influence the level of demand for a particular good or service. For example, the **weather** can affect the demand for ice cream, beach resort holidays, winter jackets and umbrellas. The size and the demographics of the **population** (such as age, gender, ethnicity and religious beliefs) can also have an effect on the level of demand for goods and services. For example, adults and children have different buying habits.

Price and quantity demanded: the demand curve

Diagrammatically, the demand curve is shown as a downward-sloping line to indicate the inverse relationship between price and quantity demanded (see Figure 6.1).

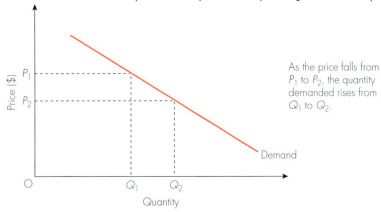

As the price falls from P_1 to P_2, the quantity demanded rises from Q_1 to Q_2.

▲ **Figure 6.1** The demand curve

Movements along a demand curve

A change in the price of a good or service causes a movement along the demand curve. A price rise will cause a **contraction in demand** for the product – that is, the quantity demanded falls. By contrast, a reduction in price will cause an **extension in demand**, as shown in Figure 6.2.

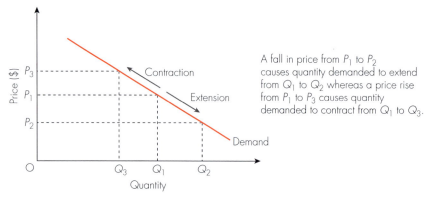

A fall in price from P_1 to P_2 causes quantity demanded to extend from Q_1 to Q_2 whereas a price rise from P_1 to P_3 causes quantity demanded to contract from Q_1 to Q_3.

▲ **Figure 6.2** Movements along the demand curve

Individual demand and market demand

The **market demand** refers to the aggregation of all individual demand for a product at different prices. We calculate it by adding up all individual demand at each price level (see Figure 6.3). For instance, suppose that a cinema charges $10 for its movie tickets. The demand for tickets from adults totals 500 per week and 400 teenagers buy tickets per week. The market demand for cinema tickets at $10 per ticket is therefore 900 tickets per week.

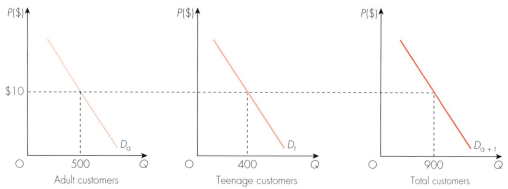

▲ **Figure 6.3** The market demand curve

Conditions of demand

While a movement in demand is caused by price changes only, a change in all other (non-price) factors that affect demand, such as income, will cause a **shift in demand**. For example, BMW recorded higher than expected profits in 2024 due to higher demand for its cars in various regions of the world. Hence, the demand for BMW's cars was higher at all price levels.

An **increase in demand** (rather than an increase in the quantity demanded) is represented by a rightward shift in the demand curve, from D_1 to D_3 in Figure 6.4. When the demand curve shifts from D_1 to D_3 at a price of P_1, the quantity demanded increases from Q_1 to Q_3.

▲ BMW's profits in 2024 were higher than expected thanks to higher demand in Europe, the USA and China

By contrast, a **decrease in demand** (rather than a fall in the quantity demanded) is shown by shifting the demand curve to the left, from D_1 to D_2 in Figure 6.4. This results in lower quantity demanded at all price levels. At the price of P_1, demand falls from Q_1 to Q_2. For example, financial problems and rising unemployment in the economy will tend to decrease the demand for cars.

Study tip

Remember the difference between **changes in demand** and **changes in the quantity demanded**.

- A shift in demand is caused by changes in non-price factors that affect demand.
- A movement along a demand curve is caused by changes in the price of the product.

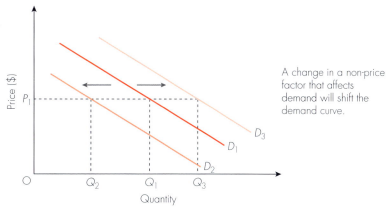

A change in a non-price factor that affects demand will shift the demand curve.

▲ **Figure 6.4** Shifts in the demand curve

Activity

France and Spain tend to be among the most visited tourist countries in the world.

a Investigate the most popular tourist cities in Asia or Europe.
b Using demand theory, explain the factors that make these cities so popular.

Activity

Using an appropriate demand diagram each time, explain the impact on the demand for Apple smartphones in the following cases.

a An increase in the price of Apple smartphones.
b An increase in the price of Samsung smartphones.
c An increase in consumer incomes.
d A successful advertising campaign promoting Samsung's latest smartphones.

Practice questions: multiple choice

1 What is the law of demand? [1]
   A the assumption that both price and non-price factors affect the level of demand for a good or service
   B the influence of non-price factors on the demand for a good or service
   C the inverse relationship between the price of a good or service and the quantity demanded of that product
   D the positive relationship between the price of a good or service and the quantity demanded of that product
2 What does a rightwards shift of the demand curve for a good or service show? [1]
   A a higher level of demand at all given price levels
   B a highly successful advertising campaign for the product
   C a lower price charged for the product
   D a reduction in the demand for the good or service

❓ Chapter review questions

1   What is meant by demand?
2   What is the law of demand?
3   What are the two reasons for the inverse relationship between price and quantity demanded?
4   What are the main determinants of demand?
5   How does the cause of a movement along a demand curve differ from the cause of a shift in a demand curve?
6   How does a contraction in demand differ from an extension in demand?
7   What is meant by market demand?
8   How does a fall in quantity demanded differ from a fall in demand?

Revision checklist

✔ Demand refers to the willingness and the ability of customers to pay a given price to buy a good or service.
✔ The market demand refers to the sum of all individual demand for a product at given prices.
✔ The amount of a good or service demanded at each price level is called the quantity demanded.
✔ The law of demand states there is an inverse relationship between the price of a good or service and the quantity demanded.
✔ The demand curve is drawn as downward sloping from left to right, showing the inverse relationship between price and quantity demanded.
✔ A change in the price of a good or service causes a movement along the demand curve.
✔ A price rise causes a contraction in demand, whereas a reduction in price causes an extension in demand for the product.
✔ The non-price determinants of demand can be remembered by the acronym HIS AGE: Habits, fashions and tastes; Income levels; Substitutes and complements (price and availability); Advertising; Government policies (such as taxes, regulations and subsidies); and the state of the Economy (for example, boom or recession).
✔ A change in all non-price factors that affect demand will cause a shift in demand.

7 Supply

This chapter will cover:

★ a definition of supply
★ how to draw and interpret appropriate supply diagrams
★ the link between individual and market supply
★ movements (contractions and extensions) along a supply curve and how to construct diagrams that illustrate these
★ the causes of shifts in a supply curve and how to construct diagrams that illustrate these.

Defining supply

Supply refers to the quantity of goods and services that firms are **able** and **willing** to provide at various prices over a given period of time. Firms will have more incentive to supply their products at higher prices. Therefore, the higher the price, the greater supply tends to be. There are two reasons for this positive relationship between price and supply:

»» Existing firms can earn higher profits if they supply more at a higher price.
»» New firms are able to join the market if the higher price allows them to cover their production costs.

> **Activity**
>
> Visit an area where there are lots of shops, such as a market, shopping street or shopping mall.
>
> a Investigate the number of stalls, stores or shops which cater specifically (or primarily) for women. Compare this with the number which cater only (or mainly) for men. Is there a difference?
> b Using supply theory, explain what you have found.

> **Activities**
>
> 1 Investigate the factors that affect the supply of one of the following products:
>   a coffee   c tea   e oil
>   b chocolate   d sugar
> 2 Organise your findings as a PowerPoint document and be prepared to present it to the class.

Determinants of supply

Although price is regarded as the key determinant of the level of supply of a good or service, it is not the only factor that affects the quantity supplied. Non-price factors that affect the level of supply of a product can be remembered by the acronym TWO TIPS:

»» **Time** – the shorter the time period in question, the less time suppliers have to increase their output, so the lower the supply tends to be. For example, it is not possible for a farmer to increase the supply of agricultural products in a short time period, even if they are offered a higher price. Output can only be increased over time.

▲ In China, the government heavily subsidises tuition costs for medical students

Definition

The **law of supply** states that there is a positive relationship between price and the quantity supplied of a product.

» **Weather** – the supply of certain goods and services can depend on the weather. For example, favourable weather conditions will shift the supply of agricultural output to the right. Some service providers, such as airline carriers, may also limit or close their operations during adverse weather conditions. This will shift the supply curve to the left.

» **Opportunity cost** – price acts as a signal to producers. It encourages them to allocate their resources to providing goods and services with higher profits. For example, if the market price of corn falls while the price of apples increases, then farmers are likely to reduce their supply of corn (due to the higher opportunity cost) and raise their supply of apples.

» **Taxes** – taxes imposed on the supplier of a product add to the costs of production. Therefore, the imposition of taxes on a product reduces its supply. This will shift the supply curve to the left.

» **Innovations** – technological advances, such as automation and digital technologies, mean that there can be greater levels of output at every price level. Hence, innovations will tend to shift the supply curve of a product to the right.

» **Production costs** – if the cost of raw materials and other factors of production falls, then the supply curve will shift to the right, ceteris paribus. Hence, there is an increase in supply at each price level. By contrast, an increase in production costs will reduce the supply of a product at each price.

» **Subsidies** – subsidies are a type of financial assistance from the government to help encourage output by reducing the costs of production for firms. Governments usually provide subsidies to reduce the costs of supplying goods and services that are beneficial to society as a whole, such as education, training and healthcare.

Price and quantity supplied: the supply curve

The **law of supply** states that there is a positive relationship between price and the quantity supplied of a product. Hence, a supply curve is drawn as upward sloping from left to right. In Figure 7.1, as the price increases from P_1 to P_2, the quantity supplied rises from Q_1 to Q_2.

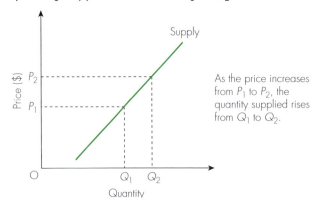

As the price increases from P_1 to P_2, the quantity supplied rises from Q_1 to Q_2.

▲ **Figure 7.1** The supply curve

Definitions

An **extension in supply** means an increase in the quantity supplied of a product following an increase in its price.
A **contraction in supply** means a fall in the quantity supplied of a product following a fall in its price.

Movements along a supply curve

A **movement along** a supply curve occurs only if the price of the product changes. A change in price alone causes a change in the **quantity supplied**. There is an **extension in supply** if the price increases. A **contraction in supply** occurs if the price of the product falls (see Figure 7.2). For example, higher prices for Apple's iPhone in China led to an extension in supply as the company opened its 57th Apple Store in China in 2024.

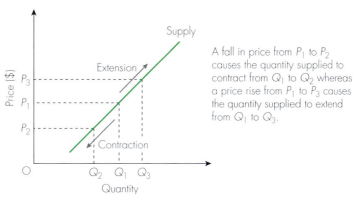

A fall in price from P_1 to P_2 causes the quantity supplied to contract from Q_1 to Q_2 whereas a price rise from P_1 to P_3 causes the quantity supplied to extend from Q_1 to Q_3.

▲ **Figure 7.2** Movements along the supply curve

Individual supply and market supply

The **market supply curve** is the aggregation of all supply at each price level, as shown in Figure 7.3. Suppose that at a price of $300 million per unit Airbus is willing and able to supply 300 aircraft per time period. In the same time period its rival, Boeing, supplies 320 aircraft. At this price, the total market supply is 620 aircraft. Hence, the market supply is found by adding up all individual supply at each price level.

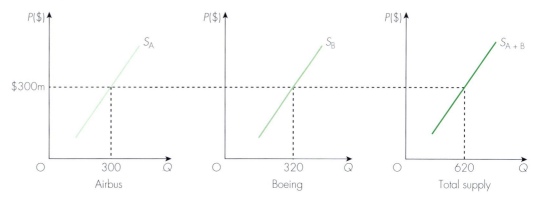

▲ **Figure 7.3** The market supply curve

Conditions of supply

A change in any of the non-price factors that affect the supply of a good or service will cause a **shift** in the supply curve. In Figure 7.4, a rightward shift of the supply curve from S_1 to S_2 is described as an **increase in supply** (rather than an increase in the quantity supplied). By contrast, a leftward shift of the supply curve from S_1 to S_3 results in a **decrease in supply** (rather than a fall in the quantity supplied). For example, the magnitude 7.6 earthquake that struck off the northern coast of Japan in January 2024 reduced the supply of parts to major manufacturers such as Hitachi, Sony, Panasonic, Toyota and Honda.

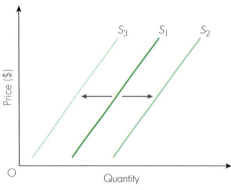

An increase in supply is shown by a rightward shift of the supply curve from S_1 to S_2.
Similarly, a fall in supply is represented by a leftward shift of the supply curve from S_1 to S_3.

▲ **Figure 7.4** Shifts in the supply curve

Activity

Discuss as a class how supply theory can be used to explain the way that natural disasters, such as earthquakes in Japan, affect the output of manufactured goods, such as Toyota cars.

Activities

1 Using an appropriate supply diagram, explain the impact on the supply of educational computer games in the following cases.
   a The government provides subsidies to producers of educational computer games.
   b There is an increase in the rate of commission paid to creators and distributors of educational computer games.
   c The government introduces a 15 per cent sales tax on all computer games.
   d There are technological advances in the production of educational computer games.
   e There is an increase in the market price of educational computer games due to higher demand from schools.

2 Using an appropriate diagram, explain how the following changes affect the supply or the quantity supplied in each scenario.
   a The Chinese government raises the minimum wage for factory workers by 20 per cent.
   b A severe drought causes vegetable prices to soar in France.
   c New technology boosts productivity at Tata Motors, India's largest car maker.
   d The US government subsidises the production of electric vehicles.
   e South Korea's Samsung launches new smartphones to rival Apple's latest iPhone.

Practice question: structured question

During the summer months, the demand for ice cream increases significantly. Explain, with the aid of a fully labelled diagram, how an increase in the price of ice creams affects the market supply curve.   [4]

Practice questions: multiple choice

1 What is the law of supply? [1]
  A the assumption that both price and non-price factors affect the level of supply of a good or service
  B the influence of non-price factors on the market supply of a given good or service
  C the inverse relationship between the price of a good or service and the quantity supplied of that product
  D the positive relationship between the price of a good or service and the quantity supplied of that product

2 What does a leftward shift of the market supply curve for a good or service show? [1]
  A a higher level of supply at all given price levels
  B a higher price charged for the product
  C an increase in production costs for suppliers
  D an unsuccessful advertising campaign for the product

? Chapter review questions

1 What is meant by supply?
2 Why is the supply curve upward sloping?
3 What are the main determinants of supply?
4 What is the law of supply?
5 How does a contraction in supply differ from an extension in supply?
6 How does market supply differ from individual supply?
7 What is the difference between the cause of a movement along a supply curve and the cause of a shift in a supply curve?
8 What are the causes of shifts in the supply curve?

Revision checklist

✔ Supply refers to the quantity of goods and services that firms are able and willing to provide at various prices over a given period of time.
✔ The determinants of supply can be remembered by the acronym TWO TIPS: Time; Weather; Opportunity cost of production options; Taxes; Innovations; Production costs and Subsidies.
✔ The law of supply states there is a positive relationship between price and the quantity supplied of a product.
✔ A movement along a supply curve is caused by a change in price.
✔ A contraction in supply means a lower quantity is supplied due to a fall in price.
✔ An extension in supply means a higher quantity is supplied due to an increase in price.
✔ The market supply is the sum of all individual supply at each price level.
✔ A change in non-price factors affecting the supply of a good or service will cause a shift in the supply curve.

Price determination

This chapter will cover:

★ a definition of the price mechanism
★ how the price mechanism answers decisions about resource allocation
★ a definition of market equilibrium
★ how to draw and interpret demand and supply schedules and curves to establish equilibrium
★ how to define market disequilibrium
★ how to draw and interpret demand and supply schedules and curves to show shortages (excess demand) and surpluses (excess supply).

Defining the price mechanism

Definition

The **price mechanism** refers to the system of relying on the market forces of demand and supply to allocate resources.

The **price mechanism** refers to the system of relying on the market forces of demand and supply to allocate resources. In this system the private sector (see Chapter 12) decides on the fundamental questions of what, how and for whom production should take place. For example, wage rates are determined by the forces of demand for labour (by private sector firms) and supply of labour (by workers who offer their labour services).

Features of the price mechanism include the following:

» There is no government interference in economic activities. Private economic agents are the owners of resources and they have the economic freedom to allocate scarce resources without interference from the government.
» Goods and services are allocated on the basis of price. A high price tends to encourage more supply whereas a low price tends to encourage more consumer spending. Goods and services are sold to those who are willing and able to pay.
» The allocation of factor resources is based on financial incentives. For example, agricultural land is used for harvesting crops with the greatest financial return, while unprofitable products are no longer produced.
» Competition creates opportunities for firms and choice for private individuals. Consumers can thus benefit from a variety of innovative products, at competitive prices and of high quality.

Practice question: multiple choice

Which option is **not** a feature of the price mechanism? [1]

A Competition creates choice and opportunities for firms and private individuals.
B Goods and services are allocated on the basis of price.
C Resources are owned by private economic agents who have the economic freedom to allocate scarce resources.
D Rules and regulations are imposed to correct market failures, such as the overconsumption of demerit goods.

Study tip

To better understand the concept of the price mechanism, refer to Chapters 6 and 7 on demand and supply.

Market equilibrium

Market equilibrium refers to the position where the demand for a product is equal to the supply of the product. At this point, an **equilibrium price** (also known as the **market clearing price**) is established. At the equilibrium price, there is neither excess quantity demanded nor excess quantity supplied (see Figure 8.1).

Definitions

Market equilibrium occurs when the quantity demanded of a product is equal to the quantity supplied of the product, i.e. there are no shortages or surpluses.

Equilibrium price is the price at which the demand curve for a product intersects the supply curve for the product. The market is therefore cleared of any excess demand or supply.

Market disequilibrium occurs when the quantity demanded of a product is unequal to the quantity supplied of the product, i.e. there are shortages or surpluses in the market.

Excess demand refers to a situation where the market price is below the equilibrium price, thus creating a shortage in the market.

A **shortage** occurs when demand exceeds supply because the price is lower than the market equilibrium.

A **surplus** is created when supply exceeds demand because the price is higher than the market equilibrium price.

Excess supply refers to a situation where the market price is above the equilibrium price, thus creating a surplus in the market.

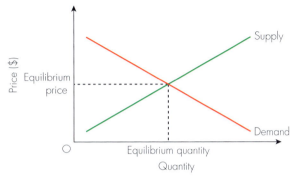

▲ **Figure 8.1** Market equilibrium

Market disequilibrium

Market disequilibrium occurs when the quantity demanded for a product is either higher or lower than the quantity supplied. Disequilibrium is inefficient, because it means there are either shortages or surpluses.

Shortages

If the selling price of a product is set too low (that is, below the equilibrium price), then demand will exceed supply (see Figure 8.2). This **excess demand** creates a **shortage** in the market. At a price of P_1, quantity demanded is Q_d, while quantity supplied is only Q_s. Hence, quantity demanded exceeds quantity supplied at this price. The excess demand will tend to cause price to rise back towards the equilibrium price of P_e.

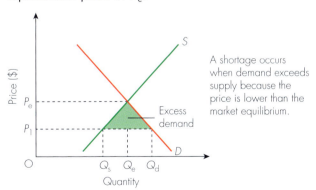

A shortage occurs when demand exceeds supply because the price is lower than the market equilibrium.

▲ **Figure 8.2** Excess demand (shortage)

Surpluses

If the price is set too high (above the market clearing price), then quantity supplied will exceed quantity demanded, as shown in Figure 8.3. This results in a **surplus**, known as **excess supply**. In order for firms to get rid of their excess supply (shown by the distance between Q_s and Q_d at each price level above the equilibrium price), they will need to reduce price (from P_1 to P_e). This is a key reason why, for example, unsold summer clothes go on sale during the autumn.

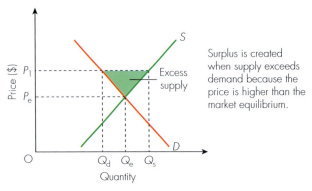

▲ **Figure 8.3** Excess supply (surplus)

Activity

The table below shows the demand and supply schedule for a particular product.

P ($)	Q_d (000s)	Q_s (000s)
0	80	0
10	60	20
20	40	40
30	20	60
40	0	80

a Identify the equilibrium price.
b Calculate and identify the value of excess demand or supply if the price is $10.
c Calculate and identify the value of excess demand or supply if the price is $40.

Practice question: multiple choice

Study the demand and supply schedule below; then answer the questions.

Price ($)	Quantity demanded (units per week, in 000s)	Quantity supplied (units per week, in 000s)
15	9	2
20	8	4
25	7	6
30	6	8
35	5	10

a At a price of $25, what situation does the market show? [1]
  A excess demand   **C** market equilibrium
  B excess supply   **D** stockpiling
b If the average price is $30 over a four-week period of trading, how much excess will suppliers accumulate? [1]
  A 2,000 units   **C** 24,000 units
  B 8,000 units   **D** 32,000 units

Practice question: structured question

Mexico is the world's biggest producer of avocados, supplying a significant amount of the planet's avocados. In May 2024, avocado prices reached a record high due to reduced harvests from major producers in Mexico, Peru and California. Prices also surged due to higher global demand in places such as the US, Europe and China. The industry has become very profitable for Mexican farmers, with avocados being nicknamed Mexico's green gold.

a Define 'supply'.   [2]
b Explain, using a demand and supply diagram, why reduced harvests caused avocado prices to reach a record high.   [4]
c Analyse the reasons why the global demand for avocados may have increased.   [6]

Activities

1 Investigate the economic reasons behind the European Union's Common Agricultural Policy (CAP) for EU farmers. Why does this policy tend to encourage excess supply of agricultural output?
2 Using demand and supply theory, discuss the reasons why property prices are extremely high in cities such as Shanghai, New York City, London and Tokyo.

? Chapter review questions

1 What is the price mechanism?
2 What are the key features of the price mechanism?
3 What is meant by market equilibrium?
4 What is meant by equilibrium price?
5 What is meant by market disequilibrium?
6 What is the difference between excess demand and excess supply?
7 When do surpluses occur?
8 When do shortages occur?

Revision checklist

✔ The price mechanism refers to the system of relying on the market forces of demand and supply to allocate resources.
✔ Features of the price mechanism include no government interference in economic activity, the allocation of resources based on price and financial incentives, and competition creating choice and opportunities for firms and private individuals.
✔ Market equilibrium refers to the position where the demand for a product is equal to the supply of the product.
✔ At the equilibrium price, there is neither excess quantity demanded nor excess quantity supplied.
✔ Market disequilibrium occurs when the quantity demanded for a product is either higher or lower than the quantity supplied.
✔ Excess demand refers to a situation where the market price is below the equilibrium price. This results in shortages.
✔ Excess supply refers to a situation where the market price is above the equilibrium price. This results in surpluses.

Price changes

This chapter will cover:

★ the causes of price changes
★ the consequences of price changes
★ how to use demand and supply diagrams to illustrate the impact of price changes.

Causes of price changes

Changes in non-price factors that affect demand or supply will cause a change in the equilibrium price and quantity traded. For example, in Figure 9.1, a sales tax imposed on tobacco products will shift the supply curve of cigarettes to the left. This raises the market equilibrium price from P_1 to P_2 and reduces the equilibrium quantity traded from Q_1 to Q_2.

Figure 9.1 could represent any factor that shifts the market supply curve to the left (see Chapter 7). For example, adverse weather conditions could reduce the level of agricultural output and subsequently force up the equilibrium price.

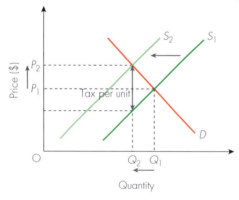

▲ **Figure 9.1** Impact of imposing a sales tax

By contrast, any factor that shifts the market supply curve to the right can be represented by Figure 9.2. For example, a subsidy for farmers or favourable weather conditions will shift the supply of agricultural output to the right. This reduces the equilibrium price of agricultural output from P_1 to P_2 and increases the quantity traded from Q_1 to Q_2.

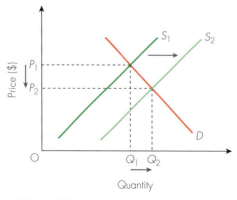

▲ **Figure 9.2** Impact of favourable weather conditions on agricultural output

Price changes can also occur due to shifts in the market demand curve (see Chapter 6). For example, any factor that shifts the demand curve to the right – such as higher levels of disposable income or effective persuasive advertising – will lead to higher prices as well as higher levels of quantity traded. In Figure 9.3, higher household incomes lead to an increase in the demand for new cars, thus shifting the demand curve from D_1 to D_2. This results in a higher equilibrium price of P_2 and a higher equilibrium quantity of Q_2.

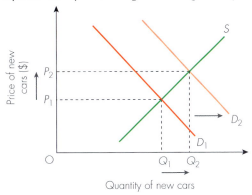

▲ **Figure 9.3** Impact of higher household income on the market for new cars

By contrast, a fall in market demand – perhaps due to negative publicity, lower prices of substitute products, or lower household income due to a recession (see Chapter 26) – will cause the demand curve to shift to the left. This will result in a fall in the price and a fall in the quantity traded. In Figure 9.4, mass unemployment in the economy leads to a fall in the demand for helium balloons. This causes the equilibrium quantity traded to fall to Q_2 and the equilibrium price to fall to P_2 ceteris paribus.

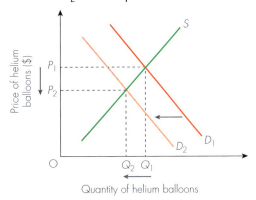

▲ **Figure 9.4** Impact of mass unemployment on the market for helium balloons

> ## ▶ Activity
>
> Investigate the various ways that different governments use to reduce the demand for cigarettes. For example, you could compare and contrast the different levels of sales taxes used in countries such as Japan, China, the UK and Australia. Explain how these government actions will have an impact on prices.

> ### Activity
>
> Using an appropriate demand and supply diagram, explain the impact on the market price and quantity traded in each of the following cases.
>
> **a** The market for air travel following the imposition of higher fuel taxes.
> **b** The market for Pepsi Cola following a fall in price of Coca-Cola.
> **c** The market for sushi (Japanese cuisine) following a successful marketing campaign promoting the health benefits of eating rice and fish.
> **d** The market for Samsung smartphones following new technologies that improve productivity in its factories.

Effects of price changes on sales

Price changes affect sales by influencing the level of consumer demand. A price increase typically leads to a decrease in sales as fewer consumers are willing and/or able to purchase the good or service. Conversely, a reduction in price generally boosts sales by making the good or service more affordable to a larger customer base. See Figure 6.2 in Chapter 6.

▲ Price reductions make goods more affordable and boost sales

Practice question: structured question

In 2012, Danish toy maker LEGO® launched LEGO® Friends to appeal primarily to girls. The products included mini-doll figures, pink and purple coloured scheme toy sets, and pets. Founded in 1949, LEGO's popular toy construction bricks had traditionally been targeted mainly at boys with theme sets such as LEGO® Racers, LEGO® *Star Wars*™, LEGO® Batman™ and LEGO® Ninjago. By early 2013, LEGO had sold twice as many of the LEGO Friends toys as had been expected. The company said that demand from children and their families was overwhelmingly positive. LEGO had spent $40 million in its global marketing of LEGO Friends, which proved to be a huge success as the company's net profit rose 35 per cent in the same year. According to LEGO, boys accounted for 90 per cent of its customers before the launch of LEGO Friends. In 2022, the company reported that LEGO Friends was among the top six earning product lines for the business.

Sources: Adapted from The LEGO® Group annual reports 2013 and 2022, and 'LEGO® Group's revenue jumps as classic sets thrive', 7 March 2023, Bloomberg

a Define 'demand'.   [2]
b Explain two possible reasons for the higher-than-expected demand for LEGO Friends toy construction bricks.   [4]

Practice questions: multiple choice

1 Which statement explains why there might be a decrease in the demand for petrol (oil)? [1]

A An increasing number of drivers buy electric-powered cars.

B Demand for new cars has increased.

C New technologies reduce the time needed to extract oil.

D There is an increase in world oil supplies.

2 The diagram below shows a change in the market for agricultural output. What is likely to have caused the change in supply? [1]

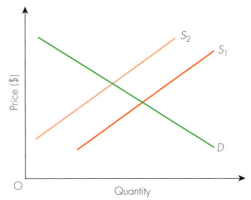

A an increase in income tax rates

B favourable weather conditions

C higher cost of fertilisers

D subsidies provided to farmers

3 The diagram below shows a change in the market for smartphones. What is likely to have caused the change in demand? [1]

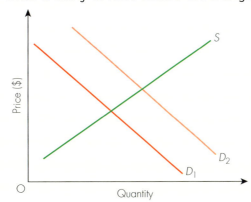

A a fall in the price of laptops

B a lower sales tax imposed on goods

C a reduction in income tax rates

D a significant fall in the price of smartphones

4 Which factor is **most** likely to shift the demand curve to the right?

A a recession in the economy

B higher levels of disposable income

C lower prices of substitute products

D negative economic growth

❓ Chapter review questions

1   Which factors cause a change in the equilibrium price and quantity traded for any given product?
2   What is the consequence of sales taxes on equilibrium price and quantity?
3   What is the impact of favourable weather conditions on the equilibrium price and quantity of agricultural output?
4   State three factors that can shift the demand curve for a given product.
5   State three factors that can shift the supply curve of a given product.

Revision checklist

✔ Changes in non-price factors that affect the demand for or supply of a product will cause a change in the equilibrium price and quantity.
✔ Price changes can occur due to shifts in supply, such as changes in the costs of production.
✔ Lower supply causes equilibrium price to rise and equilibrium quantity to fall. An increase in supply causes equilibrium quantity to rise, thus causing equilibrium price to fall.
✔ Price changes can also occur due to shifts in demand, such as changes in real incomes.
✔ Lower demand causes equilibrium quantity to fall and the price to fall. By contrast, higher demand causes both equilibrium price and quantity to rise.

10 Price elasticity of demand

By the end of this chapter, students should be able to:

★ define and calculate price elasticity of demand (PED)
★ draw and interpret demand curve diagrams to show different values of PED
★ understand the determinants of PED
★ explain the relationship between price changes, consumer spending and revenue
★ demonstrate the significance of PED for decision-makers.

Price elasticity of demand

The law of demand (see Chapter 6) states that as the price of a good or service increases, the quantity demanded will tend to fall. However, the degree of responsiveness of change in the quantity demanded may vary depending on the customer's ability and willingness to pay different prices. For example, a rise in the price of a product with plenty of substitutes (such as bananas, greeting cards or chocolate bars) will have a larger impact on its quantity demanded than a product that has fewer substitutes (such as petrol, toothpaste or haircuts).

▲ Demand for soft drinks is price elastic because there are many substitute products

Definitions

Price elasticity of demand (PED) measures the extent to which the quantity demanded for a product changes due to a change in its price.

Price inelastic demand describes demand for a product that is relatively unresponsive to changes in price, mainly because of the lack of substitutes for the product.

Price elastic demand describes demand for a product that is relatively responsive to changes in price, usually due to substitutes being readily available.

Price elasticity of demand (PED) measures the degree of responsiveness of the quantity demanded of a product following a change in its price. If a price change causes a relatively small change in the quantity demanded, then demand is said to be **price inelastic** – that is, buyers are not highly responsive to changes in price. For example, if the price of rice increases slightly, it is unlikely to have a large effect on the demand for rice in countries like China, India, Bangladesh, Indonesia and Vietnam.

By contrast, demand is said to be **price elastic** if there is a relatively large change in the quantity demanded of a product following a price change – that is, buyers are very responsive to changes in price. For example, a small rise in the price of Pepsi Cola is likely to reduce the quantity demanded quite drastically as consumers switch to buying rival brands such as Coca-Cola.

▲ The demand for rice is highly price inelastic in many countries.

Practice question: structured question

Explain whether the price elasticity of demand (PED) for the following products is likely to be price elastic or price inelastic. Justify your answers.

a	Pineapples	[4]
b	Tobacco products	[4]
c	Overseas holidays	[4]
d	International GCSE textbooks	[4]

Calculation of price elasticity of demand

Price elasticity of demand is calculated using the formula:

$$\frac{\text{Percentage change in quantity demanded}}{\text{Percentage change in price}}$$

or annotated as:

$$\frac{\%\Delta\, Q_D}{\%\Delta\, P}$$

For example, if a cinema increases its average ticket price from $10 to $11 and this leads to demand falling from 3500 to 3325 customers per week, then the PED for cinema tickets is calculated as:

» Percentage change in quantity demanded = [(3325 − 3500)/3500] × 100 = −5%
» Percentage change in price = [(11 − 10/10)] × 100 = +10%
» PED = −5/10 = −0.5

⊙ Worked example

Calculating PED

Assume the demand for football match tickets at $50 is 50,000 per week. If the football club raises its price to $60 per ticket and demand subsequently falls to 45,000 per week, what is the value of price elasticity of demand?

→ First, calculate the percentage change in the quantity demanded: demand falls by 10 per cent from 50,000 to 45,000 match tickets per week.

→ Next, calculate the percentage change in the price of match tickets: prices rise by 20 per cent from $50 to $60 per match ticket.

→ Then, substitute these figures into the PED formula: 10/20 = –0.5.

As the PED for match tickets is less than 1 (ignoring the minus sign), the demand for match tickets is price inelastic, i.e. football fans are not very responsive to the increase in match ticket prices. Subsequently, there is a smaller fall in the quantity demanded compared to the price rise.

Interpretation of the significance of the PED value

So what does a PED value of –0.5 actually mean? The above example suggests that the demand for cinema tickets is *price inelastic* – that is, relatively unresponsive to changes in price. This is because a 10 per cent increase in the price (from $10 to $11) only caused quantity demanded to fall by 5 per cent (from 3500 tickets per week to 3325).

The value of PED is negative due to the **law of demand** (see Chapter 6) – an increase in the price of a product will tend to reduce its quantity demanded. The inverse relationship between price and quantity demanded applies in the case of a price reduction – a price fall tends to lead to an increase in the quantity demanded.

The calculation of PED generally has two possible outcomes:

» If the PED for a product is less than 1 (ignoring the minus sign), then demand is **price inelastic** – that is, demand is relatively unresponsive to changes in price. This is because the percentage change in quantity demanded is smaller than the percentage change in the price (see Figure 10.1).

As the price rises from P_1 to P_2, the quantity demanded falls by a smaller proportion from Q_1 to Q_2. Examples of products with low PED are salt, alcohol, electricity, cigarettes and nail clippers.

▲ **Figure 10.1** A price inelastic demand curve

» If the PED for a product is greater than 1 (ignoring the minus sign), then demand is **price elastic** – that is, demand is relatively responsive to changes in price. This is because the percentage change in quantity demanded is larger than the percentage change in the price of the product (see Figure 10.2).

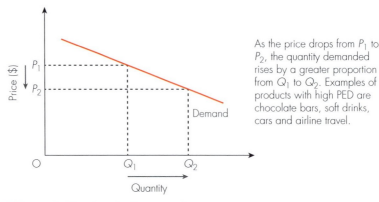

As the price drops from P_1 to P_2, the quantity demanded rises by a greater proportion from Q_1 to Q_2. Examples of products with high PED are chocolate bars, soft drinks, cars and airline travel.

▲ **Figure 10.2** A price elastic demand curve

However, there are three special cases which are theoretical possibilities:

» If the PED value for a product is equal to 0, then demand is **perfectly price inelastic** – that is, a change in price has no impact on the quantity demanded. This suggests that there is absolutely no substitute for such a product, so the quantity demanded is independent of the price (see Figure 10.3).

Definitions

Perfectly price inelastic demand means that the quantity demanded of a product is independent of its price.
Perfectly price elastic demand means that consumers are indefinitely responsive to a change in the price.

As the price increases from P_1 to P_2, the quantity demanded remains unchanged at Q_e. Realistically, demand will never be completely independent of the price level, but the demand for prescription drugs, anti-venom or water would be very price inelastic.

▲ **Figure 10.3** The perfectly price inelastic demand curve

» If the PED value for a product is equal to infinity (∞) then demand is **perfectly price elastic** – that is, a change in price leads to zero quantity demanded. This suggests that customers switch to buying other substitute products if suppliers raise their price (see Figure 10.4).

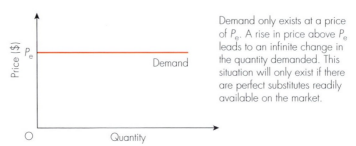

Demand only exists at a price of P_e. A rise in price above P_e leads to an infinite change in the quantity demanded. This situation will only exist if there are perfect substitutes readily available on the market.

▲ **Figure 10.4** The perfectly price elastic demand curve

Definition

Unitary elastic demand occurs when the percentage change in the quantity demanded is proportional to the change in the price, so there is no change in the sales revenue.

» If the PED value for a product is equal to 1 (ignoring the minus sign), then demand is said to be **unitary elastic** – that is, the percentage change in the quantity demanded is proportional to the change in the price (see Figure 10.5).

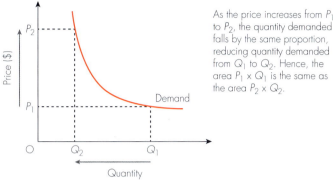

As the price increases from P_1 to P_2, the quantity demanded falls by the same proportion, reducing quantity demanded from Q_1 to Q_2. Hence, the area $P_1 \times Q_1$ is the same as the area $P_2 \times Q_2$.

▲ **Figure 10.5** The unitary price elasticity demand curve

Activity

Many governments around the world regularly raise the taxes on tobacco, alcohol and petrol. In small groups, discuss the economic reasons for doing so. Use the theory of price elasticity of demand (PED) in your answers.

Practice questions: structured questions

1 Assume the price of a sack of rice falls from $25 to $24, resulting in an increase in quantity demanded from 850 sacks to 875 sacks per month.
   a Calculate the value of price elasticity of demand for the product. [2]
   b Explain your answer. [2]
2 Explain two reasons why the demand for rice is price inelastic in countries like India, Vietnam and China. [4]

Determinants of price elasticity of demand

There are several interlinked determinants of the PED for a good or service. These factors include the following:

» **Substitution** – this is the key determinant of the PED value for a product. In general, the greater the number and availability of close substitutes there are for a good or service, the higher the value of its PED will tend to be. This is because such products are easily replaced if the price increases, due to the large number of close substitutes that are readily available. By contrast, products with few substitutes, such as toothpicks, private education and prescribed medicines, have relatively price inelastic demand.

» **Income** – the proportion of a consumer's income that is spent on a product also affects the value of its PED. If the price of a box of toothpicks or a packet of salt were to double (100 per cent increase), the percentage change in price would be so insignificant to the consumer's overall income that the quantity demanded would be hardly affected, if at all. By contrast, if the price of an overseas cruise holiday were to rise by 20 per cent from $12,000 to $14,400 per person, this would discourage many customers because the extra $2,400 per ticket has a larger impact on a person's disposable income (even though the percentage increase in the price of a cruise holiday is much lower than that of a box of toothpicks or a packet of salt). Therefore, the larger the proportion of income that the price of a product represents, the greater the value of its PED tends to be. Of course, those on extremely high levels of income (such as Mark Zuckerberg, Jeff Bezos and Larry Page – currently three of the richest men on the planet – and Françoise Bettencourt Meyers, the world's richest woman) are probably not responsive to any change in the market price of goods and services!

» **Necessity** – the degree of necessity of a good or service will affect the value of its PED. Products that are regarded as essential (such as food, fuel, medicines, housing and transportation) tend to be relatively price inelastic because households need these goods and services, and so will continue to purchase them even if their prices rise. By contrast, the demand for luxury products (such as Gucci suits, Chanel handbags and Omega watches) is price elastic as these are not necessities for most households. The degree of necessity also depends on the timeframe in question. For example, demand for fresh flowers on Valentine's Day and Mother's Day is highly price inelastic compared to other days. Many countries operate public transport systems that charge more for travelling during peak time. This is partly due to overcrowding problems during such times, but also because the transport operators know that peak-time travel is more of a necessity than off-peak travel.

▲ Demand for fresh flowers on special days is relatively price inelastic compared with other days

» **Habits, addictions, fashions and tastes** – if a product is habit forming (such as tobacco) or highly fashionable, its PED value tends to be relatively price inelastic. Similarly, people who are extremely devoted to a particular hobby (such as sports or music) are more willing to pay, even at higher prices. Hence, the demand from these people is less sensitive to changes in price.

» **Advertising and brand loyalty** – marketing can have a huge impact on the buying habits of customers. Effective advertising campaigns for certain products not only help to shift the demand curve outwards to the right, but can also reduce the PED value for the product. Customers who are loyal to particular brands are less sensitive to a change in their prices, partly because these brands are demanded out of habit and personal preference – in other words, they are the default choice over rival brands. Examples of brands with a loyal customer following include Coca-Cola, HSBC, Apple, Samsung, Chanel, Toyota and Tesla.

» **Time** – the period of time under consideration can affect the value of PED because people need time to change their spending habits and behavioural norms. Over time, they can adjust their demand based on more permanent price changes by seeking out alternative products. For example, parents with children in private fee-paying schools are unlikely to withdraw their children from school if these establishments raise school fees because this would be very disruptive to their children's education. Similarly, owners of private motor vehicles are not likely to get rid of their vehicles simply because of higher fuel prices. However, if there is a continual increase in prices over time, both parents and vehicle owners may seek alternatives. Hence, demand tends to be more price elastic in the long run.

» **Durability** – some products, such as fresh milk, are perishable (do not last very long) but need to be replaced, so they will continue to be bought even if prices rise. By contrast, if the price of consumer durable products (such as household furniture, televisions or smartphones) increases, then households may decide to postpone replacing these items due to the high prices involved in such purchases. Therefore, the more durable a product is, the more price elastic its demand tends to be.

▲ Even if prices rise, people will tend to carry on buying perishable products like milk

>> **The costs of switching** – there may be costs involved for customers who wish to switch between brands or products. If there are high switching costs, the demand for the product is less sensitive to changes in price – that is, it tends to be relatively price inelastic. For example, manufacturers of smartphones and laptops make it more difficult for their customers to switch between rival brands by supplying different power chargers, accessories and subscription software packages. Similarly, subscribers to broadband, Wi-Fi and television streaming services can be bound by lengthy contracts, so that switching between rival brands or service providers is less easy. Such barriers to switching therefore make customers less responsive to higher product prices.

>> **The breadth of definition of the product** – if a good or service is very broadly defined (such as food rather than fruit, meat, apples or salmon), then demand will be more price inelastic. For example, there is clearly no real substitute for food or housing, so demand for these products will be extremely price inelastic. However, it is perhaps more useful to measure the PED value for specific brands or products, such as carbonated soft drinks and textbooks.

Practice question: multiple choice

The price elasticity of demand for a product is known to be –0.3.
The product is **most** likely to be: [1]

A breakfast cereal
B electricity
C running shoes
D soft drinks

Activity

Volkswagen (VW) is a Germany-based multinational motor manufacturer. It produces passenger cars, trucks and light commercial vehicles such as buses. VW also owns luxury brands Audi, Bentley, Lamborghini and Porsche. It is one of the world's largest motor vehicle manufacturers. VW's best-selling cars are the Golf and Polo.

Discuss how the price elasticity of demand (PED) and its determinants can help to explain why Volkswagen is one of the world's largest motor vehicle manufacturers.

PED, consumer expenditure and firms' revenue

Knowledge of the price elasticity of demand for a product can be used to assess the effect of price changes on the amount spent by consumers and revenue raised due to changes in price. **Sales revenue** (sometimes referred to as **total revenue**) is the amount of money received by a firm from the sale of a good or service. It is calculated by multiplying the price charged (P) for each product by the quantity demanded (Q):

Sales revenue = Price × Quantity demanded = P × Q

Note that this is not the same as **profit**, which is the numerical difference between a firm's total sales revenues and its total costs of production.

For example, if a retailer sells 5000 laptops at $700 each, then its sales revenue is $3.5 million. Suppose the retailer reduces its price to $650 and quantity demanded rises to 5500 units in the following quarter. Was this a good business decision? A quick calculation of PED reveals that the demand for the laptops is relatively price elastic:

» Percentage change in quantity demanded = (5500 − 5000)/5000 = +10%
» Percentage change in price = ($650 − $700)/$700 = −7.14%
» Thus, PED = −1.4

This means the demand for the laptops is price elastic. Hence a fall in price causes a relatively large increase in the quantity demanded, so sales revenues should increase. This can be checked as follows:

Original sales revenue	= $700 × 5000	= $3,500,000
New sales revenue	= $650 × 5500	= $3,575,000
Difference in sales revenue	= $3.575m − $3.5m	= +$75,000

Given that demand for laptops in the above example is price elastic, a reduction in price was a sensible business decision. Therefore, it can be seen that knowledge of PED for a product can inform firms about their pricing strategy in order to maximise sales revenues.

The relationship between PED and revenue is summarised in Table 10.1 and Figures 10.6 and 10.7.

Table 10.1 The relationship between PED and revenues

Price change	Inelastic demand	Unitary demand	Elastic demand
Increase price	Revenues rise	No change in revenues	Revenues fall
Reduce price	Revenues fall	No change in revenues	Revenues rise

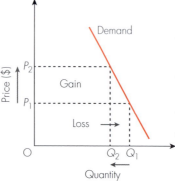

In this case, the demand curve is relatively price inelastic (rather unresponsive to changes in price). If the firm raises its price from P_1 to P_2, the percentage increase in price is far greater than the subsequent fall in demand from Q_1 to Q_2. Hence, the firm's revenue will increase (as the area of the gain in revenue, due to the higher price, is larger than that for the loss due to lower quantity demanded). The opposite is true for a price fall.

▲ **Figure 10.6** Price inelastic demand and revenue

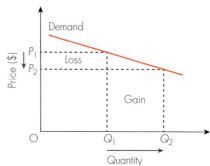

In this case, the demand curve is relatively price elastic (somewhat responsive to changes in price). A fall in price from P_1 to P_2 will therefore lead to a net gain in revenue. This is because the area of the loss (due to the lower price) is less than the area of the gain (from the higher quantity demanded). By contrast, if the price were to increase, customers would simply switch to substitutes, thereby generating a net loss in revenue.

▲ **Figure 10.7** Price elastic demand and revenue

The significance of price elasticity of demand for decision-makers

Knowledge of PED has implications for decision-making by consumers, workers, producers (firms) and the government. Essentially, it can provide valuable information about how the demand for different products is likely to change if prices are adjusted. This information can be used in several ways, such as the following:

» **Helping producers to decide on their pricing strategy** – for example, a business with price inelastic demand for its products is likely to increase prices, knowing that the quantity demanded will hardly be affected. Therefore, the business will benefit from higher sales revenue by selling its products at a higher price (see Figure 10.6).

» **Predicting the impact on producers following changes in the exchange rate** (see Chapter 35) – for instance, firms that rely on exports will generally benefit from lower exchange rates (as the price of exports becomes cheaper) and thus they become more price competitive. This assumes that the PED value for exports is price elastic, of course.

» **Price discrimination** – this occurs when firms are able to charge different customers different prices for essentially the same product because of differences in their PED. For example, theme park operators charge adult visitors different prices from children and they also offer discounts for families and annual pass holders.

» **Deciding which products to impose sales taxes on** – taxing products that are price inelastic ensures the government can collect large sums of tax revenue without seriously affecting the overall demand for the product (so there is minimal impact on revenues for firms and jobs for workers). Producers can also decide how much of the tax can be passed on to customers. For example, products such as alcohol, tobacco and petrol are price inelastic in demand, so taxes on these products can quite easily be passed on to consumers without much impact on the quantity demanded.

» **Determining taxation policies** – knowledge of PED can help governments to determine taxation policies. For example, the government can impose heavy taxes on **demerit goods** (see Chapter 13), such as petrol and cigarettes, knowing that the demand for these products is price inelastic. As demerit goods are harmful to society as a whole, the government needs to impose very high levels of taxes on such products in order to reduce the quantity demanded.

» **Wage negotiations** – workers may consider PED when negotiating wages. For example, if the demand for the product they produce is highly price inelastic, meaning consumers are indifferent to price changes, then a larger wage increase can be negotiated as any increase in price is unlikely to lead to a significant fall in quantity demanded.

Definition

Price discrimination occurs when firms charge different customers different prices for essentially the same product due to differences in PED.

▲ The different prices that theme parks charge for essentially the same service is explained by PED

Practice question: structured question

Sharma Fabrics sells 1350 units of wool per month at $4.00 each. Following an increase in price to $4.60 per unit, the firm discovers that the quantity demanded falls to 1215 units per month.

a Calculate the price elasticity of demand for wool sold at Sharma Fabrics. [2]
b Calculate the change in the total revenue following the increase in price of wool. [2]
c Explain how knowledge of price elasticity of demand can be of use to Sharma Fabrics. [4]

❓ Chapter review questions

1 What is meant by price elasticity of demand (PED) and how is it calculated?
2 Why should firms raise prices for products with price inelastic demand, and reduce prices for products with price elastic demand?
3 Use a diagram to show the difference between perfectly price elastic demand, unitary PED and perfectly price inelastic demand.
4 What are the key determinants of PED?
5 How might knowledge of PED be of value to consumers?
6 How might knowledge of PED be of value to producers (firms)?
7 How might knowledge of PED be of value to workers?
8 How might knowledge of PED be of value to the government?

Revision checklist

✔ Price elasticity of demand (PED) measures the degree of responsiveness of the quantity demanded of a product following a change in its price.

✔ PED is calculated using the formula: $\%\Delta Q_D / \%\Delta P$.

✔ Demand is price elastic if there is a relatively large change in the quantity demanded of a product following a relatively small change in its price. Hence, if demand is price elastic, firms will tend to reduce prices to increase sales revenue.

✔ Demand is price inelastic if there is a relatively small change in the quantity demanded for a product following a relatively large change in its price. Hence, if demand is price inelastic, firms will tend to raise prices to increase sales revenue.

✔ Determinants of PED include time, habits and tastes, income, the degree of necessity and the availability of substitutes.

✔ Knowledge of PED enables producers to determine their pricing strategies (to maximise sales revenues) and governments to determine their tax policies (to maximise tax revenues).

✔ Workers can use their knowledge of PED in wage negotiations.

✔ Knowledge of PED also enables firms to determine whether they can use price discrimination (charge different customers different prices for essentially the same product because of differences in their PED).

11 Price elasticity of supply

This chapter will cover:

★ a definition of price elasticity of supply (PES)
★ how to calculate PES
★ how to draw and interpret supply curve diagrams to show different PES
★ how to interpret the significance of PES values: perfectly inelastic, inelastic, unitary elastic, elastic and perfectly elastic
★ the main determinants of PES.

Defining price elasticity of supply

Definition

Price elasticity of supply (PES) measures the degree of responsiveness of the quantity supplied of a product following a change in its price. Supply is said to be **price elastic** if producers can quite easily increase supply without a time delay if there is an increase in the price of the product. Supply is **price inelastic** if firms find it difficult to change production in a given time period due to a change in the market price.

Price elasticity of supply (PES) measures the degree of responsiveness of the quantity supplied of a product following a change in its price. Supply is said to be **price elastic** if producers can quite easily increase supply without a time delay if there is an increase in the price of the product. This can help to give such firms a competitive advantage as they are able to respond quickly to changes in price. By contrast, supply is **price inelastic** if firms find it difficult to change production in a given time period due to a change in the market price.

Calculating price elasticity of supply

Price elasticity of supply is calculated using the formula:

$$\frac{\text{Percentage change in quantity supplied}}{\text{Percentage change in price}}$$

or annotated as:

$$\frac{\%\Delta Q_S}{\%\Delta P}$$

For example, if the market price of beans increases from $2 per kilo to $2.20 per kilo, causing quantity supplied to rise from 10,000 kilos to 10,500 kilos per week, then the PES is calculated as:

» Percentage change in quantity supplied = (10,500 − 10,000)/10,000 = +5%
» Percentage change in price = ($2.20 − $2)/$2 = +10%
» PES = +5%/+10% = 0.5

What this means is that the supply of beans is only slightly affected by the change in price – that is, supply is relatively price inelastic. Note that the value of PES is positive due to the law of supply – an increase in price tends to increase the quantity supplied (and vice versa).

Practice question: structured question

Suppose in Country X that higher demand for mangoes causes an increase in the price from $1 to $1.45 per unit. This results in an increase in quantity supplied from 110 kilos to 120 kilos each month.

a Calculate the price elasticity of supply (PES) for mangoes in Country X.　[2]
b Explain one reason for the value of PES for mangoes in Country X.　[2]

Interpreting supply curve diagrams and price elasticity of supply

The value of PES reveals the degree to which the quantity supplied of a product responds to changes in price. The calculation of PES generally has two possible outcomes:

» If the PES value is greater than 1, supply is **price elastic** – that is, quantity supplied is responsive to changes in price. This is because the percentage change in quantity supplied is greater than the percentage change in price (see Figure 11.1).

» If the PES value is less than 1, supply is **price inelastic** – that is, quantity supplied is relatively unresponsive to changes in price. This is because the percentage change in quantity supplied is less than the percentage change in price (see Figure 11.2).

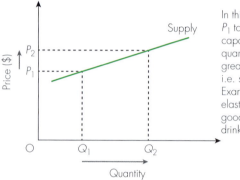

In this case, when price rises from P_1 to P_2, there is plenty of spare capacity for the firm, so the quantity supplied can increase by a greater proportion from Q_1 to Q_2, i.e. supply is price elastic. Examples of products with price elastic supply are mass-produced goods such as carbonated soft drinks and toothpaste.

▲ **Figure 11.1** A price elastic supply curve

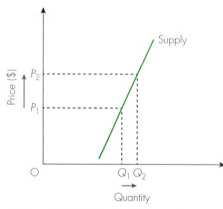

In this case, when price rises from P_1 to P_2, there is very little spare capacity for the firm, so the quantity supplied can only rise by a smaller proportion from Q_1 to Q_2. Examples are fresh fruit and vegetables that take time to grow (so supply is relatively unresponsive to changes in price).

▲ **Figure 11.2** A price inelastic supply curve

However, there are three special cases which are theoretical possibilities for PES:

» If the PES of a product is equal to 0, then supply is **perfectly price inelastic** – that is, a change in price has no impact on the quantity supplied. This suggests that there is absolutely no spare capacity for suppliers to raise output, irrespective of increases in price (see Figure 11.3).

» If the PES of a product is equal to infinity (∞), then supply is **perfectly price elastic** – that is, the quantity supplied can change without any corresponding change in price. For example, a software developer selling products online can very easily increase supply to match higher levels of demand, without any impact on the price level. Due to the spare capacity that exists, suppliers are able to raise output at the current price level (see Figure 11.4).

» If the PES for a product is equal to 1, then supply has **unitary price elasticity** – that is, the percentage change in the quantity supplied matches the percentage change in price (see Figure 11.5). Any upward-sloping supply curve that starts at the origin will have unitary price elasticity.

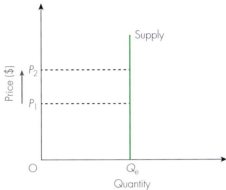

Here, supply is perfectly price inelastic at Q_e. Irrespective of price changes, the firm can only supply a maximum of Q_e, so changes in price have no impact on the quantity supplied, i.e. PES = 0. An example is a football stadium or a concert hall that cannot accommodate more than the seating capacity.

▲ **Figure 11.3** The perfectly price inelastic supply curve

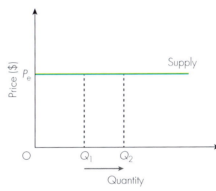

Here, supply is perfectly price elastic at a price of P_e. For example, Duracell might have a huge stock of batteries, so any increase in demand will simply result in more Duracell batteries being sold, without the price being raised. Hence, as quantity supplied can increase from Q_1 to Q_2 irrespective of a price change, the PES = ∞.

▲ **Figure 11.4** The perfectly price elastic supply curve

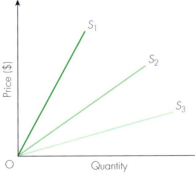

Any supply curve that starts at the origin (such as S_1, S_2 or S_3) has a PES value equal to 1. This theoretical outcome means that a change in price causes the same proportional change in quantity supplied.

▲ **Figure 11.5** The unitary price elasticity supply curve

Study tip

In reality, supply curves are likely to be non-linear, so will have a different PES value at different points. Supply is more price elastic at lower prices and more price inelastic at higher prices.

Activity

Discuss in pairs why the price elasticity of supply of the following products will differ:

a smartphones
b organic vegetables
c fresh flowers

d hotel buildings and related facilities
e Ferrari cars

Practice question: structured question

Angry Birds is a highly popular video game created by Finnish company Rovio in December 2009 for the iPhone. Since then, over 300 million customers have paid $0.99 each to download the game from Apple's App Store. The game has become available for other platforms such as Android and Windows operating systems and available for both video games consoles and personal computers. Rovio has since launched variations of the video game, such as *Angry Birds Seasons*, *Angry Birds Rio*, *Angry Birds Space* and *Angry Birds Star Wars*. According to its website, in 2022 more than 200 million people played *Angry Birds* every month, and by July 2015 the *Angry Birds* games had been downloaded over 3 billion times across all platforms.

a Explain, with the use of an appropriate diagram, why the high level of demand for *Angry Birds* games has no effect on the selling price. [6]

b Analyse, in the context of the case study, the significance of the value of PES. [6]

Determinants of price elasticity of supply

There are several interlinked determinants of the PES for a product. These factors include the following:

» **The degree of spare capacity** – if a firm has plenty of spare capacity, then it can increase supply easily, without increasing its costs of production. This means that supply is relatively price elastic. For example, Coca-Cola's bottling plants can produce thousands of bottles per minute, so it is very easy for the world's largest beverage company with plenty of spare production capacity to respond to changes in price. In general, the supply of goods and services is highly price elastic during an economic recession (see Chapter 26) when there are spare (unused) resources such as land, capital and labour.

» **The level of stocks** – if a firm has unused raw materials, components and finished products (collectively known as **stocks** or **inventories**) that are available for use, then the firm is more able to respond quickly to a change in price, as it can supply these stocks on to the market. Not all inventories are sold to consumers – raw materials and components (parts such as gearboxes and motors for cars) are used in the production process. In addition, some types of stock (such as pencils and ball bearings) are easier to store than others (such as fresh milk or organic vegetables), so it will be easier to increase their supply if prices increase. This means that the higher the level of stocks of finished goods (such as cars) that are ready for sale, the more price elastic supply tends to be.

» **The number of producers in the industry** – the more suppliers of a product there are in the industry, the easier it tends to be for firms to increase their output in response to a price increase. For example, there is plenty of competition in the restaurant trade, so suppliers will be highly responsive to increases in price. Hence, the greater the number of firms in an industry, the more price elastic supply tends to be. By contrast, high barriers to entry in the pharmaceutical industry mean that there are very few suppliers in the industry, so supply tends to be price inelastic.

Definition

Stocks (or **inventories**) are the raw materials, components and finished goods (ready for sale) used in the production process.

»» **The time period** – in the short run, most firms are not able to change their factor inputs, such as the size of their workforce or the fixed amount of capital equipment they employ. For example, in agriculture and horticulture, the supply of fresh fruit and vegetables is dependent on the time it takes to grow and harvest the products and climatic conditions beyond the control of the suppliers. Hence, supply is less responsive to changes in price in the short run. Supply is more likely to be price elastic in the long run because firms can adjust their levels of production according to price changes in the market.

»» **The ease and cost of factor substitution** – this refers to how easy and affordable it is for firms to replace one factor of production (such as labour or capital) with another in the production process. If capital and labour resources are occupationally mobile, this means they can be substituted easily in the production process. For example, capital is occupationally mobile in a printing press that can switch production quite easily between printing textbooks, magazines, trade journals, calendars and greetings cards. This means the ease of factor substitution in the printing press makes supply highly price elastic. By contrast, the PES for a product where capital equipment and labour cannot easily be switched, as the production process is inflexible, will be very low.

Activity

With the use of an appropriate diagram, explain whether the PES of the following products is relatively price elastic or price inelastic in supply.

a Bananas
b Fresh bread
c Computers
d Coal

? Chapter review questions

1 What is meant by PES?
2 How is PES calculated?
3 Use a diagram to show the difference between perfectly price elastic supply, unitary PES and perfectly price inelastic supply.
4 Use a diagram to distinguish between price elastic PES and price inelastic PES.
5 What are the key determinants of PES?
6 If a product has a PES value of 0, what does this actually mean? What about PES = 1 and PES = ∞?
7 What is the difference between perfectly elastic and perfectly inelastic supply?
8 Why is supply generally less responsive to changes in price in the short term?
9 Why is supply generally more responsive to changes in price in the long term?

Revision checklist

✔ Price elasticity of supply (PES) measures the degree of responsiveness of the quantity supplied of a product following a change in its price.
✔ PES is calculated using the formula: $\%\Delta Q_S/\%\Delta P$.
✔ PES is positive due to the law of supply – that is, the positive relationship between price and quantity supplied.
✔ If PES is greater than 1, supply is price elastic – that is, quantity supplied is relatively responsive to changes in price.
✔ If PES is less than 1, supply is price inelastic – that is, quantity supplied is relatively unresponsive to changes in price.
✔ If the PES of a product is equal to 0, supply is perfectly price inelastic – a change in price has no impact on the quantity supplied.
✔ If the PES of a product is equal to infinity (∞), supply is perfectly price elastic – the quantity supplied can change without any corresponding change in price.
✔ Determinants of PES include spare capacity, inventory (stock) levels, the number of firms in the industry, the ease and the cost of factor substitution, and the time period.

12 Market economic system

This chapter will cover:

★ the market economic system
★ the advantages of the market economic system
★ the disadvantages of the market economic system.

Defining the market economic system

An **economic system** describes the way in which an economy is organised and run. This includes alternative views of how to best allocate scarce resources. A key question in economics is the extent to which a government should intervene in the economy or leave economic agents (households and firms) to operate freely.

There are two main types of economic systems.

Definition

A **market economy** relies on the market forces of demand and supply (in the private sector) to allocate resources with minimal government intervention.

1 **Market economy** – this economic system relies on the market forces of demand and supply (in the private sector) to allocate resources. There is minimal government intervention. Hence, it is also known as the **free market economic system**. In this system, economic agents are driven by incentives, such as wages, salaries or profits. Singapore, Switzerland and Ireland are examples of market economies.

▲ Singapore is widely accepted as the world's freest market economy

2 **Mixed economy** – as its name suggests, this economic system is a combination of government-controlled resource allocation with the market economic system. Some resources are owned and controlled by private individuals and firms, while others are owned and controlled by the government (public sector). Examples of mixed economies are Belgium, Indonesia and Mexico. The USA is often given as an example of running a market economic system. However, in reality the state and federal governments do get involved in providing some

basic services. In effect, the USA is a mixed economic system (see Chapter 14) but with a much larger private sector than many other nations.

The market economy is central to supply-side economics (see Chapter 25) and the associated gains from free international trade (see Chapter 33).

The Heritage Foundation compiles an annual index of economic freedom for all countries (see Table 12.1).

Table 12.1 Top ten countries in the index of economic freedom world rankings, 2023

Country	Ranking	Economic freedom scoring key
Singapore	83.5	80–100 Free
Switzerland	83.0	70–79.9 Mostly free
Ireland	82.6	60–69.9 Moderately free
Taiwan (Republic of China)	80.0	50–59.9 Mostly unfree
Luxembourg	79.2	0–49.9 Repressed
New Zealand	77.8	
Denmark	77.8	
Estonia	77.8	
Sweden	77.5	
Norway	77.5	

Source: The Index of Economic Freedom, Heritage Foundation, October 2023, Heritage Foundation website

According to the Heritage Foundation, there is a high correlation between a country's level of economic freedom and its standard of living (see Chapter 29). Its research data suggest that market economies substantially outperform others in terms of economic growth, healthcare, education, protection of the environment and the reduction of poverty.

> **Activity**
>
> Refer to the countries in Table 12.1. Research the latest data on the real gross domestic product (GDP) per capita of these countries. Discuss whether there is a correlation between real GDP per capita and the level of economic freedom in these countries.

Advantages of the market economic system

The market economic system offers the following advantages:

» **Efficiency** – competition helps to ensure private individuals and firms pay attention to what consumers want. This helps to stimulate innovation, thereby making market economies more responsive and dynamic.
» **Freedom of choice** – individuals can choose which goods and services to purchase and which careers to pursue. They are not restricted by excessive government regulations.
» **Incentives** – the profit motive for firms and the possibility for individuals to earn unlimited wealth create incentives to work hard. This helps to boost productivity, economic growth and living standards in the country.

Disadvantages of the market economic system

The market economic system suffers from the following disadvantages:

» **Income and wealth inequalities** – in a market economic system, the rich have far more choice and economic freedom. Production is geared to meet the needs and wants of the wealthy. Thus, basic services for the poorer members of society may be neglected.

» **Environmental issues** – there are negative consequences of economic prosperity under the market economic system. These include resource depletion (especially of non-renewable resources), pollution and climate change.

» **Social hardship** – the absence of government control means that public goods (see Chapter 13), such as street lighting, public roads and national defence, may not be provided. Poverty relief in society might only be done through voluntary charities. This creates social hardship for those who have limited resources and lack economic opportunities.

» **Wasteful competition** – competitive pressures can mean that firms use up unnecessary resources, such as excess packaging and advertising clutter, to gain competitive advantages over their rivals. Consumers might be exploited by marketing tactics, such as pester power (see the activity below). The lack of government involvement could also mean that products are less safe for consumers.

> ### Activity
>
> **Pester power** is the marketing term used to describe the ability that children in some societies have to persuade their parents to buy certain items.
>
> **a** Use the internet to find examples of pester power and be prepared to share your findings with the class.

Study tip

To better understand the contents of this topic, also read Chapters 13 (Market failure) and 14 (Mixed economic system).

Practice questions: multiple choice

1 Which economic system enables individuals and firms to pursue their own best interests? [1]
   A market economic system
   B market failure
   C market structures
   D mixed economic system

2 What is an advantage of the market economic system? [1]
   A government provision of essential services
   B incentives to work
   C maximum prices
   D minimum prices

Chapter review questions

1. What is meant by an economic system?
2. What are the two main types of economic system?
3. What are the key features of the market economic system?
4. What are the advantages of operating a market economy?
5. What are the disadvantages of operating a market economy?

Revision checklist

- ✔ An economic system refers to the way in which an economy is organised in terms of how it best allocates scarce resources.
- ✔ There are two main types of economic system: a market economy and a mixed economy.
- ✔ A market economy relies on the market forces of demand and supply (in the private sector) to allocate resources, with minimal government intervention. In this system, economic agents are driven by incentives, such as wages, salaries or profits.
- ✔ Advantages of the market economy include efficiency in the use and allocation of resources, freedom of choice and incentives to work.
- ✔ Disadvantages of the market economy include income and wealth inequalities, environmental degradation, depletion of non-renewable resources, social hardship and wasteful competition.

13 Market failure

This chapter will cover:

★ a definition of the concept of market failure
★ a definition of terms associated with market failure
★ the causes of market failure
★ the consequences of market failure.

Defining market failure

Market failure occurs when the production and/or consumption of a good or service causes positive or negative side-effects to a third party not involved in the economic activity. In other words, the market forces of demand and supply fail to allocate resources efficiently. For example, in a free market the following situations may arise:

» Education and healthcare services are only provided to those who are willing and able to pay, despite the benefits these services bring to society as a whole. This means poorer people do not benefit.
» Street lighting and public roads are underprovided as producers cannot exclude those who do not pay from benefiting once these services are provided.
» Products or activities that can be harmful, such as cigarettes, are overprovided as there is a lack of government intervention to regulate production and consumption levels in these markets.
» Activities such as extracting oil and constructing office buildings cause damage to the natural physical environment and the loss of ecosystems.
» Monopolists (see Chapter 21) can abuse their market power by charging customers higher prices or supplying lower quantities than if they were faced with competition.

Private and social costs

The **private costs** of production and consumption are the actual costs of an individual firm, household or government. For example, the owner of a car pays for the insurance, licence, fuel and cost of purchasing the car.

The **external costs** are the negative spillover effects (or side-effects) of production or consumption incurred by third parties for which no compensation is paid. For example, a car owner does not pay for the cost of the congestion and air pollution created when driving the car. This is an example of market failure as the private costs (of driving) do not represent the true costs (of driving) to society. The true cost of an economic activity is called the **social cost**.

Social costs = Private costs + External costs

For example, in 2023 methane emissions from agriculture and energy production caused about 30 per cent of the rise in global temperatures leading to climate change.

Source: 'Understanding methane emissions', by Global Methane Tracker, IEA.org website

---

Definitions

Market failure occurs when the market forces of demand and supply are unsuccessful in allocating resources efficiently and cause external costs or external benefits.

Private costs of production and consumption are the actual costs for a firm, individual or government.

External costs are the negative side-effects of production or consumption incurred by third parties, for which no compensation is paid to these third parties.

Social costs are the true (or full) costs of consumption or production to society as a whole, i.e. the sum of private costs and external costs.

Methane emissions are becoming an increasing problem and create external costs. Other examples of external costs are:

» air pollution caused by fumes from a factory
» noise pollution from a construction site
» cigarette smoke
» advertising clutter (which causes visual blight, i.e. an unsightly landscape)
» litter.

▲ Litter is an example of an external cost

Private and social benefits

Private benefits are the positive aspects of production and consumption experienced by an individual firm, household or government. For example, a car owner gains the benefit of driving the car and owning it as a means of private transportation. Similarly, a person who owns a garden enjoys the personal benefits of having green space and plants, flowers and possibly vegetables.

External benefits are the positive side-effects of production or consumption experienced by third parties for which no money is paid by the beneficiary. For example, the sight and smell of a well-kept garden might give pleasure to a neighbour or a person walking by. The flowers in the garden attract bees and other insects, which act as pollinators and are essential for biodiversity. The plants and trees also absorb carbon dioxide and therefore are good for the natural environment. Other examples of services with external benefits are education, training, law enforcement and vaccinations.

When a person has a vaccination against tuberculosis, for example, they receive the private benefit of being immune to the disease. However, the individual getting the vaccination also helps to protect third parties and society as a whole from this highly contagious illness. To eradicate diseases, many governments make it a legal requirement for children to be vaccinated against certain diseases before they can start school. Many governments provide vaccines free of charge to children and the elderly due to the external benefits the vaccinations bring.

Vaccination programmes are an example of market failure, as they offer external benefits to society. If vaccinations were left to the choice of individuals, in a free market, they would be under-consumed. This is mainly due to the price that

Definitions

Private benefits are the positive aspects of production and consumption enjoyed by a firm, individual or government.

External benefits are the positive side-effects of production or consumption experienced by third parties for which no money is paid by the beneficiary.

Definition

Social benefits are the true (or full) benefits of consumption or production, i.e. the sum of private benefits and external benefits.

would be charged for such vaccinations in the free market. The true benefit of the vaccination is called the **social benefit**.

Social benefit = Private benefit + External benefit

Another example is training programmes, such as first aid or coaching skills for employees, which create benefits that can be enjoyed by others in society.

➡ Case study: Tourism in Machu Picchu

Machu Picchu, the ancient city of the Incas, is a famous tourist destination in Peru. It attracts thousands of tourists per day. Tourism brings many private benefits to the local community, businesses in the travel industry and the Peruvian government. Tourism also creates benefits in the form of increasing cultural awareness and education about the history of the site and surrounding areas. However, in September 2023, three parts of the ancient structure were closed to visitors because of erosion and damage caused by the number of visiting tourists. A new airport built nearby may increase air pollution. One suggestion is to invest some of the profits made from tourism into improving conservation and preservation of the site.

▲ Machu Picchu

▶ Activity

a Identify the private and external costs and benefits of tourism in Machu Picchu.
b Investigate the impact of tourism in your country or a country of your choice.

▶ Activity

Discuss with a partner which of the following are examples of products/services that incur social costs or social benefits. Make sure you can explain your answers to each other.

- Dental health check-ups
- Art museums
- Consumption of soda/fizzy drinks
- Overuse of antibiotics
- A person using a phone while driving
- Single-use plastic bags
- Reusable straws

▶ Activity

Copy the table and in each column state a private and external cost and private and external benefit of smartphones.

Private costs of smartphones	Private benefits of smartphones	External costs of smartphones	External benefits of smartphones
Purchase price	Online maps	Excessive screen time	Self-education

Case study: Subsidised rooftop solar panels in India

In February 2024, the Indian government launched a scheme to provide eligible citizens with a subsidy of up to 40 per cent of installation costs to encourage them to install solar panels on their rooftops. The aims of the scheme are to provide free electricity to households, reduce carbon emissions, reduce costs of electricity for the government and increase the use of renewable energy. Households can also sell excess electricity generated back to the national grid. The subsidy scheme therefore brings private benefits to households and several external benefits to society.

Source: PM Surya Ghar: Muft Bijli Yojana, 2024, Ministry of New and Renewable Energy, myScheme website

Causes and consequences of market failure

The free market fails to allocate resources efficiently in relation to public goods, merit goods, demerit goods and the abuse of monopoly power. Their existence in an economy causes market failure.

Public goods

Definition

Public goods are goods and services that are non-excludable and non-rivalrous, and which are a cause of market failure as there is a lack of a profit motive to produce them.

The private sector fails to provide certain goods and services due to the lack of a profit motive. In other words, the private sector (the market) fails to provide **public goods** because they cannot charge people for using them. The non-provision of public goods by the private sector is a misallocation of resources. If the government did not step in and provide public goods, there would be a missing market and essential goods and services would not be provided to society. Examples are:

» street lighting
» road signs
» law and order
» flood control systems
» national defence
» lighthouses
» online search engines
» public roads.

Public goods are non-excludable and non-rivalrous in consumption. This means that those who do not pay can still enjoy access to the product (non-excludable) and there is no competition to purchase or use the product (non-rivalrous).

 Case study: Flooding in Bangladesh

Bangladesh is a country that suffers from frequent flooding. The flooding is caused by a range of factors, such as the country's geographical location, increased rainfall due to climate change, deforestation and illegal dumping of materials in rivers. The government has put in place flood defence systems. These include embankments, drainage systems to remove excess water and planting grasses to hold slopes together.

Practice question: structured question

Explain why flood defence systems are an example of public goods. [4]

Merit goods

Merit goods are deemed to have social benefits yet are underprovided and under-consumed without government intervention or provision. Consumption of merit goods creates external benefits (positive spillover effects) for a third party. Hence, the social benefits of producing and consuming merit goods outweigh the private benefits. Examples are:

» education
» healthcare services
» vaccinations
» research and development
» work-related training schemes
» subsidised housing
» museums
» public libraries.

Both the public and private sectors of the economy can provide merit goods and services. For example, there are private independent schools and people can buy their own private healthcare insurance. Many governments provide public hospitals and schools so that all members of society can have access to healthcare and education.

  Under-consumption of merit goods, such as education, and under-production of goods which create external benefits to society, such as growing a garden, represent a misallocation of resources. This would lead to beneficial (and sometimes essential) goods and services not being available to society.

Practice questions: structured questions

1 Explain the difference between public goods and merit goods.   [4]
2 Analyse the reasons why a government might choose to provide public goods and merit goods.   [6]

Demerit goods

Demerit goods are goods or services which when produced or consumed cause external costs (negative spillover effects) in an economy. They are a source of market failure because, without government intervention, demerit goods are over-produced and over-consumed. Examples of demerit goods are:

» cigarettes and e-cigarettes
» alcohol
» junk food
» soda/sugary drinks
» gambling.

Overconsumption of these goods cause negative social consequences and can result in costs to the government in terms of healthcare and rehabilitation services.

Activity

Discuss whether you think drones are demerit goods.

Case study: External costs of drones

In May 2023, it was reported that 12 incoming flights were disrupted at London's Gatwick Airport due to a suspected drone being seen close to the airport. The drone sighting caused delays of almost an hour and flights to be diverted to other airports. Back in December 2018, drone sightings at Gatwick Airport caused chaos as more than 1000 flights and about 140,000 passengers were affected.

▲ Do drones cause external costs?

Source: 'Flights into Gatwick diverted after reports of drone near airport', *The Guardian*, 14 May 2023, The Guardian website

Abuse of monopoly power

The existence of a monopoly market (see Chapter 21) can also cause market failure. Without government control, certain private sector firms could grow to become monopolies and exploit their market power by charging higher prices or reducing supply. In general, profit-maximising monopolists lack incentives to be competitive, so create inefficiencies in the market.

Case study: United States government versus Apple Inc.

On 21 March 2024, the US government filed a lawsuit against Apple, accusing it of monopolistic practices in the smartphone market. Apple has created a system which means that it is easier for Apple users to connect with other Apple products, e.g. the Apple Watch and iPhone, than competitors' products. These anti-competitive practices keep prices high and restrict choices. They also prevent smaller firms from entering the market, and therefore stifle competition and innovation in the market.

Source: 'Apple sued in a landmark iPhone monopoly lawsuit' by Brian Fung, Hannah Rabinowitz and Evan Perez, 21 March 2024, CNN website

See Chapter 21 to read about the advantages and disadvantages of monopolies.

Activity

Read the case study about the oil spill in the Philippines and identify as many examples of market failure and economic concepts as possible.

Case study: Oil spill in the Philippines

On 28 February 2023, an oil tanker called the *MT Princess Empress*, carrying 800,000 litres of industrial oil, sank off the coast of Mindoro in the Philippines. The oil slick extended 75 miles across the island region and negatively impacted the livelihoods of 21,000 families who relied on fishing for both income and nutrition. The Pola region was badly affected. There, toxic oil pollution caused some people to become ill with vomiting, dizziness and breathing difficulties. Businesses in the tourism industries experienced a fall in the number of visitors. The spillage threatened to damage biodiversity in more than 20 protected marine areas. The clean-up operation was expensive and required specialist equipment and skills. Local people received some cash from the government in return for helping with the clean-up process, but many complained that it did not match the income they received from fishing.

Source: 'Residents hit by dizziness and fever as oil spill blankets coast of Philippine island' by Kathleen Magramo, 9 March 2023, CNN website

Practice question: multiple choice

Which item is **not** a public good? [1]

A lighthouse
B museum
C public road
D street lighting

? Chapter review questions

1 When and why does market failure occur?
2 Give three examples of market failure.
3 What are the differences between private, external and social costs?
4 What are the differences between private, external and social benefits?
5 What are public goods?
6 What are the differences between merit and demerit goods?
7 What are the social benefits of public provision of education?
8 What is meant by the abuse of monopoly power?
9 Why do governments provide public goods such as street lighting and lighthouses?
10 What are the external costs of over-consumption of single-use plastics?

Revision checklist

✔ Market failure occurs when the production and/or consumption of a good or service causes positive or negative side-effects to a third party.
✔ Private costs (of production and consumption) are the actual costs of an individual firm, household or government.
✔ External costs are the negative spillover effects (or harmful side-effects) of production or consumption incurred by third parties, without any compensation paid to these third parties.
✔ The true cost of an economic activity is called the social cost, which comprises both private and external costs.
✔ Private benefits are the benefits of production and consumption experienced by an individual firm, household or government.
✔ External benefits are the positive side-effects of production or consumption experienced by third parties.
✔ The true value of an economic activity is called the social benefit, which comprises both private and external benefits.
✔ Causes of market failure include public goods, merit goods, demerit goods and abuse of monopoly power.
✔ Over-consumption of demerit goods, such as smoking cigarettes, and over-production of goods which create external costs to society, such as single-use plastics, represent a misallocation of resources. These have negative implications for society as a whole.
✔ Under-consumption of merit goods, such as education, and under-production of goods which create external benefits to society, such as growing a garden, represent a misallocation of resources. These goods are beneficial to society as a whole, so their under-consumption has negative implications for society.

14 Mixed economic system

This chapter will cover:

★ a definition of the mixed economic system
★ the advantages and disadvantages of the mixed economic system
★ maximum and minimum prices
★ government intervention to address market failure.

Defining the mixed economic system

Definition

The **mixed economic system** is a combination of government-controlled resource allocation and a market economic system.

In a **mixed economic system**, resources are allocated by the private and public sectors (see Chapter 12). The government determines the degree of public and private sector involvement in economic activity. The public sector provides essential services, such as state education, healthcare and postal services. The government aims to redistribute income and wealth by providing unemployment benefits and state pensions, for example. In the private sector, profit acts as the motive for firms to provide the goods and services demanded by consumers.

In the UK and France, the public sector accounts for a significant portion of gross domestic product (GDP), so both are good examples of mixed economies. Other examples are Australia, Iceland, Sweden and Italy.

Arguments for and against the mixed economic system

The mixed economic system achieves the best of both the public and private sectors. For example, the government provides necessary services for everyone while most other goods and services are competitively marketed. Producers and workers have incentives to work hard, to invest and to save. There is a large degree of economic freedom with plenty of choice for private individuals and firms.

The disadvantages of the market economic system also apply to the mixed economy. For example, consumers still pay higher prices due to the profit motive of private sector businesses, such as private healthcare and private education. Public sector activities must also be funded by taxes and other government fees and charges. This creates opportunity costs (see Chapter 3) for both taxpayers and the government.

Practice questions: structured questions

The Organisation for Economic Co-operation and Development (OECD) acknowledges that there is more to human life than economic statistics such as gross domestic product (GDP). The OECD's Better Life Index allows for a comparison of well-being and the quality of life based on different metrics, such as education, in the areas of material living conditions. Education in Finland is 100 per cent state funded and is rather unorthodox given that students do not start schooling until 7 and rarely have tests or homework until their teenage years. By contrast, in South Korea and Japan, education is crucial for success, so there are huge pressures placed on students, who can start school aged 3. Testing is regular and rigorous, making after-school private tuition classes extremely popular. According to the OECD Better Life Index, the top 10 countries were ranked as follows in 2024:

1 Finland
2 Australia
3 Sweden
4 Estonia
5 Slovenia

6 Poland
7 Denmark
8 Belgium
9 Czechia
10 Canada

Source: OECD Better Life Index: Education, 2024, OECD website

1 Explain how scarce resources are allocated in a mixed economy. [4]
2 Discuss whether education should be funded by the government. [8]

> **Study tip**
>
> Countries rarely fall perfectly into the categories of government-run and market economies. In reality, most countries tend to be mixed economies with a stronger element of either public or private sector economic activity.

> **Activity**
>
> Use the internet to find relevant economic data for two different countries (for example, North Korea and Singapore) to distinguish between the two main types of economic system. You might also find it useful to look at newspaper articles on current topics related to economic systems.

Government intervention to address market failure

Governments can intervene to correct market failure by setting maximum or minimum prices. Governments can also use a combination of other methods: indirect taxation, subsidies, regulation, privatisation, nationalisation, direct provision of goods and services, and quotas.

Maximum prices

A **maximum price** is a method of price control which involves the government setting the price of a particular good or service below the market equilibrium price in order to make the product more affordable and encourage consumption. It is also used to protect the interests of consumers from soaring prices, such as escalating rents or significantly higher food prices.

In Figure 14.1, the imposition of a maximum price of P_2 (below the market equilibrium price of P_e) reduces the quantity supplied to S_1, while demand expands to D_1. This results in excess demand for the product – in other words, there is a shortage.

> **Definition**
>
> A **maximum price** occurs when the government sets a price below the market equilibrium price in order to encourage consumption.

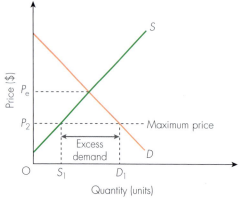

▲ **Figure 14.1** Imposition of a maximum price

Consumers can benefit from the lower price after the imposition of the maximum price. For example, they can benefit from the lower prices of food products or rent on housing. For exporters, a maximum price imposed on the exchange rate (see Chapter 35) can help to improve their international competitiveness.

However, price ceilings distort market forces and therefore can result in an inefficient allocation of scarce resources. For example, a maximum price to control residential rents would result in more demand (D_1) than is supplied at the lower price (P_2). This results in excess demand, as shown in Figure 14.1. This shortage is made up by government supplying housing at a price of P_2 to stabilise rents in the economy. It also increases the likelihood of long waiting lists for government housing.

In product markets, one drawback of imposing maximum prices is that they can cause unofficial or parallel markets to appear due to the resulting shortages in supply.

Minimum prices

A **minimum price** refers to the imposition of a price guarantee set above the market price to encourage supply of a certain good or service. For example, farmers could be offered prices above the market equilibrium to boost the supply of agricultural output. Alternatively, workers could be offered a wage rate higher than the market rate to create incentives to work or to enable them to earn a liveable minimum wage (see Chapter 17).

In Figure 14.2, a minimum price is offered to farmers, giving them an incentive to increase the quantity supplied (S_1) beyond the market equilibrium (Q_e). At a price higher than the equilibrium, demand contracts from Q_e to D_1, but supply extends to S_1. This results in excess supply, as shown by the shaded area. The surplus is bought by the government to support the agricultural farmers and released onto the market during times of bad harvests to stabilise food prices.

Definition

A **minimum price** occurs when the government sets a price above the market equilibrium price in order to encourage output of a certain good or service.

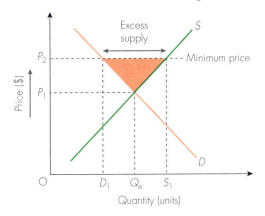

▲ **Figure 14.2** Imposition of a minimum price

This also applies in the labour market, where more workers supply their labour services if there is a minimum wage (see Figure 14.3). The national minimum wage (NMW) is imposed above the equilibrium wage rate, to ensure all workers have a decent liveable income. However, this results in the supply of labour (S_L) exceeding the demand for labour (D_L). The NMW results in higher costs of labour, which in theory can cause unemployment.

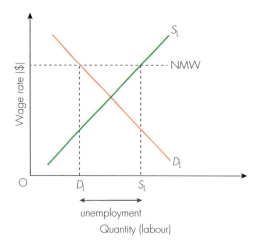

▲ **Figure 14.3** Consequences of a minimum wage in the labour market

Indirect taxation

One way to solve market failure is to place an indirect tax (see Chapter 23) on demerit goods, such as cigarettes, with the aim of reducing the demand for these products.

In Figure 14.4, the indirect tax imposed on a packet of cigarettes causes the supply curve to shift from S_1 to S_{tax}. As a result, the price increases from P_1 to P_2 and the quantity of cigarettes demanded falls from Q_1 to Q_2. The demand for cigarettes tends to be price inelastic (see Chapter 10) and therefore the percentage change in quantity demanded is less than the percentage increase in price. This means the tax has to be very high to have any impact on reducing the consumption of cigarettes.

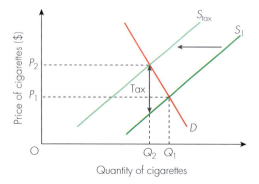

▲ **Figure 14.4** The impact of an indirect tax on cigarettes

The advantages of imposing an indirect tax on a good or service include the following:

» It increases the price, so should reduce the quantity demanded, ceteris paribus.
» It generates tax revenue for the government which can be used to fund the provision of important goods and services.

The disadvantages of imposing an indirect tax on a good or service are as follows:

» The demand for cigarettes, alcohol and petrol (gasoline) tends to be highly price inelastic. This means that the increase in price may have little impact on the consumption level of many people. In the case of cigarettes, the nicotine in tobacco makes smoking highly addictive. Therefore, most smokers will pay the higher price, so consumption will change only slightly.
» The indirect tax will be regressive (see Chapter 23), so will have a greater impact on low-income earners than high-income earners.

Practice question: structured question

Traffic congestion in central London has fallen since the introduction of a congestion charge for driving into the central business district. In 2024 it cost £12.50 (approximately $16) each day to drive into the restricted area during peak hours (between 7 a.m. and 6 p.m. on weekdays and 12 p.m. and 6 p.m. during the weekend and public holidays). There is a penalty for failure to pay the congestion charge.

a Explain, using an example, an external cost of driving a car. [2]
b Analyse the advantages and disadvantages of the congestion charge for two different stakeholders. [6]
c Discuss whether you think the congestion charge is a long-term or short-term solution to the problem of traffic congestion in London. [8]

Subsidies

Governments often provide subsidies to encourage the consumption of certain goods and services. For example, the government might subsidise public transport to discourage people from using private cars. Figure 14.5 shows the impact of a subsidy on the market for public transport. The bus and railway firms receive a sum of money from the government. This lowers their production costs and causes the supply curve to shift from S_1 (before subsidy) to S_2 (after subsidy). Price falls from P_1 to P_2 and the quantity demanded increases from Q_1 to Q_2. An increase in the use of public transport should lower congestion and reduce the amount of pollution caused by driving cars. Therefore, the subsidy helps to reduce the external costs created by driving.

The main disadvantages of providing subsidies involve the opportunity cost for taxpayers and the government. Subsidies place a financial burden on the government budget, often necessitating higher taxes or increased borrowing. This can result in budget deficits and higher national debts. In addition, the opportunity cost of subsidies is significant, as the funds used could otherwise be invested in other goods and services such as education, healthcare and infrastructure. Another disadvantage is that government subsidies can distort market forces by artificially lowering the costs of certain goods or services. This can lead to overproduction and inefficiencies, as firms may rely on subsidies instead of improving their own competitiveness and productivity.

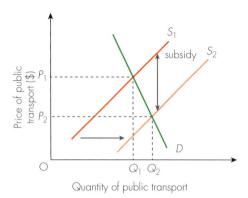

▲ **Figure 14.5** The effects of a producer subsidy

Case study: Flu vaccines in Hong Kong

The Hong Kong government subsidises the cost of annual flu vaccines for the very young and the elderly to encourage people in high-risk age groups to get vaccinated. The aim is to reduce the amount of flu in the wider community by targeting these age groups, so that fewer people need to be hospitalised for the treatment of flu. Vaccinations create positive spillover effects for the rest of the economy and result in less pressure on healthcare services.

Rules and regulations

Governments can also impose rules and regulations in an attempt to solve market failures. For example, imposing laws on the minimum age that people must be before they are legally allowed to purchase cigarettes or alcohol helps to reduce the consumption of such demerit goods. Laws can also restrict where people can smoke. In many countries, smoking is banned in public places such as shopping centres, bars, restaurants, airports, railway stations and at the beach.

▲ Laws restrict where people are allowed to smoke

Figure 14.6 illustrates the impact of a ban on smoking in public places. The inconvenience causes the demand curve for cigarettes to shift to the left from D_1 to D_2, resulting in the quantity of cigarettes demanded falling from Q_1 to Q_2.

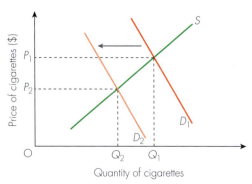

▲ **Figure 14.6** Impact of rules and regulations on the demand for cigarettes

Other examples of laws and regulations imposed to correct market failures are:

» laws regulating where people can drive, cycle and gamble
» regulations imposed to make sure children are vaccinated against certain diseases
» laws making it illegal for people to eat or to talk on a mobile phone while driving
» motorcyclists being made to wear a helmet and car passengers having to wear seat belts
» airport authorities regulating the number of night flights
» laws banning the sale of alcohol.

Activity

If alcohol creates negative spillover effects, discuss why more countries do not ban the sale of alcohol.

 ### Case study: Compulsory education

Parents in the UK could face high fines if they do not send their children to school. This strict rule is designed to improve the uptake of education. Since 2015, full-time education in the UK has been compulsory for children up to 18 years of age.

Activity

Investigate the laws and regulations in your country that are used to correct market failures. How effective have these laws and regulations been?

The advantages of imposing rules and regulations to correct market failures are as follows:

» People may consume less of the good or service.
» People may become more aware of the negative impacts of demerit goods (such as drinking and driving). This can help to change the behaviour of people in the long term.
» People may become more aware of the positive impacts of consuming merit goods (such as education).

The disadvantages of imposing rules and regulations to correct market failures are as follows:

» Restrictions can cause unofficial or parallel markets to provide the good or service, often at a very high price.
» The government has no control over the quality of the goods produced in parallel markets. In some cases, these goods can be dangerous, for example illegally distilled alcohol or tainted baby milk powder.
» People might break the rules. For example, under-age smokers and alcohol drinkers can bypass the law by obtaining false ID cards.
» The fine or punishment for ignoring the rules and regulations must be enforced. It must also be set sufficiently high to discourage consumption of the demerit good or service.

Education

To correct market failures, the government can insist that schools educate students about the negative side-effects of demerit goods, such as smoking and passive smoking. In many countries, cigarette packets must carry a government health warning which clearly explains the dangers of smoking. The Australian government has made it a legal requirement for cigarettes to be sold in packets covered with negative images about smoking. The images are graphic with the aim of educating and shocking people in order to discourage them from smoking. If these methods are successful, the raised awareness of the dangers of smoking should reduce the demand for cigarettes (or any other demerit good).

Another example is the government using informative advertising and education to explain the benefits of eating at least five portions of fruits and vegetables each day. In Figure 14.7, the demand curve for fresh fruit and vegetables shifts from D_1 to D_2 and the equilibrium quantity increases from Q_1 to Q_2. Healthier people in the economy should mean less absence from work and school, resulting in improved productivity and output. Therefore, healthy eating produces an external benefit for the rest of society.

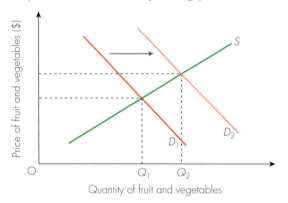

▲ **Figure 14.7** The impact of positive advertising on the market for fruit and vegetables

Schools around the world educate students about issues such as healthy eating, the negative impacts of driving gas/petrol-fuelled cars, and the importance of conserving energy and recycling. Regulating such educational programmes should change the pattern of demand, thus helping to correct market failures.

Activity

Consider whether smoking is a problem in your country. Assess the degree of effectiveness of the measures taken by the government to reduce the number of smokers. What possible improvements could be made to the current situation? Take action by writing a letter to a local politician or a local newspaper explaining your suggestions.

Privatisation and nationalisation

Definition

Privatisation is the transfer of the ownership of assets from the public sector to the private sector.

Privatisation refers to the transfer of the ownership of assets from the public sector to the private sector. For example, Hong Kong's MTRC (see case study below) was wholly owned by the Hong Kong government, but was privatised on 5 October 2000, raising significant funds from the sale to shareholders. This decision was part of the government's plan to wind down its interest in public utilities.

> ## Case study: Privatisation in Hong Kong
>
> The MTR Corporation Limited (MTRC) is a publicly listed company on the Hong Kong Stock Exchange. The MTRC operates Hong Kong's railway services, as well as being a major property developer. The company was privatised in October 2000. The MTRC also has investments in railways in Beijing, Hangzhou, London, Melbourne, Shenzhen, Stockholm and Sydney.
>
>

Advantages of privatisation include the following:

» The government can earn one-off privatisation proceeds from the sale of state-owned assets.

» Privatisation helps to reduce government debt in three ways: the government no longer has to maintain the operation of state-owned enterprises, it earns revenue from the sale of the privatised business, and the private sector firm pays corporate taxes.

» Privatisation reduces costs to taxpayers, who no longer have to pay to finance the operations of the business.

» Private sector businesses have the incentive to improve efficiency, as they need to remain competitive. This can also promote an enterprising culture of risk-taking and innovation.

Disadvantages of privatisation include the following:

» The process creates a private sector monopoly, which is not always a positive outcome for customers, who may face higher prices (see Chapter 21).
» Government regulation and intervention may still be needed to protect the public interest.
» There is a trade-off (opportunity cost) as state-owned enterprises can provide social benefits, such as education, housing, postal services and public transport.

> ### ▶ Activities
>
> 1 In small groups, discuss whether countries should privatise their postal services and telecommunications services in the digital twenty-first century.
> 2 Do you think that all schools and universities in your country should be privatised? Consider the impact of privatising education on different stakeholders: consumers, workers, firms, the government and the economy (society) as a whole.

The 2008 global financial crisis caused many banks to be bailed out (nationalised), making nationalisation popular again as a method of correcting market failure and inefficiencies in the economy. **Nationalisation** is when the government purchases private sector assets, bringing them into the ownership and control of the public sector. This can protect employment and promote economic stability in key industries. Industries that are usually nationalised include public transport, telecommunication networks, energy, utilities and natural resources. There is a rather large opportunity cost, however. For example, the UK spent a significant portion of its GDP on bank bailouts following the global financial crisis. The COVID-19 pandemic had similar impacts, as many businesses and key industries across the world struggled to survive the worst global crisis in living memory.

Direct provision

In many countries, governments provide certain goods and services free of charge to their citizens, even though people may have indirectly paid for these through income tax. Examples are education, healthcare, public libraries, parks, museums, public roads and motorways (highways), garbage or refuse collection, street lighting, street signs and national defence.

▲ In the UK, battleships are funded by the public sector from its national defence budget. HMS *Belfast* was used during the Second World War but has been decommissioned and is now used as a museum on the River Thames in London

There is a conflict between providing goods and services directly to people and asking them to pay for the goods and services. The law of demand (see Chapter 6) dictates that as the price of a good or service rises, people will consume less. Healthcare and education are under-consumed in many countries because people cannot afford to pay. This has a negative effect on the quality of their lives in the short term, and in the long term causes a potential decrease in life expectancy and earning potential. This has a negative impact on the whole of society, as human resources are not being used to their full capacity.

The advantages of direct government provision of goods and services are as follows:

» The goods and services are accessible to all people in society, regardless of their income or social status.
» Consumption of the good or service has private benefits for the individual and external benefits for third parties in society.
» Government oversight and regulation can help maintain high-quality standards in the provision of services such as healthcare and education. By establishing standards, conducting inspections and enforcing quality assurance measures, the government can help ensure consistent and reliable service outcomes for consumers.

The disadvantages of government provision of goods and services are as follows:

» There is an opportunity cost, as the money could have been spent on something else, such as paying off government debt or possibly reducing rates of taxation.
» Goods and services which are free of charge may be over-consumed, so long queues or shortages may arise. For example, the waiting list for operations in a government hospital may be very long.
» In the case of a shortage of supply caused by excess demand, it can be difficult to decide who should be entitled to take advantage of the free government service.
» Some people (known as **free riders**) are able to take advantage of free goods and services without contributing to government revenue by paying taxes.

Definition

Free riders benefit from public goods without paying for them

Quotas

Quotas are government-imposed limits on the quantity of a good or service that can be produced, consumed or traded within a given period of time. They are often used as a form of government intervention to address market failures, particularly in the case of natural resource extraction.

An example of quotas imposed on natural resource extraction is in the fishing industry. Governments may impose quotas on the amount of fish that can be caught during a given time period, such as per month, in order to prevent overfishing and the depletion of fish stocks. By limiting the quantity of fish that can be harvested, quotas aim to ensure the sustainability of fish populations and maintain ecological balance in marine ecosystems.

Similarly, quotas can be applied to the extraction of minerals or fossil fuels. For instance, governments may set quotas on the amount of oil that can be drilled from a particular oil field each year to prevent resource depletion and environmental degradation. The same can apply in the forestry industry in order to protect tree species and deforestation.

The advantages of using quotas for natural resource extraction are as follows:

▲ Quotas are often imposed on the extraction of natural resources from the planet

» **Resource conservation** – quotas help to prevent the overexploitation and depletion of natural resources.

They do this by limiting the quantity that can be extracted, ensuring the sustainability of these resources.

» **Environmental protection** – by regulating the volume of extraction of natural resources, quotas can mitigate environmental damage caused by resource extraction operations, such as the destruction of natural habitat as well as noise and air pollution.

The disadvantages of using quotas for natural resource extraction are as follows:

» **Market distortions** – quotas can lead to market distortions and inefficiencies, as they may artificially restrict supply and therefore push up prices for consumers.
» **Monitoring and enforcement costs** – implementing and enforcing quotas require significant administrative and enforcement efforts, including monitoring extraction activities of firms in the primary sector. This can be costly for the government.

? Chapter review questions

1 What is meant by a mixed economic system?
2 What are the advantages and disadvantages of operating a mixed economic system?
3 What is meant by a maximum price, and why might governments impose this?
4 What is meant by a minimum price, and why might governments impose this?
5 How does indirect taxation work to correct certain market failures?
6 How might subsidies be used to correct certain market failures?
7 How might the use of rules and regulations help to correct certain market failures?
8 What is the difference between privatisation and nationalisation with regard to the correction of market failure?
9 What are quotas and why might governments use these?

Revision checklist

✔ The mixed economic system is a combination of both government-controlled resource allocation and a market economy.
✔ A maximum price is a price control system that involves setting the price below the market equilibrium price in order to make products more affordable.
✔ A minimum price is a price guarantee set above the market price to encourage supply of a certain good or service.
✔ Excess supply occurs when a minimum price is imposed above the market equilibrium price, as supply exceeds demand at higher prices.
✔ Consumers tend to pay higher prices if minimum prices are imposed.
✔ An indirect tax causes costs of production to increase, thereby shifting the supply curve of demerit goods to the left. This results in a higher equilibrium price and a contraction in demand.
✔ Subsidies can be used to lower the cost of providing merit goods and services. This helps to cut prices and encourage demand for such socially beneficial products.

✔ Rules and regulations can limit access to certain goods and services that have negative externalities, such as tobacco, alcohol and gambling.
✔ Privatisation is the transfer of the ownership of assets from the public sector to the private sector. It can help to correct market failures by making resource allocation more efficient, as the private sector has incentives to be innovative and competitive.
✔ Nationalisation is the purchase of private sector assets by the government, bringing these into the ownership and control of the public sector. This can protect employment and promote economic stability in key industries.
✔ Quotas are government-imposed limits on the quantity of a good or service that can be produced, consumed or traded. They are used to address market failures and to conserve natural resources in particular.

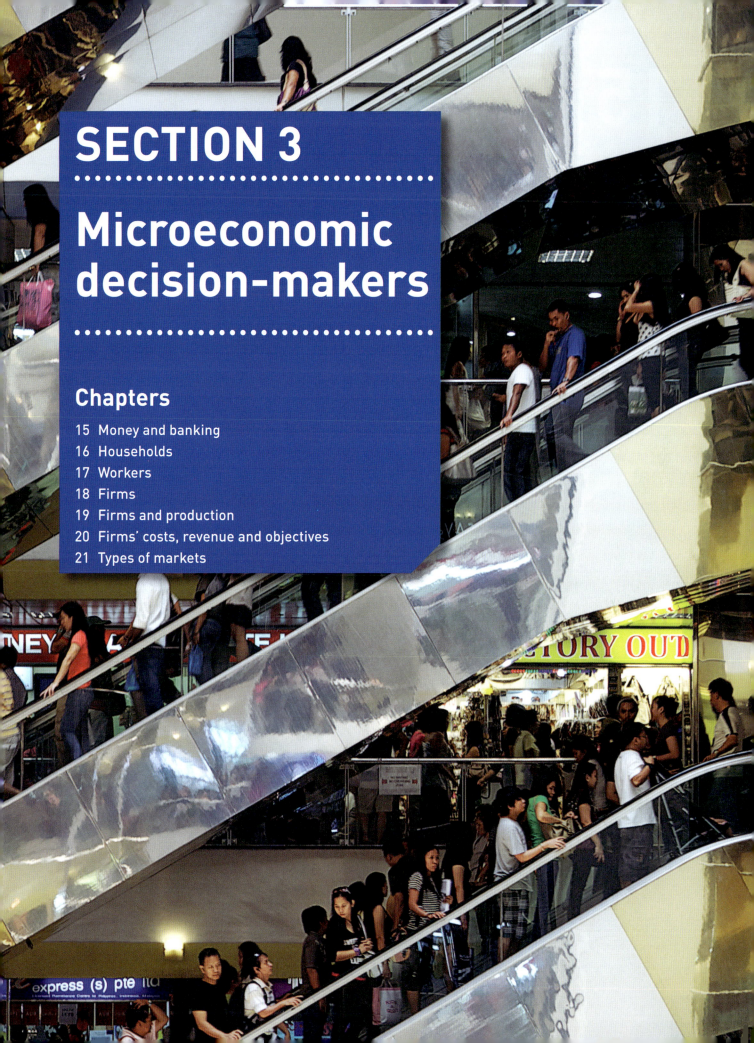

SECTION 3

Microeconomic decision-makers

Chapters

15 Money and banking

This chapter will cover:

★ the forms, functions and characteristics of money
★ the role and importance of central banks
★ the role and importance of commercial banks.

The meaning of money

Definition

Money is any commodity that can be used as a medium of exchange for the purchase of goods and services, e.g. banknotes and coins.

Money refers to any commodity that can be used as a medium of exchange that is widely accepted for the purchase of goods and services.

Forms of money

Money can take different forms. People have used commodities such as cloth, shells and even salt as money in the past in different parts of the world. Today, the main forms of money include the following:

» **Cash** – banknotes and coins (collectively called **legal tender**) are a physical form of money. While cash is convenient for many transactions, it is inconvenient and risky to use cash for larger transactions. Hence, in the UK for example, in 2024 cash accounted for less than 3 per cent of the country's total money supply.
» **Bank deposits** – these are money reserves placed in commercial bank accounts. This form of money accounts for the vast majority of all money in modern economies. Commercial bank money is in electronic form, rather than physical form. Instead of carrying large amounts of cash, customers use credit and debit cards or make online bank transfers, which allow money to be transferred electronically between bank accounts.
» **Central bank reserves** – these consist of the money held by the central bank and used by commercial banks to make payments between themselves. Like bank deposits, central bank reserves are electronic forms of money.

Study tip

Money is not simply cash (notes and coins) in circulation. In fact, most of an economy's money exists as bank deposits and reserves, not in the form of cash.

Functions of money

There are four key functions of money:

» Money acts as a **medium of exchange** – as a way to conduct trade. It is widely recognised and accepted as a means of payment for goods and services.
» Money is a **measure of value** (or **unit of account**) – it measures the market value of different goods and services. It is far more efficient for trading purposes to express the price of goods and services in a currency (such as dollars) rather than using products such as cloth, shells, salt or livestock. All of these were forms of money in the past.
» Money is a **store of value** – it can be stored and used at some time in the future. In other words, money must be able to hold its purchasing power over time. Money therefore gives firms and households flexibility in the timing of their sales and their purchases, removing the urgency to trade straightaway.
» Money is a **standard of deferred payment** – this means that money is used as the standard for future (deferred) payments of debt. For example, loans taken out today are repaid in the foreseeable future. Thus, money is used as the standard to pay off debts.

Activities

1 To appreciate the need for money, try to explain why many economists argue that the invention of money is one of the greatest inventions of all time.
2 List the methods of payment that you can use in your economy.

Characteristics of money

Money has certain characteristics:

» **Durability** – money, such as banknotes and coins, should be long lasting yet easily replaced if it becomes worn. In many instances, modern-day banknotes are made from polymer rather than paper. Polymer banknotes are significantly more durable and are used extensively in many countries, including India, China, Brazil, Mexico, Romania, Australia and Vietnam.

▲ Polymer banknotes are widely used in Egypt, Australia, Singapore, Brunei and Hong Kong

» **Acceptability** – money is widely recognised and accepted as a medium of payment for goods and services. Legal tender is the official money of a country (such as India's rupee or the UK's pound sterling). Other forms of money might also be accepted, such as tourists using US dollars. Gold is universally accepted as a form of money. By contrast, the Zimbabwean dollar ceased to be accepted as a medium of exchange in 2009 when the country, which was suffering from civil unrest, experienced hyperinflation.

» **Divisibility** – as money is a measure of the value of goods and services, it must be divisible. Many economists and historians believe that cattle are the oldest form of money, with cows being used for trade as far back as 9000BC. Some African nations were using cattle as money during the latter half of the twentieth century. However, cattle and livestock are not 'useful' forms of money as they are not truly divisible: a third of a goat is not really useful for any trader!

▲ Gold is universally accepted as a form of money

» **Uniformity** – for money to be easily recognisable there must be uniformity. This means that all legal tender denominations of banknotes and coins will look identical in terms of shape, size and design. Cows come in many shapes and sizes and each has a different value; this means that cows are not a uniform form of money. The first consistent form of money, cowrie shells, was used in China over 3000 years ago. These seashells were used mainly for trading food, livestock and textiles.

» **Scarcity** – money must be limited in supply in order to keep its value. Both seashells and salt have been used as money in the past, although the high levels of supply meant they soon lost much of their appeal as a medium of exchange. By contrast, silver and gold are better types of money due to their scarcity. The supply of money, including banknotes and coins, is regulated by the country's central bank. This ensures that the money retains its value over time by being relatively scarce.

▲ Cowrie shells were first used as money in China during the Shang Dynasty (c.1600–1050BC)

» **Portability** – money must be conveniently portable. For example, the approximate weight of a banknote, regardless of its denomination, is just 1 gram. While almost every country uses government-issued banknotes and coins as their official currency, there are other forms of money. For example, money in bank accounts, the use of credit cards and mobile payment systems, such as Alipay and Google Pay, enable payment to be made electronically, without the customer having to use physical cash. The first coins used as money appeared around 2000BC. In those days, the value of coins was determined by their weight, which hindered their effectiveness as money due to the difficulties of portability.

Case study: Venezuela drops six zeros from its currency

On 1 October 2021, Nicolás Maduro, the leader of Venezuela, removed six zeros from the bolívar, the Venezuelan currency, and new banknotes were printed. The name of the new currency is the 'digital bolívar'. The reason for the new banknotes was hyperinflation. Before the change, citizens had to carry around huge quantities of notes if they wanted to pay for goods and services using cash. The Venezuelan economy suffered from very high rates of inflation from 2013, with rates reaching a high of approximately 344,509 per cent in February 2019. In 2020, the rate of inflation was almost 3000 per cent. It fell to around 680 per cent in 2021. The depreciation of the currency has caused many people to use US dollars to pay for goods and services instead of the bolívar.

Bartering

Definition

Bartering is the act of swapping items in exchange for other items through a process of bargaining and negotiation, due to the absence of money in the economy.

In the absence of money, people have to use a barter system in order to trade goods and services. **Bartering** is the act of swapping items in exchange for other items through a process of bargaining and negotiation. For example, someone might trade five sacks of rice for one camel, or four chickens for a sheep.

The barter system is problematic in several ways:

» The key problem with a barter system is the need for a **double coincidence of wants** – that is, the person with chickens must find a trader who wants four chickens in exchange for a sheep. As two people engaged in a transaction must both want what the other person is offering, bartering is highly inefficient.

» A second problem with bartering is that of **divisibility** – half a sheep or two-thirds of a chicken is not very useful for traders.

» A third problem is that of **portability** – compare the portability of a sheep or fish with that of paper money (banknotes).

Hence, due to the problems associated with bartering, countries around the world eventually developed the use of commodity money, such as cowrie shells, grain and cloth. For much of history, precious metals such as gold and silver have served a monetary role.

Activity

Bartering still takes place in some parts of the world today. Discuss with a partner the problems associated with bartering as a means of trade and exchange in your country.

▲ This print shows Scandinavian and Russian traders bartering their wares

Practice question: structured question

a Define 'bartering'. [2]

b Analyse, with reference to the functions of money, why bartering is an ineffective method for trading. [6]

The functions of central banks

The **central bank** of a country is the monetary authority that oversees and manages the nation's money supply and banking system. Examples of central banks include the European Central Bank (for the Eurozone countries), the People's Bank of China, the Reserve Bank of India, the USA's Federal Reserve and the Bank of England. These banks are responsible for overseeing the **monetary policies** (see Chapter 24) of their respective countries. They are also responsible for the nation's entire money supply and the manipulation of interest rates to affect the economy.

 Case study: The Central Bank of Egypt's modernisation efforts

The Central Bank of Egypt (CBE), based in Cairo, plays a vital role in managing the country's monetary policy. It is responsible for the economy's financial stability and oversees the issuance of Egypt's national currency, the Egyptian pound (EGP). In recent years, the CBE has taken significant steps to modernise its currency and operations.

In 2022, the CBE introduced Egypt's first polymer banknotes, starting with the EGP10 denomination, followed by the EGP20 in 2023. These banknotes are printed at a state-of-the-art facility in the New Administrative Capital located just outside of Cairo, using advanced security features such as holograms and watermarks. The transition to polymer notes aims to enhance durability, reduce counterfeit risks and support environmental sustainability by lowering the frequency of reprinting. Polymer notes are water-resistant, less prone to wear and tear and recyclable, aligning with Egypt's Vision 2030 sustainability goals.

Besides issuing currency, the CBE is pivotal to Egypt's financial system, managing foreign reserves, acting as a banker to the government and implementing monetary policy to stabilise the economy.

Activity

What interesting facts and figures can you find out about the central bank in your country?

Central banks tend to have the following four key functions:

» **The sole issuer of banknotes and coins** – in almost every country, the central bank has the sole rights to issue legal tender in its own country. That is, it is the only authority that can print banknotes and mint coins. This helps to bring uniformity to and improves public confidence in the country's monetary system. One rare exception to this function is Hong Kong, a special administrative region of China, where three commercial banks (Standard Chartered, HSBC and Bank of China) have note-issuing rights, although the Hong Kong Monetary Authority maintains overall control of the banking system, including the circulation of banknotes and coins.

» **The government's bank** – the central bank operates as a banker to the government, performing the same functions as a commercial bank does for its customers. Hence, as the government's bank, it maintains the bank accounts of the central government, such as receiving deposits from government, making short-term loans to the government and making payments for items of government expenditure (see Chapter 23). The central bank also manages public sector debt and represents the government in international financial markets such as foreign exchange. This has become an important function of central banks because such intervention can help to stabilise the external value of a nation's currency (see Chapter 35).

» **The bankers' bank** – the central bank acts as the bank for other banks in the country. This function includes overseeing the cash reserves of commercial banks. This means that all banks in the country must have their accounts with the central bank, enabling the central monetary authority to easily manage the claims made by banks against each other. For example, payment made by a Citibank customer writing a cheque to another customer with an HSBC account goes through the central bank's clearing system – that is, the central bank debits the account of the Citibank customer and credits the account of the HSBC customer. This function of the central bank reduces the need for cash withdrawals, thus enabling commercial banks to function more efficiently. In addition, it also allows the central bank to have a better overview of the liquidity position (the ability to convert assets into cash) of the country's commercial banks.

» **The lender of last resort** – the authorities require all commercial banks to keep a certain percentage of their cash balances as deposits with the central bank, and these cash reserves can be used by the country's banking system during financial emergencies. This function helps to build public confidence in the country's banking system. For example, if a certain commercial bank faces temporary financial difficulties, it can, as a last resort, seek financial assistance from the central bank. This helps to ensure the commercial bank does not collapse, protects jobs, and safeguards the nation's banking system and economic welfare.

➡ Case study: Bank bailouts

A bailout refers to a loan or financial assistance provided to a company (or country) which faces major financial difficulties or the threat of bankruptcy. The global financial crises of 1997 and 2008 caused the collapse of hundreds of banks all over the world, over a number of years. The financial bailout by central banks was seen as necessary to prevent job losses and socioeconomic failures on a mass scale.

Central banks can do this through various means, such as providing subsidies or low-interest loans to commercial banks in need of liquidity (cash assets). Bailouts in

Indonesia (1997) and Cyprus (2012) proved to be the most expensive in economic history. Cyprus spent $10 billion bailing out its banks – this represents a huge 56 per cent of Cyprus's $18 billion GDP (see Figure 15.1). In March 2023, the Silicon Valley Bank in the USA went bankrupt (literally). The Federal Reserve, the US Central Bank, promised to return to customers the money that they had deposited in the bank. They did this to restore confidence in the banking system and prevent people and businesses withdrawing their money from the bank.

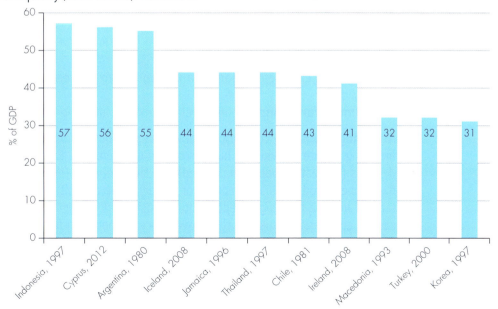

▲ **Figure 15.1** The biggest bank bailouts as a percentage of GDP

The functions of commercial banks

A **commercial bank** is a retail bank that provides financial services to its customers, such as accepting savings deposits and approving bank loans or mortgages. Examples of commercial banks are shown in Table 15.1. All commercial banks are responsible for maintaining the deposits of their account holders. Their transactions are socially and legally governed by the central bank. Commercial banking started over 200 years ago when goldsmiths (metal workers specialising in precious metals such as gold) operated as banks. Banking itself can be traced as far back as 2000BC when merchants in Assyria and Babylonia gave grain loans to farmers and other traders. Modern-day commercial online banking did not start until 1995.

Table 15.1 The world's largest commercial banks, October 2024

Rank	Bank	Country
1	JPMorgan Chase	USA
2	Bank of America	USA
3	Industrial and Commercial Bank of China Limited (ICBC)	China
4	Agricultural Bank of China (ABC)	China
5	China Construction Bank	China
6	Bank of China	China
7	Wells Fargo	USA
8	Royal Bank of Canada	Canada
9	Morgan Stanley	USA
10	HSBC	UK

Source: 'The 10 largest banks in the world in 2024', Forbes India, 4 October 2024, Forbes India website

The functions of commercial banks can be split into two categories: primary and secondary.

The **primary functions** of commercial banks include the following:

» **Accepting deposits** – commercial banks accept deposits from their customers, including private individuals, businesses and governments. Examples are sight deposits (deposits payable on demand) and time deposits (deposits payable after a fixed time period, such as 6 months or a year). Time deposits tend to attract higher rates of interest than sight deposits for deposit holders. Businesses also deposit their cash in commercial banks for the convenience of their own financial operations, such as paying their suppliers and employees.

» **Making advances** – commercial banks provide advances (loans) to their customers. These advances include overdrafts (a banking service that allows approved customers to withdraw more money than they actually have in their account) and mortgages (long-term secured loans for the purchase of assets such as commercial and residential property).

» **Credit creation** – this describes the process by which banks increase the money supply in an economy by making money available to borrowers. Credit allows the borrower (or debtor) to gain purchasing power (money) by promising to pay the lender (or creditor) at a future time. Credit creation enables commercial banks to generate considerable additional purchasing power from their cash deposits. While central banks can print money, they do not create credit. This is done by commercial banks. It is a key factor that distinguishes commercial banks from other financial institutions, such as insurance companies and investment banks.

The **secondary functions** of commercial banks include the following:

» Collecting and transferring funds on behalf of their clients.
» Offering additional financial services such as foreign exchange dealings, overseas remittances and wealth management.
» Providing safety deposit boxes for customers to safeguard highly valued possessions, including jewellery and important documents such as wills.
» Providing money transfer facilities, such as transferring money to an overseas bank account or to pay various bills, such as telephone, electricity, gas and water bills.
» Offering credit card facilities for the convenience of customers (private individuals and commercial clients).
» Offering internet banking facilities, such as online bill payments, wired bank transfers between bank accounts, and the online purchase of shares and foreign currencies (see Chapter 35).

▲ A safety deposit box in a bank vault

Practice questions: structured questions

The Industrial and Commercial Bank of China Ltd (ICBC) and the China Construction Bank Corporation (CCB) are among the largest banks in the world. Commercial banks, such as the ICBC and CCB, have an important role in the development of the Chinese economy. Nevertheless, the trading of the renminbi, China's official currency, is still closely monitored by the People's Bank of China, the central bank.

1 Describe one function of a commercial bank such as ICBC or CCB. [2]
2 Explain two key functions of central banks such as the People's Bank of China. [4]

Practice questions: multiple choice

1 Which option is a characteristic of money?   [1]
   A medium of exchange
   B portability
   C store of value
   D unit of account

2 Which term describes the act of swapping items in exchange for other items in the absence of money?   [1]
   A bartering
   B double coincidence of wants
   C negotiation
   D unit of account

? Chapter review questions

1 What is meant by money?
2 What are the various forms of money?
3 What are the key functions of money?
4 What are the main characteristics of money?
5 What is a central bank?
6 What are the key functions of a central bank?
7 How does a central bank differ from commercial banks?
8 What are the main functions of commercial banks?

Revision checklist

✔ Money is any commodity that people can use as a medium of exchange for the purchase of goods and services, such as banknotes and coins.

✔ Forms of money include cash (notes and coins), commercial bank deposits and central bank reserves.

✔ There are four functions of money: a medium of exchange, a measure of value (unit of account), a store of value and a standard for deferred payment.

✔ Characteristics of money include durability, acceptability, divisibility, uniformity, scarcity and portability.

✔ The central bank of a country is the monetary authority that oversees and manages the economy's money supply and the banking system.

✔ Central banks have four key functions: the sole issuer of legal tender, the government's bank, the bankers' bank and the lender of last resort.

✔ Commercial banks are retail banks that provide financial services to their customers, such as savings accounts, bank loans and mortgages.

✔ Functions of commercial banks include accepting deposits, making (approving) advances, credit creation and a range of other banking services (such as cheque clearance, foreign exchange dealings, money transfer facilities and online banking).

16 Households

This chapter will cover:

★ the factors that influence household spending, savings and borrowing.

Influences on household spending

Income

The amount of money that individuals spend on goods and services largely depends upon their level of income. The main source of income for most people is wages or salaries (see Chapter 17). However, people can earn income from other sources, including:

» interest on savings (return on capital)
» rent earned from leasing property (return on land)
» dividends – a share of a company's profits from shares owned in a company (return on enterprise)
» profit earned from running a business (return on enterprise).

Households are not able to spend all of the income they earn; they can only spend their disposable income. **Disposable income** refers to the income earned by an individual after income tax and other charges such as pension contributions have been deducted. It is therefore the amount of income a person has available to spend on goods and services. This is the single largest determinant of how much an individual or household spends, saves or borrows.

There is a positive relationship between the level of spending and the income earned – that is, higher levels of disposable income usually lead to higher spending and higher savings. Direct taxation (see Chapter 23) reduces the amount of income a person receives, so higher income tax rates can lower the level of disposable income and therefore consumption.

> **Definition**
>
> **Disposable income** is the amount of income a person has available to spend on goods and services after compulsory deductions such as income tax.

▲ There is a positive relationship between a person's level of spending and the income they earn

Different income levels affect different types of expenditure. For example, low-income earners will spend a greater proportion of their income on food and necessities whereas high-income earners will spend a lower proportion of their income on food and necessities. Table 16.1 shows the reasons why different income groups have different expenditure patterns (spending, saving and borrowing).

Definitions

Current expenditure is money spent on goods and services consumed within the current year. Unlike capital expenditure, it is often recurrent, such as the spending on food, clothing, entertainment and haircuts.

Capital expenditure is money spent on fixed assets (items owned by an individual or firm which last more than 12 months), such as computers, cars, furniture, buildings and equipment.

Table 16.1 Reasons for different expenditure patterns

Income group	Spending	Saving	Borrowing
Low	Spend most of their income on necessities, e.g. food, clothing and housing	Tends to be low as there is not much income left over after spending on necessities	Borrow to fund their expenditure on capital items, e.g. furniture, cars and home appliances In extreme circumstances, people may borrow to fund **current expenditure** on necessities Banks less likely to lend money to low-income earners as they represent higher risk
Middle	Spend a lower proportion of their income on food and other necessities than low-income earners Spend on some luxuries	Able to save some money from their wages or salaries	Borrow money to fund expenditure on capital items, e.g. furniture, new cars and home appliances Use credit cards to pay for both capital and current expenditure Take out a mortgage (long-term secured loan) to purchase a home
High	Spend the smallest proportion of income on necessities Purchase luxury goods and services	High level of savings possible Save a greater proportion of their income than middle-income earners	Borrowing occurs but there is only a small risk of not being able to repay loans for **capital expenditure** and mortgages Generally, there is less need to borrow money to fund purchase of capital expenditure items

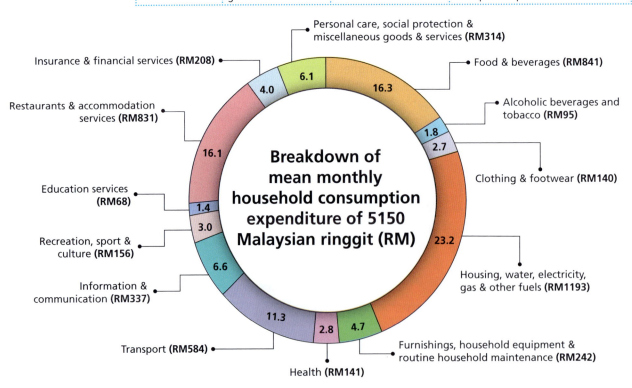

Source: Department of Statistics Malaysia (DOSM)

▲ **Figure 16.1** What Malaysians spent their money on in 2022. RM = Malaysian ringgit (currency)

Activities

1 With reference to Figures 16.2–16.4, compare the trends in real household disposable income and consumer spending in the USA, Japan and the United Kingdom from 2014 to 2024.
2 Determine whether there is a positive relationship (trend) between the two variables.

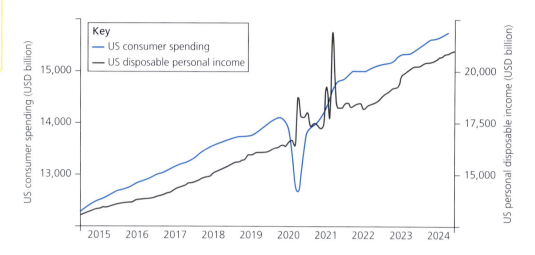

Source: United States consumer spending and personal disposable income, 2014–2024, US Bureau of Economic Analysis, August 2024

▲ **Figure 16.2** Consumer spending and real disposable income in the USA, 2014–2024

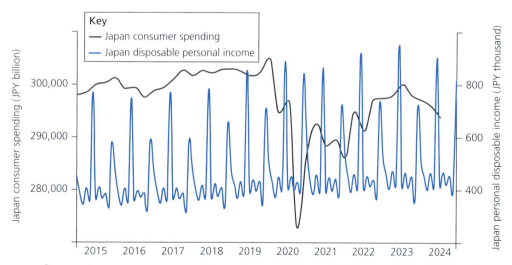

Source: Japan consumer spending and personal disposable income, Cabinet Office, Japan, 2014–2024, August 2024, Trading Economics website

▲ **Figure 16.3** Consumer spending and real disposable income in Japan, 2014–2024

Study tip

How to describe a trend:

1 Describe the overall trend from the beginning period to the end period.

2 Describe any variations to the trend.

3 Describe the magnitude (size) of any variations to the trend.

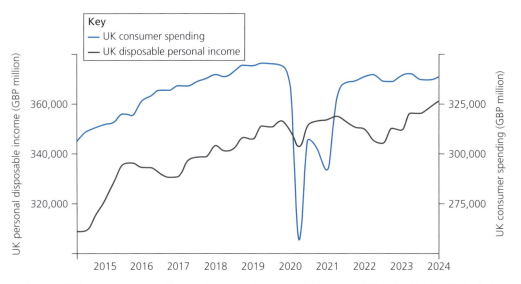

Source: UK consumer spending and personal disposable income, Office for National Statistics, 2014–2024, August 2024, Trading Economics website

▲ **Figure 16.4** Consumer spending and real disposable income in the UK, 2014–2024

The **wealth** of an individual is measured by the amount of assets they own minus their liabilities (the amount they owe). When the value of assets, such as property and other investments, increases there is said to be a **positive wealth effect**. This causes people to spend more. In some cases, it also causes owners of assets to borrow against the value of their existing assets, such as residential or commercial property.

Conspicuous consumption occurs when people purchase goods and services that they feel increase their status or image. For example, a person may buy a very expensive car, yacht, diamond ring or designer handbag as a status symbol. Some wealthy people engage in conspicuous consumption.

By contrast, if the value of an asset decreases, the wealth effect can become negative. For example, a severe recession (Chapter 26) can cause some people to experience **negative equity** – when the value of their secured loan or mortgage exceeds the market value of their property. In a recession, consumer spending falls.

▲ A queue for a luxury brand. Luxury brands restrict the number of customers who can enter the shop at one time which adds to the prestige and exclusivity of the products

Case study: Negative equity

Yoshie Sano bought an apartment in Los Angeles for $1,000,000 in 2007. She borrowed $800,000 from the bank and paid a deposit of $200,000. In December 2008 the property market crashed due to the global financial crisis, causing Yoshie's apartment to fall in value to $700,000. She is in negative equity as the value of the existing mortgage is greater than the value of the property.

Activity

With reference to the case study on negative equity, discuss in pairs:

a the impact of negative equity on Yoshie's spending, saving and borrowing
b the options available to Yoshie to repay her mortgage.

We will now consider some of the other determinants of the level of spending, saving and borrowing, besides income.

The rate of interest

Interest rates determine the cost of borrowing or lending money. An increase in interest rates (see Chapter 24) may lead to decreased consumer spending, less borrowing and more saving for the following reasons:

» Borrowing becomes more expensive and therefore the demand for loans falls, which leads to less consumer spending.
» Savings may become more attractive due to the higher return, so individuals may save more and spend less.
» If an individual has an existing loan or mortgage, the increase in interest repayments is likely to cause a fall in disposable income, so spending falls.

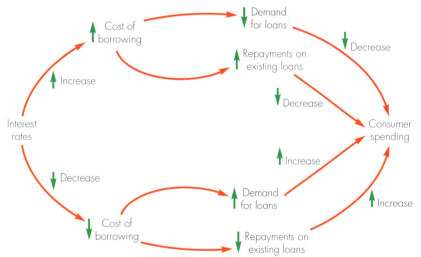

▲ **Figure 16.5** The effects of a change in interest rates on consumer spending

Confidence levels

The level of spending in an economy is heavily influenced by the level of consumer and business confidence in an economy. During a recession or a period of low economic growth (see Chapter 26), people may prefer to save rather than spend as they lack confidence about the future of the economy. For example, they might fear that they may lose their job.

▲ The sale of luxury items such as bespoke jewellery increases during an economic boom or period of high economic growth

By contrast, during an economic boom or a period of high economic growth, people and firms feel confident about the future and therefore purchase more goods and services. The sale of luxury items such as restaurant meals, spa treatments and foreign holidays increases. Firms may invest more in new equipment and technology because they feel confident about the future. This creates jobs and fuels spending, borrowing and saving.

Inflation

The general level of prices in the economy influences consumer spending because an increase in inflation (see Chapter 28) reduces the purchasing power of individuals. Therefore, inflation tends to cause reduced spending, less savings and more borrowing, and vice versa.

Age

A person's age impacts upon their level of consumer spending. A young single person may earn a relatively low income and spend most of it on goods and services to support their lifestyle. As a person gets older their earnings will typically rise and they may start to save a greater proportion of their income to buy a property or in anticipation of marriage and children. During the family stage of a person's life, they will spend more of their income on their children but might also have to save for their children's university education and to build up a pension to support themselves when they retire. After retirement, people dissave (the opposite of saving) as they have no earned income, so must spend from their savings.

> ### Activity
>
> Copy and complete the following table using the words high, low or moderate.
>
> | Age | Spending | Saving | Borrowing | Dissaving |
> |-----|----------|--------|-----------|-----------|
> | 16–25 | High | Low | Low | – |
> | 26–35 | Moderate | | | |
> | 36–45 | Moderate | | | |
> | 46–65 | Moderate | | | |
> | 66 onwards | | | | Yes |

The size of households (culture)

The average size of households has changed over time and is reflective of the culture of the economy. In economically developed countries, birth rates are falling (see Chapter 31) as people choose to marry later in life and have fewer children. There has also been an increase in single households. This influences expenditure patterns because, for example, a family with three children will usually consume more goods and services than a single-person household.

Practice question: structured question

The chart below shows the average weekly household expenditure in the UK, financial year ending 2023.

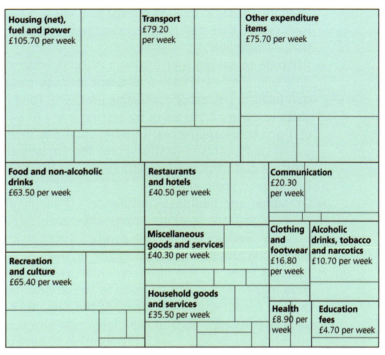

Housing (net), fuel and power £105.70 per week	Transport £79.20 per week	Other expenditure items £75.70 per week

| Food and non-alcoholic drinks £63.50 per week | Restaurants and hotels £40.50 per week | Communication £20.30 per week |

| | Miscellaneous goods and services £40.30 per week | Clothing and footwear £16.80 per week | Alcoholic drinks, tobacco and narcotics £10.70 per week |

| Recreation and culture £65.40 per week | Household goods and services £35.50 per week | Health £8.90 per week | Education fees £4.70 per week |

▲ **Figure 16.6** Family spending in the UK, financial year ending March 2023

Source: Living costs and food survey, Office for National Statistics, UK

a Describe, with reference to the chart, how spending patterns in the UK might be different from those in less economically developed countries such as Bangladesh. [2]

b Spending on education and health is a small proportion of overall spending in the UK. Explain two reasons why this might be the case. [4]

c Identify one reason why a person on a low income may spend a higher proportion of their income on food than those on higher incomes. [1]

Definition

Saving occurs when a person puts away part of their current income for future spending.

▲ There are numerous reasons why people save money

Influences on household savings

Saving occurs when a person puts away part of their current income for future spending. The reasons for saving include the following:

» A person decides to sacrifice current spending so that they have funds to spend in the future. For example, people save for a holiday or for their retirement. Parents may save money for their children's education.

» A person may choose to save a portion of their income in a bank or other financial institution in order to earn interest. Banks also provide a secure place for depositing savings.

» A person may save for precautionary reasons so that they have money put aside in case of an emergency such as an accident, job loss or unforeseen event in the future.

The level of savings is affected by the following factors:

» **Age of a person** – in many modern economies, from about the age of 25 people start to save for their future. They will be likely to have secured permanent employment. The amount a person will save is influenced by the amount of support a government gives its citizens in terms of old-age pensions and healthcare provision. If people have to fund their own healthcare and pensions, they will have to save more during their working lives.

» **Attitude to saving** (personal and cultural influences) – as every person is different, they each have a different attitude to saving. For example, in the USA and the UK, many consumers borrow to fund expenditure by using credit cards to make purchases or by getting loans to buy expensive items such as cars and home appliances. In other countries such as Japan and Germany, the use of credit cards is relatively low. The Chinese and Japanese are generally cautious and conservative with money, so like to save for a 'rainy day' (unforeseen emergencies).

» **Consumer and business confidence** – if people and firms have confidence in the economy, the level of savings will usually fall as people spend money more willingly. Savings tend to rise during an economic slowdown when consumers are feeling less optimistic about the future.

» **Interest rates** – a rise in interest rates means that people with existing debts have higher repayments to make to the lender. This will therefore reduce their level of spending in other areas. At the same time, people may save more in a bank to take advantage of the higher rate of return. By contrast, when interest rates are low, people have a disincentive to save and may choose to spend their money instead or find an alternative means of increasing the value of their savings, such as by purchasing shares or making other investments.

» **Income levels** – in general, the more money a person earns, the higher their savings tend to be. This is because a wealthy individual is more able to save a higher proportion of each extra dollar earned. By contrast, less wealthy people are unable to reach their target wealth, so are less able to save money.

> **Case study:** China, an economy with a culture for saving
>
> In China, the level of gross savings as a proportion of GDP was approximately 46 per cent in 2022.
>
> Reasons for China's high level of savings are as follows:
>
> * Household incomes have risen due to China's phenomenal economic growth over recent decades. Many people have a surplus of income over their expenditure, so are able to save more.
> * The one-child policy, which was in place from 1979 until 2015, reduced family size and therefore the level of household spending (and hence encouraged higher levels of saving).
> * People are accustomed to saving to buy large items they wish to own instead of borrowing money from banks. Culturally, Chinese people buy what they can afford, with cash, preferring not to get into debt to make purchases.
> * People are saving for their retirement to add to any pension they will receive.
>
> Source: China – Gross saving (% of GDP), World Bank, 2023, Trading Economics website

Influences on household borrowing

Borrowing occurs when an individual, firm or the government takes out a loan from a bank or financial institution, paying it back over a period of time with interest. Borrowing leads to debt, which is manageable if monthly repayments are affordable and interest rates are relatively low. An increase in interest rates causes repayments to rise and this can affect the purchasing power of individuals, firms and governments.

Case study: The cost of borrowing

Laura Brown borrows $500,000 to buy a property when current mortgage interest rates are 6 per cent. In the first year, interest repayments are $30,000 (or $2500 per month). In the second year of the mortgage, interest rates increase to 7 per cent and interest repayments rise to $35,000 (which increases Laura Brown's monthly loan repayments to around $2917). The higher cost of borrowing will therefore reduce her disposable income.

Individuals and firms may borrow for different reasons, including:

» to fund expensive items such as a car or an overseas holiday
» to fund private and tertiary education
» to purchase property or land, such as a factory, office or home
» to start up a new business
» to fund large projects, such as business expansion in a foreign country.

▲ Many students borrow money to fund their university education

Factors that affect the level of borrowing in an economy include the following:

» **Interest rates** – the higher the level of interest, the more expensive borrowing is. Hence, there is a negative correlation between the level of interest rates and the amount of borrowing in the economy.
» **Confidence levels** – firms and individuals will tend to borrow more if confidence in the economy is high. For example, firms will borrow to invest in long-term capital projects if they believe economic prospects are good.

» **Availability of funds** – banks and other financial institutions lend money to individuals and firms in the form of loans and mortgages. The central bank of a country (see Chapter 15) controls the amount of funds which are available for borrowing by setting the cash reserve ratio (the percentage of a bank's assets which must be kept in cash in bank vaults or with the central bank). A decrease in the cash reserve ratio means that more funds are available for lending, resulting in an increase in the money supply and more money being available for borrowing.

» **Credit cards** – credit allows individuals and firms to purchase goods and services with deferred payment. People or firms take ownership of the goods and services immediately and must repay the amount to the credit card company several weeks later – they 'buy now and pay later'. If the full amount owed to the credit card company is repaid in full each month, then no interest is charged, but if only a portion is repaid then interest is charged on the remainder. Interest rate charges on credit card borrowing are extremely high, typically as high as 30 per cent per annum.

» **Store cards** – these are issued to regular customers of large retail stores in many countries to encourage spending. Store cards act as a credit card that can be used only in the individual retail outlet. Firms offer discounts and free gifts as an incentive for people to sign up for a store card. Customers can also accumulate loyalty points on the card, which can be used in the future to purchase goods and services within the store. Store cards can give people an incentive to overspend and can raise their level of debt. If debts are cleared when payment is requested, no interest is charged, but just as in the case of credit cards, if repayments are not made then interest is charged on the outstanding debt.

» **Wealth** – the wealth of a person may affect their level of borrowing as a bank will be more willing to lend money to wealthier individuals or highly profitable firms. This is because they have valuable assets and so are more likely to repay the loan, whereas less wealthy customers have a higher risk of **defaulting** on the loan (being unable to repay their borrowing). To avoid **bad debts** (debts which cannot be repaid), banks often make sure that they have some guarantee of getting their money back. A large business may own several stores or have valuable assets which can be used as **collateral** (security) for a loan. In the case of a mortgage, the property purchased provides security for the loan, and therefore if the borrower defaults on the loan, the bank will take ownership of the property.

Practice question: structured question

The 'household debt to disposable income' ratio in Canada was 178 per cent in December 2023. It is one of the highest in the world. The reason for the high levels of debt is the boom in house prices. Vancouver and Toronto are among the most expensive cities in the world to live. The acceleration in house prices provided an incentive for people to increase their borrowing to buy property as they believed that prices would continue to rise.

Source: Canada households credit market debt to disposable income, July 2024, Statistics Canada

a Identify two reasons why borrowing might have increased in Canada. [2]

b Analyse the effect on the economy of a high ratio of borrowing to disposable income. [6]

c Discuss reasons why some people spend more of their income and others save more of their income. [8]

? Chapter review questions

1. What are the main factors that affect the level of consumer spending in an economy?
2. How will the spending, borrowing and saving patterns of a young family with two children under the age of 5 compare with those of an old-aged pensioner?
3. How do spending and saving patterns of low-income earners differ from those of high-income earners?
4. How does wealth affect a person's level of spending, saving and borrowing?
5. How do changes in interest rates influence consumer spending, saving and borrowing?
6. What are the main determinants of the level of savings in an economy?
7. What factors affect the level of borrowing in an economy?
8. Why might one person save more of their income than another?

Revision checklist

✔ The amount of money that individuals spend on goods and services is largely dependent upon their level of disposable income.

✔ Disposable income is the amount of income a person has available to spend on goods and services after compulsory deductions such as income tax.

✔ Direct taxation reduces the amount of disposable income and therefore the amount of spending and saving in the economy.

✔ Current expenditure is money spent on goods and services consumed within the current year. Capital expenditure is money spent on fixed assets.

✔ The wealth of an individual is measured by the amount of assets they own minus their liabilities (the amount they owe). A positive wealth effect causes people to spend more.

✔ Apart from levels of income, other determinants of the level of spending include interest rates, confidence levels, inflation, age and the size of households.

✔ Saving occurs when a person puts away part of their current income for future spending.

✔ Determinants of saving include the level of disposable income, age, attitudes towards saving (culture), size of households, confidence levels and interest rates.

✔ Borrowing occurs when an individual, firm or the government takes out a loan, paying it back to the financial lender over a period of time, with interest payments.

✔ Factors that affect the level of borrowing in an economy include the level of disposable income, interest rates, confidence levels, the availability of funds (money supply), attitudes towards borrowing (culture), credit (including store cards) and wealth.

17 Workers

This chapter will cover:

★ the wage and non-wage factors affecting an individual's choice of occupation
★ the factors that influence the demand for and supply of labour, including drawing and interpretation of diagrams
★ trade unions and their relative bargaining power
★ the role of government policy, including national minimum wage (NMW), in wage determination, including drawing and interpretation of the NMW diagram
★ the reasons for differences in earnings
★ the causes and consequences of changes in the occupational and geographical mobility of labour
★ the advantages and disadvantages of division of labour (worker specialisation).

Factors affecting an individual's choice of occupation

An individual's choice of occupation depends on many factors, which can be categorised as wage- and non-wage factors.

Wage factors refer to the financial rewards that workers receive in return for their labour services. These are a major influence on their choice of occupation. Table 17.1 outlines the different types of payment a worker may receive in return for their labour.

Table 17.1 Financial payment methods for labour services

Methods of payment	Explanation	Examples
Wages	Wages are time-based, paid hourly, daily or weekly, so are a variable cost to firms	Part-time workers in a shop or restaurant receiving $10 per hour
Salary	Salaries are paid monthly at a fixed rate irrespective of the amount of work done, so are fixed costs	Full-time workers, such as teachers, accountants, shop managers and nurses
Piece rate	A fixed amount paid per item produced or sold	Workers producing individual items in a factory receiving $2 per garment made
Commission	A percentage of the value of products or services sold	Real estate agents receiving 1% of the value of each property they sell
Bonus	An additional lump sum of money paid during the year, usually dependent upon performance	Bank managers earning end-of-year bonuses based on the bank's profits
Profit-related pay	Additional payment to workers, based on the value of profits made by a firm	A partner in a law firm receiving 15% of the annual profits
Share options	Workers receive shares in the firm to give them an incentive to work hard, so that the firm is profitable	Public limited companies offering share options to employees
Fringe benefits (or perks)	Additional benefits, which have a monetary value	Pensions, health insurance, company car, laptop, mobile phone, education for children or membership of a health club

Non-wage factors are also a major influence on an individual's choice of occupation. While people may be motivated by money in the short term, they will also want to feel happy, valued and motivated at work in the long term. Non-wage factors that influence an individual's choice of occupation include the following:

» **Level of challenge** – does the job require thinking and creativity skills or is it repetitive and boring?
» **Career prospects** – are there opportunities for progression within the firm, or will a person have to change jobs to be promoted?
» **Level of danger involved** – is the job dangerous? For example, some people face a high degree of risk at work, such as lifeboat rescue teams, firefighters, window cleaners and miners.
» **Length of training required** – some jobs require few skills, such as cleaning or shop work. By contrast, other jobs require many years of training, such as civil engineers, plastic surgeons, pilots, accountants and lawyers.
» **Level of education required** – some jobs require no or minimal education whereas other jobs require postgraduate levels of education (for example, university professors, architects and dentists).
» **Recognition in the job** – does the worker receive praise and recognition for their performance at work? If a worker feels valued and respected at work, then they may be motivated to work harder and remain in the job.
» **Personal satisfaction gained from the job** – if a worker feels satisfied and happy in their work, they may work harder and stay in the job longer. For example, people who are happy to work for no or low pay may do voluntary work. The intrinsic reward they get is the personal satisfaction of working for a charity, such as taking care of the elderly, sick or those in need.
» **Level of experience required** – some jobs require no or minimal experience whereas other jobs, such as judges and law makers, require a minimum amount of experience.

▲ Firefighters face a high degree of risk at work

Case study: Fringe benefits

- Yahoo! employees get discounts to ski resorts and amusement parks.
- Visa rewards workers who use public transportation to get to work.
- Southwest Airlines employees get free flights for themselves, their family and friends.
- Mattel allows its employees to take paid time off to attend their children's school field trips.
- Google offers free food, a staff gym, bowling alleys and an on-site library.
- Campbell Soup Company has an on-site kindergarten and after-school programmes for staff with young children.

Activity

Interview several adults and ask them about the financial and non-financial reasons why they chose their occupation. Share your findings with the rest of the class.

Study tip

When you are answering questions about the demand for and supply of labour, remember that workers supply labour services to firms, and firms demand workers to produce goods and services.

Wage determination

Wages are determined by the interaction of the demand for labour and the supply of labour. For example, the combination of high demand (ability and willingness to pay) for neurosurgeons and their low supply means their pay is very high.

The demand for labour

The **demand for labour** refers to the number of workers that firms are willing and able to employ at a given wage rate. As with all factors of production, the demand for labour is a **derived demand**. This means that labour is demanded for the goods and services it produces, and not for itself. For example, bakers are demanded for the bread they bake, rather than for the sake of hiring bakers.

Figure 17.1 shows a downward-sloping demand for labour (D_L) curve. When the wage rate falls from W_1 to W_2, the quantity of workers demanded increases from N_1 to N_2. This is because firms (employers) are able to hire more workers when the wage rate is lower.

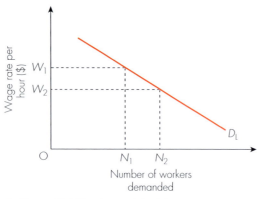

▲ **Figure 17.1** The demand for labour curve

The factors that influence the demand for labour include the following:

» The **level of total demand** in the economy – during a boom or period of economic growth, the demand for goods and services, and therefore the demand for labour to produce them, will be higher. By contrast, the demand for labour falls during a recession.

» The **productivity of labour** (output per worker over a period of time) – the demand for workers increases as their productivity increases through training and changes to production methods. For example, allowing workers to make suggestions about how their working practices can be improved and putting the suggestions into practice can motivate workers as they feel empowered to make changes. Recognition of workers' achievements can also be motivational and increase productivity. Consider how praise from your teachers or parents can impact upon your own attitude to learning!

» The **cost of labour** as compared with the cost of machinery and technology that could replace the labour – technology and machinery, such as the use of artificial intelligence, can often perform the tasks carried out by workers. Although technology and machinery are expensive to purchase in the short run, they can save money for the business in the long run. For example, many firms have cut back on the number of security guards they hire and replaced them with security cameras. Cameras are cheaper in the long run and they do not need toilet or meal breaks, although they do break down occasionally! Similarly, car manufacturers use robotic equipment and machinery that can operate 24 hours a day.

▲ Security cameras can be more cost-effective than security guards in the long run

The supply of labour

The **supply of labour** in an economy consists of people who are of working age and who are both willing and able to work at different wage rates. This does not include those who are in full-time education or those who do not work by choice, such as a housewife or househusband.

Figure 17.2 shows an upward-sloping supply of labour (S_L) curve. If the wage rate in an industry increases from W_1 to W_2, the number of people willing to work will increase from N_1 to N_2 because more workers are attracted by higher wages, ceteris paribus.

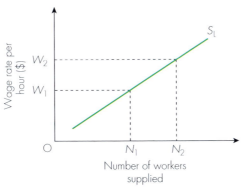

▲ **Figure 17.2** The supply of labour curve

It is possible, at least in theory, for the S_L curve to be backward bending. Figure 17.3 shows that high wage rates will cause workers to work longer hours to increase their earnings, but only up to a certain point. As wage rates increase from W_1 to W_2 the number of hours worked increases from H_1 to H_2. However, as wages increase from W_2 to W_3 the number of hours worked falls from H_2 to H_3 because there is a trade-off between work and leisure time. At W_3 a person can work fewer hours yet have a higher income than at W_2. The **backward-bending supply of labour curve** therefore occurs when wage rates rise to a high enough point to allow people to work less and enjoy more leisure hours.

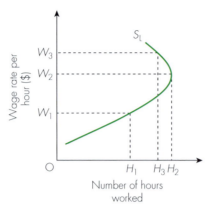

▲ **Figure 17.3** The backward-bending supply of labour curve

The structure of the labour supply varies between countries and depends on the following factors.

Labour force participation rate

The labour force participation rate is the percentage of the working population that is working, rather than unemployed. Table 17.2 shows the participation rate in a selection of countries. This is influenced by:

» the number of full-time and part-time workers in the labour force
» the number of women in the workforce
» the age distribution of the workforce
» the official retirement age of the country.

Availability and level of welfare benefits

In many countries, welfare benefits are provided to the unemployed. However, if welfare benefits are high and readily available, this can discourage people from seeking employment (supplying their labour services) as the opportunity cost of not working and receiving welfare payments is too great. Governments try to regulate who can receive benefits to prevent disincentives to work. For example, in the UK an eligible person must prove that they are actively seeking work if they are to continue to receive welfare payments.

Changing social attitudes

In many countries, more women are entering the workforce and delaying having families (thereby increasing the supply of labour). In addition, more men are looking after the home and children while their wives work. This affects the composition of the workforce as well as the overall supply of labour. Also, as a result of falling birth rates some countries have ageing populations (see Chapter 31). This means such countries may have to rely on immigration to ensure that they have workers with the required skills in the future.

Table 17.2 Labour participation rates (% of population aged 15+ in selected countries), 2023

Country	Labour participation rate (%)
United Arab Emirates	83
Nigeria	59
Vietnam	73
Thailand	67
Japan	63
Bangladesh	58
France	56
Pakistan	53
Mauritius	56
Jordan	39

Source: Labor force participation rate, total (% of total population ages 15+) (modeled ILO estimate), by International Labour Organization, 6 February 2024, World Bank Group website

Equilibrium wage rate

For the vast majority of jobs in a market economy, the equilibrium wage rate is determined by the interaction of the demand for and supply of labour (see Figure 17.4).

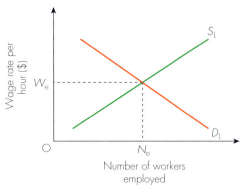

▲ **Figure 17.4** Equilibrium wage rate determination

The **equilibrium wage rate** is determined when the wage rate employees are willing to work for equals the wage rate that firms (employers) are prepared to pay – that is, when the demand for labour is equal to the supply of labour. In Figure 17.4, the equilibrium wage rate is W_e and N_e workers are employed. Changes in the demand for or supply of labour in an industry will therefore change the equilibrium wage rate.

> ### Activity
>
> Draw and interpret a demand and supply of labour diagram for each of the scenarios below. Include the correct labels for the axes in each diagram.
>
> **a** An increase in the demand for skilled labour in the technology sector.
> **b** A decrease in the supply of labour in the agricultural sector due to rural–urban migration.
> **c** A government-imposed minimum wage above the equilibrium wage rate in the retail sector.

Government policy

Definition

A **national minimum wage** is the lowest legal amount any firm can pay its workers and is set by the government.

Wage determination is also influenced by government policy in the form of **national minimum wage** (NMW) legislation. This is the lowest amount a firm can pay its workers, per time period, as set by the government. Any firm which pays workers less than the legal minimum wage is breaking the law.

Since May 2011, Hong Kong has had a statutory minimum wage. In 2024, the NMW in Hong Kong was HK$40 (around $5.12) per hour for all workers. In Australia, the NMW in 2024 was AU$23.23 (around $15.42) per hour. In some countries, such as the UK, the NMW is age-dependent (see Table 17.3).

Table 17.3 Minimum wage rates per hour in the UK, 2024

Age of worker	NMW	Approx. US$
Under 18	£6.40	$8.15
18–20	£8.60	$10.95
21 and over	£11.44	$14.56

Source: Compiled from Minimum wage rates for 2024, National Minimum Wage UK website

In Figure 17.5, the equilibrium wage rate before the national minimum wage is W_1 and N_1 workers are demanded and supplied.

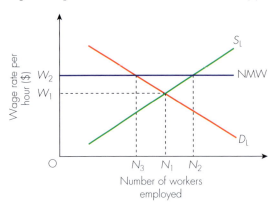

▲ **Figure 17.5** National minimum wage

If the government introduces an NMW which is above the equilibrium wage at W_2, then the quantity of labour supplied to the market increases from N_1 to N_2. This is because more workers are prepared to work for a higher wage rate.

However, the quantity of labour demanded falls from N_1 to N_3 because firms (employers) are less able or willing to pay as many workers as possible at a higher wage rate. As the quantity of labour supplied is greater than the quantity demanded, there is a surplus of labour at a wage rate of W_2. Thus, if the NMW is set too high, this may lead to unemployment in the economy, at least in the short run.

Advantages of a national minimum wage include the following:

»» Workers receive a fair (or 'liveable') wage for an hour's work and are not exploited by employers.
»» Unemployed people may have an incentive to work as the wage rate may be more attractive than relying on welfare payments.
»» Low-income earners may have more money to spend. This may increase consumption in the economy, thus easing any fears that higher wages (and hence costs of production) might cause unemployment.

Disadvantages of a minimum wage include the following:

»» Workers who earn more than the minimum wage (perhaps due to their seniority at work) may request a higher wage rate to maintain the wage differential between them and workers who earn less than they do. For example, when cleaners in an office receive a pay rise as a result of an increase in the NMW, other office staff may ask for a wage increase to maintain the difference between their wages and those of the cleaners. This causes an even larger increase in the cost of labour for firms.

>> As indicated in Figure 17.5, unemployment in the economy (see Chapter 27) may increase because firms face higher wage bills and therefore reduce their demand for labour. Firms may purchase machinery and equipment to reduce the number of workers required.

Another determinant of wages is trade unions and their relative bargaining power. A **trade union** is an organisation which exists to protect the rights of workers. They originated in the 19th century in the UK and the USA. Workers often worked in very poor conditions, so they created trade unions to bargain for better terms and working environments. A worker becomes a member of a trade union by paying a subscription fee, usually on a yearly basis. The membership fees help to pay for the administrative and legal expenses of operating the trade union.

Reasons for differences in wages

This section of the syllabus requires you to understand the reasons for differences in wages and how these reasons influence the wages of workers.

Various factors can influence differences in earnings between workers.

Level of skills of workers

In general, skilled workers earn more than unskilled workers due to their relatively high demand and low supply. As an example, Table 17.4 shows some of the highest- and lowest-paid occupations in the UK.

Table 17.4 Earnings for selected occupations in the UK, April 2024

Profession	Annual salary (£)	Profession	Annual salary (£)
Chief executive officer	113,577	Kitchen and catering assistant	10,220
Information technology director	91,810	Cleaner and domestic work	10,023
Marketing, sales and advertising director	87,050	Elementary services	9,707
Public relations and communications director	77,351	Care worker	9,397
Director in logistics, warehousing and transport	71,271	Bar staff	7,928

Note: all figures are expressed as pre-tax earnings for the median full-time worker
Source: Labour market overview, UK: April 2024, released by the Office for National Statistics website

Workers in the primary sector industries of agriculture, fishing and forestry tend to earn the lowest wages in the economy, as much of their work is unskilled. In addition, the output of these industries, such as fish and food products, has a low sales value. In general, as the value of a good or service produced increases, so will the wage of the person who produced it. A rise in the price of minerals and metals is likely to lead to higher earnings for people working in mining and quarrying.

In the UK, electricians and gas technicians have been in short supply in recent years. The short supply and the necessary training period are likely to lead to higher earnings for workers in these trades.

Occupations in the finance, insurance, information and communication industries typically earn the highest wages. These tertiary sector occupations produce services of a higher value than in the primary sector, and workers are rewarded accordingly. People in tertiary sector professions tend to have high earnings because to become a fully qualified accountant, doctor or lawyer requires postgraduate-level study, professional examinations and many years of experience. The reward for this time and effort is higher wages, which attracts people to these professions. In many countries, students have to take out loans for university and postgraduate training, and they would only be prepared to do this because of the potential reward of high future earnings.

> ### ▶ Activity
>
> In small groups, investigate the differences in earnings between different occupations in your country, or a country of your choice. Each group could research the differences in earnings based on:
>
> - the level of skills of workers (skilled versus unskilled)
> - discrimination between workers, e.g. male versus female workers
> - whether the worker is working in the private sector or public sector
> - primary versus secondary versus tertiary sectors of production.
>
> Compare your findings with those of the other groups in your class.

Relative bargaining strengths

The ability of workers to achieve higher wages depends partly on their ability to negotiate and bargain with their employers. This is affected by several factors:

» **Trade unions** – in general, trade unions will use their bargaining strength to negotiate on behalf of their members. The more united the trade union and the larger its membership, the more successful it is likely to be in negotiating with employer representatives. The basis for higher wages is normally based on one or more of the following in the bargaining process:
   - If there has been a rise in the cost of living due to inflation (see Chapter 28). This reduces the real wages of workers.
   - If workers in comparable occupations have received a wage increase.
   - If the firm's profits have increased and if the profits in the industry as a whole justify a higher return for labour services.
   - If the productivity of labour increases, this will further justify an increase in wages.

As part of the collective bargaining process, especially if there are disputes with employer representatives, trade unions can call upon their members to take industrial action. This refers to any measure taken by a group of workers in protest of major disagreements or disputes with their employers, such as strike action.

» **Age and experience** – earnings change over a person's lifetime. Age has a direct impact on workers' bargaining power in achieving higher wages. Inexperienced workers, such as graduates in their first year of work, will earn less than highly experienced workers. Workers can negotiate higher salaries and wages if they have a greater degree of experience. However, in general a person's earnings potential declines after the age of about 60.

» **Level of education** – a person's level of education tends to affect their earnings and their ability to negotiate higher wages (see Table 17.5). This is because highly educated people tend to be in higher demand and lower supply in labour markets.

Table 17.5 Weekly median earnings and unemployment rate by educational attainment in the USA, 2023

	Less than college graduate	Less than college graduate	College graduate	College graduate
	Less than high school diploma	High school diploma	Bachelor's degree	Professional degree
Mean income, full-time workers	$708	$899	$1,493	$2,206
Unemployment rate	5.6%	3.9%	2.2%	1.2%

Source: US Bureau of Labor Statistics (BLS), Learning and earning and More education: Lower unemployment, higher earnings

The data in Table 17.4 show that unskilled occupations (such as bar staff and care workers) earn significantly less on average than skilled workers (such as directors of different aspects of a business). This is because there is a large supply of people able to work as waiters and care workers (relatively low-skilled occupations). By contrast, to be a doctor, lawyer or engineer, a university degree and subsequent professional training are required. Therefore, as illustrated in Figure 17.6, the supply of doctors is lower than that of waiters.

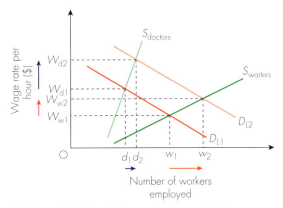

▲ **Figure 17.6** The difference in the equilibrium wage rates of waiters and doctors

Figure 17.6 shows the demand for and supply of waiters and doctors in an economy. Waiters are elastic in supply ($S_{waiters}$) because if the demand for waiters increases from D_{L1} to D_{L2}, the percentage change in quantity of waiters supplied (w_1 to w_2) will be greater than the percentage increase in wages (W_{w1} to W_{w2}) as indicated by the red arrows. This is because the job requires few skills, so it will be relatively easy to increase the supply of waiters in the short term.

By contrast, doctors are inelastic in supply ($S_{doctors}$). If demand for doctors increases from D_{L1} to D_{L2}, the percentage change in quantity of doctors supplied (d_1 to d_2) in the short term will be less than the percentage increase in wages (W_{d1} to W_{d2}). This is because the level of qualifications and length of training required both make it difficult to increase the supply of doctors in the short term. A relatively large increase in wages is required to attract people to study and train as doctors, as illustrated by the blue arrows.

 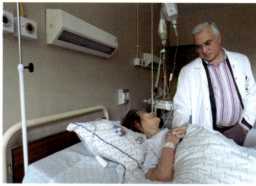

▲ Baristas and waiters are relatively elastic in supply, whereas doctors are inelastic in supply

Practice questions: structured questions

1 Explain one reason why the potential earnings of an individual tend to fall after the age of about 60. [2]
2 Explain, with reference to Table 17.5, how educational attainment impacts upon earnings of an individual. [4]

Differences between male and female workers

In all countries, there is a noticeable difference between the average wages of male and female workers (see Figure 17.7).

Possible reasons for the difference in male and female earnings are as follows:

» There are more women in part-time work than men, so their earnings are lower on average.
» Women take career breaks to have children and therefore miss out on promotional opportunities.
» Women may accept low-paid and part-time jobs as hours are flexible and can fit in with childcare arrangements.
» Women may face social and economic discrimination at work.

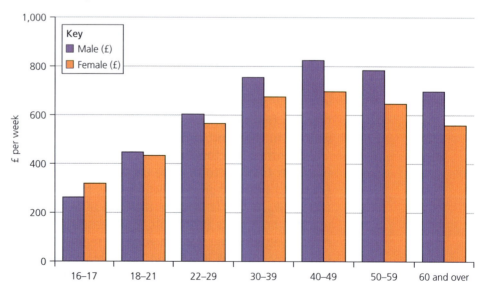

▲ **Figure 17.7** Median weekly earnings for UK full-time employees by gender and age, 2023

Source: Average weekly earnings for full-time employees in the UK 2023 by age and gender, D Clark, 4 July 2023, Statista website

▲ Female participation in the workforce is increasing in many parts of the world

However, times are changing for females, especially those in more economically developed countries. For instance, there are more females than males in the UK enrolled on veterinary science courses, and subjects associated with medicine and education, at university. Almost 70 per cent of the head teachers (principals) in the UK are females.

Differences between private and public sector workers

Workers in the private and public sectors tend to earn different wages. In theory, people in the private sector can earn more than workers in the public sector. In many countries, salaries in the public sector are typically less than those which can be earned in the private sector, but jobs are more secure and are often accompanied by a pension in retirement. Examples of public sector jobs are teachers, nurses, police officers, fire service officers and civil servants.

Private sector jobs typically have higher earning potential as private individuals and firms strive for profit maximisation (see Chapter 20). For example, average bonuses at investment bank Goldman Sachs were $199,000 on average salaries of $200,000 in 2023. Standard Chartered bankers were paid bonuses of $154,167 on average annual salaries of $176,667.

However, this often comes with more risk as jobs are less secure in the private sector and workers often have to save up for their own pensions in retirement. For example, the global financial crisis, which started in late 2008, caused huge job losses at Citibank Group and investment bank JPMorgan Chase by the end of 2013. American Airlines, the world's largest airline, also cut thousands of jobs due to the COVID-19 pandemic.

The mobility of labour

The mobility of factors of production refers to the extent to which resources can be changed for one another in the production process. For example, farming is very traditional in some parts of the world and relies heavily on labour resources. However, in other countries, farming is predominantly mechanised with a heavy reliance on capital resources.

Changes in labour and geographical occupational mobility often arise from shifts in economic conditions, technological advancements and macroeconomic policy changes. Examples include the following:

1 The decline of the coal industry in the USA due to environmental regulations and the rise of cheaper natural gas has forced many coal miners to seek employment in alternative industries. Government schemes help to retrain these workers for jobs in renewable energy, such as wind and solar power.

2 The decline of UK manufacturing industries over the past few decades has led to a shift in the workforce towards the services sector. Former factory workers have retrained and adapted to new roles in retail, hospitality and other service-oriented jobs.

3 The rapid developments in information and communications technology (ICT) has created new job opportunities in software development, cybersecurity and data analysis. Technological advances have also enabled many more people to work from home, thereby significantly increasing both occupational and geographical mobility.

Study tip

It is incorrect to assume that those in the private sector always get paid more than those in the public sector. This depends on many variables, such as the level of qualifications, skills and experience of the workers.

Study tip

Government policies affect labour markets, so have an impact on differences in earnings. For example, governments impose laws to protect the rights of workers and employers, although these vary between countries. Employment laws are designed to prevent discrimination between workers due to gender, race, religion or disability.

Study tip

Economists usually talk about labour mobility, although factor mobility can apply to any factor of production. For example:

- Land might be used for various competing purposes, such as to grow certain fruits and/ or vegetables, or to construct buildings such as housing, hospitals or schools.
- Capital equipment might be used for different purposes too. For example, the same machinery in a Coca-Cola factory can be used to produce Coca-Cola, Sprite and/or Fanta.
- Entrepreneurs can also be mobile. For example, Mary Barra, the first female chief executive officer (CEO) of General Motors, was previously on the board of directors of the Walt Disney Company.

Definitions

Geographical mobility refers to the extent to which labour is willing and able to move to different locations for employment purposes.
Occupational mobility refers to the extent to which labour is able to move between jobs.

4 Following the UK's decision to leave the European Union (EU) (often referred to as Brexit), changes in immigration policies have affected the geographical mobility of labour in the UK. Many EU workers who previously filled roles in sectors such as agriculture, construction, healthcare and hospitality have returned to their home countries or moved to other EU nations in search of employment.

The consequences of labour mobility can include changes in the composition of the labour force of a region or country, changed spending patterns and changes in the quality of life of workers.

Labour mobility can be broken down into two categories: geographical and occupational mobility.

Geographical mobility

This refers to the willingness and ability of a person to relocate from one part of a country to another for work. There are two main reasons why some people may not be geographically mobile:

» **Family ties** and related commitments – people may not want to relocate as they want to be near their family and friends. There may be other commitments such as schooling arrangements for children (relocation can be highly disruptive to the education of children who have to move to a new school in a new town or country).
» The **cost of living** may vary between regions, being too high in another location and making it uneconomical for a person to relocate there. For example, a local bus driver may find it impossible to relocate from the countryside to the city because house prices are much higher in urban areas and therefore they cannot afford to rent or purchase a home in the city. By contrast, an investment banker may be offered a relocation allowance to move to another city and the potential earnings are much higher, so the investment banker has greater **geographical mobility** than the local bus driver.

Occupational mobility

This refers to the extent to which a person is able to change between jobs. The degree of **occupational mobility** depends on the cost and length of training required to change professions. For example, an ex-banker might retrain to become an economics teacher in a relatively short time but retraining to become a civil engineer or criminal lawyer might take them longer. The more skilled and qualified a person is, the greater their occupational mobility tends to be.

Generally, the more occupationally and geographically mobile workers are in a country, the greater its international competitiveness (see Chapter 32) and economic growth (see Chapter 26) are likely to be.

Practice question: structured question

In some countries around the world there are shortages of people with particular skills. For example, the following shortages existed in 2024:

- There is a global shortage of doctors and nurses.
- Belgium and the UK have a shortage of chefs.
- Nordic countries have a shortage of psychologists.

Millions of international migrants are prepared to relocate in order to take advantage of employment opportunities. For example, many nurses trained in the Philippines seek employment opportunities in overseas countries.

a Give two reasons why there is a global shortage of doctors and nurses.   [2]
b Explain the reasons why nurses trained in the Philippines may relocate to take advantage of employment opportunities.   [4]
c Analyse how countries can attract individuals to professions in which they have a shortage of workers.   [6]

> ## Activity
>
> Use the internet to investigate global employment opportunities in selected countries around the world. Be prepared to share your findings with your teacher and fellow students.

Division of labour and specialisation of labour

Definitions

Specialisation of labour refers to workers being experts in a particular profession.

Division of labour occurs when a production process is split between different workers, who become experts in a part of the process.

Specialisation of labour occurs when a worker becomes an expert in a particular profession, such as a landscape architect, a psychiatric nurse, an electrical engineer or an economics professor. **Division of labour** occurs when a production process or task is split between different workers, who become experts in a part of the process. Examples are supermarket checkout operators, waiters serving people in a restaurant and factory workers who operate machinery.

Advantages of division of labour and specialisation of labour for the individual (workers) and firms include the following:

- » Workers become experts in their field, so their productivity and efficiency increase.
- » The quality of the product or service increases.
- » Workers can become very skilful, so their earning potential may increase.

These advantages culminate in higher motivation, productivity, output and competitiveness for firms.

Disadvantages of division of labour and specialisation of labour for the individual and firms include the following:

- » The work may become repetitive and boring.
- » Workers may become alienated, especially those specialising in low-skilled work.
- » The production process may become overspecialised – that is, too dependent on an individual worker or group of workers.
- » The workers may become deskilled in other areas – in other words, there is a lack of flexibility.

These disadvantages culminate in lower motivation, productivity and output for firms.

The advantages and disadvantages of specialisation for the economy as a whole are outlined in Chapter 33.

Case study: The rich and famous

There are some people with special talents or qualities who earn exceptionally high wages. Examples are supermodels, top footballers and tennis players, famous celebrities and A-list actors. This is because their skills are exceptional and are in short supply, and thus their labour supply curve is price inelastic as shown in Figure 17.8.

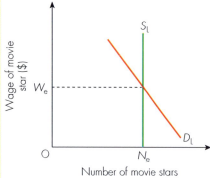

▲ **Figure 17.8** Price inelastic supply of Hollywood movie stars

There are only a finite number of top Hollywood movie stars (N_e), so the equilibrium wage rate will be relatively high (W_e). Special talents allowed Taylor Swift to be listed on Forbes' World's Billionaires List in 2024.

Activities

1 Investigate the highest-earning male and female:
   a film (movie) stars
   b tennis players
   c pop singers or rappers
   d other category of your choice.
2 Discuss possible reasons for any differences in the earnings.

Practice questions: multiple choice

1 Which term describes the lowest amount of pay that a firm can reward its employees, as stipulated by the government? [1]
   A equilibrium wage rate
   B fringe benefits
   C national minimum wage
   D wages per hour

2 Which option is a disadvantage of division of labour? [1]
   A a lack of labour flexibility
   B production processes may be overspecialised
   C unemployment as a result of higher wages
   D work may become repetitive and boring

❓ Chapter review questions

1 How do wage and non-wage factors differ, regarding a worker's choice of occupations?
2 What are fringe benefits?
3 How are wages determined?
4 What is meant by the demand for labour, and what are the factors that affect the demand for labour?
5 What is derived demand?
6 What is meant by the supply of labour, and what are the factors that affect the supply of labour?
7 Why might the supply of labour curve be backward bending after a certain wage rate is reached?
8 How are wages determined in a market economy?
9 How might a national minimum wage affect the demand for and supply of labour?
10 Why might a national minimum wage, set above the market equilibrium, cause unemployment?
11 What are the various factors that influence differences in earnings between workers?
12 What is meant by the mobility of labour?
13 How do the division of labour and specialisation of labour improve productivity and efficiency?

Revision checklist

✔ An individual's choice of occupation depends on many factors, which can be categorised as wage and non-wage factors.
✔ Wage factors are the financial rewards that workers receive.
✔ Non-wage factors are the non-financial factors that influence an individual's choice of occupation.
✔ Wages are determined by the interaction of the demand for labour and the supply of labour.
✔ The demand for labour is the number of workers that firms are willing and able to hire at a given wage rate.
✔ The supply of labour refers to everyone in an economy who is of working age and is both willing and able to work at different wage rates.
✔ The equilibrium wage rate is determined when the demand for labour is equal to the supply of labour.
✔ The national minimum wage is the lowest amount a firm can pay its workers as set by the government.
✔ The various factors that influence differences in earnings between workers include level of skills, the production sector, gender, private or public sector employment and the age of the worker.
✔ Wage determination is also dependent on trade unions and their relative bargaining power.
✔ The mobility of factors of production refers to the extent to which resources can be changed for one another in the production process.
✔ Geographical mobility refers to the extent to which a person is willing and able to move to different locations for employment purposes.
✔ Occupational mobility refers to the extent to which a person is able to switch between different jobs (occupations).
✔ Specialisation of labour refers to workers being expert in a profession.
✔ Division of labour occurs when a production process is split between different workers, who become experts in a part of the process.

Firms

Classification of firms

Economic sector

Firms can be classified according to the economic sector in which they operate:

» **Primary sector** – this sector of the economy contains firms that extract raw materials from the earth. Examples are fishing, mining and agricultural farming.
» **Secondary sector** – this sector contains firms that:
  – manufacture goods, changing raw materials into finished products
  – construct buildings, roads and bridges.
» **Tertiary sector** – this sector contains firms that provide services to the general public and other firms. Examples are retail shops, doctors, dentists, schools, hairdressers, advertising agencies, lawyers, financial advisers, insurance companies and banks.

▲ Agricultural workers operate in the primary sector

Definition

Interdependence means that the three sectors of industry depend on each other and cannot operate independently to produce goods and services.

The primary, secondary and tertiary sectors of an economy are **interdependent** (they depend on each other). This is because a firm cannot operate without using goods and services from all three sectors of industry to make and sell its goods or services to the final customer. Firms in the three sectors are linked through a process known as the **chain of production** (see the Seven Stars case study).

Case study: Seven Stars

Seven Stars is an independent children's clothes shop located in Karachi, Pakistan. The business owners design the clothes, which are made locally. They are sold to customers from its store and through the firm's website. Table 18.1 shows examples of goods and services from the primary, secondary and tertiary sectors that are necessary for Seven Stars to operate successfully. The firms in each sector represent links in the chain of production.

Table 18.1 Goods and services used by Seven Stars

Activity/sector	Examples of goods/services required
Primary	Cotton fabric, wool, thread
Secondary	Designers, machinists, pattern cutters, hand finishers
Tertiary	Advertising, insurance, banking and finance, transport of finished goods, website designers and a shop to sell the clothing to customers

Activities

Refer to the Seven Stars case study.

1 Identify the factors of production required by Seven Stars to operate its business.
2 Produce a table like the one above for:
  a a manufacturer of smartphones
  b a coffee shop
  c a shop selling kitchen equipment
  d a sheep farmer.

Public and private sectors

Firms can also be classified according to whether they operate in the private or public sector.

Private sector firms are owned by private individuals and owners. Their main aim is to earn profit. The types of private sector firm include:

» sole trader – a business owned and controlled by a single person
» partnership – a business owned by between two and twenty people, with shared ownership and risk-taking
» private limited company – a business owned by shareholders, who are unable to buy or sell shares without the consent of other shareholders
» public limited company – a business owned by shareholders, who can openly and freely buy or sell their shares on a stock exchange.

Public sector firms are owned by the government. Their main aim is to provide a service to the general public. For example, the government provides education and healthcare services for people who are unable and/or unwilling to pay for private education and private healthcare. In both France and the UK, in 2024 the public sector accounted for a large portion of gross domestic product (GDP). Both are good examples of mixed economies (see Chapter 14). Other examples are South Korea, Japan, Iceland, Denmark and Romania.

Public sector organisations are wholly owned by the government and are therefore funded through tax revenues. Examples of public sector organisations are water suppliers, sewerage providers, utilities (electricity and gas providers), the post office and state-owned news and broadcasting organisations (such as TVN in Chile and ABC in Australia).

The relative size of firms

Another way to classify firms is according to their relative size. In every economy there are firms of different sizes. Small firms, such as local grocery stores and sole traders, co-exist alongside large multinational companies such as Walmart and Volkswagen. A business may start as one store and grow over time. For example, Burger King opened its first restaurant in Florida, USA, in 1953 and today has thousands of stores across many countries. Alternatively, a business may choose to stay small, such as a wedding dress designer, a hairdresser or an owner of a small gift shop.

The relative size of a firm can be measured in different ways. The following are some examples:

» **Number of employees**
» **Market share** – this measures a firm's sales revenues as a proportion of the industry's sales revenue.
» **Market capitalisation of a firm** – this is the stock market value of a company, calculated by multiplying the total number of shares in the business by the current share price.
» **Sales revenue of a firm** – this is measured by multiplying the unit price of a product by the quantity sold (see Chapter 20).

Case study: The dominance of large firms

Firms of all sizes exist in local, national and international markets. However, large firms often dominate the industry. For example:

- The sports clothing industry is dominated by Nike, Adidas and Puma.
- The tennis racket industry is dominated by Wilson, Prince and Head.
- The chocolate industry is dominated by Mondelēz, Mars, Nestlé and Ferrero Rocher.
- The smartphone industry is dominated by Samsung, Apple, Xiaomi and Oppo.
- The market for search engines is dominated by Google, Bing and Yahoo!

Activity

Use the internet to research the market share of the largest companies in the above industries in your country.

Examples of products and services provided by small shops are made-to-measure clothing and custom-made furniture. They tend to focus on smaller markets and may cater for specific tastes and to people with higher incomes.

▲ Bespoke suits are made by small, independent firms

A **sole trader** (or **sole proprietor**) is an individual who owns his or her personal business. The owner runs and controls the business and is the sole person responsible for its success or failure. This is the most common type of business ownership. Examples are self-employed painters and decorators, plumbers, mechanics, physiotherapists and freelance photographers. Sole proprietorships are often small family-run businesses and can be set up with relatively little capital, usually obtained from personal savings and borrowing.

Case study: Sole traders into big companies

Many of today's well-known companies started as sole traders. For example, Chanel was started by Coco Chanel in 1910 and has a huge global presence today. Pierre Omidyar started AuctionWeb in 1995. It grew to become eBay, which is possibly the world's largest and most well-known online consumer-to-consumer sales platform and business-to-consumer sales platform.

The advantages and benefits of small firms include the following:

» Few legal formalities exist. This means that sole proprietorships are quite easy to set up. Start-up costs are also usually much lower than in setting up larger types of business.
» Smaller firms are easier to manage and control. Larger firms can suffer from diseconomies of scale (see below) due to coordination problems.
» The sole trader is the only owner of a firm and therefore receives all of the profits made by the business. This gives them an incentive to work hard to become successful.
» Being your own boss can have some advantages: not having to take orders from others, having flexibility in decision-making (such as dictating your working hours), and enjoying higher self-esteem from being successful.
» Small businesses are likely to know their customers on a more personal level and this can lead to better relationships. Larger firms might not have the time to get to know their customers, so their services often become impersonal. Smaller shops can also adapt quickly to changing consumer tastes – for example, a small bakery may make more sourdough bread to cater for an

increase in demand, or a small independently run book shop may order titles for individual customers.

» Smaller firms may provide unique goods and services for customers or can tailor products to meet needs of customers. For example, a small grocery store has to find a way to compete with supermarkets. It might do so by providing a range of goods which people cannot buy in a supermarket, such as speciality cheeses or vegan food. This allows them to attract customers willing to pay higher prices.

» The small grocery store may be located in a remote area and be the only local seller of provisions.

Small firms do, however, face some challenges and disadvantages:

» Small firms have limited start-up capital, which makes it difficult for them to raise finance to establish the business. Sole traders may find it difficult to secure any funds beyond their personal savings. Trying to expand the business can also be problematic due to the lack of sources of finance available to small businesses.

» Statistically, small firms have the largest risk of business failure. Even the successful ones usually face intense competition due to the vast number of small firms that exist. In addition, the presence of larger and more established businesses often threatens the survival of smaller firms.

» The success of small firms very much depends on the abilities and commitment of the owners. Sole traders often have to do their own financial accounts, marketing and management of human resources. They are unlikely to be equally effective in the different roles, and having to do all these tasks adds to the workload, stress and challenges of running a small firm.

» Small firms often suffer from a lack of continuity. The running of the business can be jeopardised if the owner is not there, maybe due to going on holiday, or due to illness.

» As they are unable to exploit the benefits of large-scale production, small firms have higher unit costs of production. Subsequently, their prices tend to be less competitive than those of larger competitors (which benefit from economies of scale – see below). This can reduce the competitiveness and profits of smaller firms.

Causes of the growth of firms

Firms can grow either internally (such as increasing their market share) or externally (such as through mergers).

External growth

External growth (or **inorganic growth**) occurs when expansion involves another organisation, such as through mergers, takeovers and franchises.

Mergers

Definition

A **merger** occurs when two or more firms join together to form one firm.

In a **merger**, two firms agree to form one new company. For example, the MTRC and KCRC railway companies in Hong Kong merged in 2007 to become one company which now is the only provider of railway and underground railways services in Hong Kong. They formed a monopoly (see Chapter 21), but any fare increases must be approved by the government. Another example is when Facebook bought WhatsApp in 2014 for $19bn.

We will consider the different types of mergers in more detail in the next section.

Definition

A **takeover** occurs when a firm is taken over by another firm. A takeover may be hostile, or the two firms might have agreed to the takeover.

Takeovers

By buying a majority stake (share) in another business, a firm can take over the target firm and instantly increase its size. For example in 2023, Mars Confectionery bought Hotel Chocolat, a British producer of chocolate and cocoa grower, to expand into the luxury chocolate market. Amazon bought One Medical in 2023 to further expand its pharmaceutical and healthcare portfolio of businesses. Microsoft spent $68.7bn on the purchase of Activision Blizzard, the creator of *Call of Duty* and *World of Warcraft*, in November 2023. **Takeovers** can be hostile, which means that the firm being taken over does not agree to the buyout. However, they can also be agreeable to both firms.

▶ Mars Confectionery's purchase of Hotel Chocolat expanded its presence in the luxury chocolate market

Types of mergers

There are three main types of mergers: horizontal, vertical and conglomerate. These types also apply to takeovers.

Horizontal mergers

Definition

A **horizontal merger** occurs when two or more firms in the same economic sector of industry integrate.

A **horizontal merger** occurs when two or more firms in the same industry integrate (join together). For example, Kraft purchased Heinz in 2015 to form the Kraft Heinz Company. Both firms manufacture food and the merged company has become one of the largest food manufacturers in the world.

▶ The merger of Kraft and Heinz created one of the world's largest food manufacturers

The merged firms can benefit from:

» having higher market share
» gaining skilled employees from each other
» operating with fewer employees (as there is no need to hire two finance managers, for example), so this may reduce costs of production
» taking advantage of economies of scale.

However, the potential costs or drawbacks of a horizontal merger include the following:

» There may be a duplication of resources, so some workers may lose their jobs. Job losses can cause anxiety, demotivate staff and lead to a fall in productivity.
» The newly formed, larger firm may face increasing costs arising from diseconomies of scale (see below).
» The new firm may suffer from culture clashes between the merged businesses. Initially, this may cause communication and organisational problems for the firm.

Vertical mergers

> **Definition**
>
> A **vertical merger** occurs when integration takes place between two firms from different economic sectors of industry.

A **vertical merger** occurs when a firm from one economic sector (primary, secondary or tertiary) merges with a firm at a different stage of production. There are two types of vertical merger: backward and forward.

Backward vertical mergers

A **backward vertical merger** occurs when a firm from the secondary sector merges with a firm from the primary sector, or when a firm from the tertiary sector merges with a firm operating in the secondary or primary sector. For example, a factory in China that makes chicken nuggets for McDonald's buys a chicken farm. The chicken farm supplies the factory with live chickens and eggs, produced for McDonald's outlets for their breakfast products.

 Backward vertical integration

The benefits of backward vertical integration in the above example include the following:

>> The firm in the secondary sector has control over the quality of raw materials with which it is supplied.
>> The price of raw materials falls as the manufacturer does not have to pay another (external) firm for the raw materials.

However, the drawbacks of backward vertical integration in the above example include the following:

>> Costs of running the farm in the primary sector increase total costs as more land, labour and capital resources are required.
>> Transport costs increase for the merged firm as raw materials were previously delivered by external suppliers.

Forward vertical mergers

A **forward vertical merger** occurs when a firm from the primary sector of industry merges with a firm in the secondary or tertiary sector, or when a firm from the secondary sector merges with a firm operating in the tertiary sector. For example, Apple, Levi's and IKEA all own shops in which to sell their manufactured products. Shell owns its entire chain of production: oil mines, oil processing plants and the petrol stations where consumers purchase fuel for their cars.

The benefits and drawbacks of forward vertical mergers are similar to those of backward vertical mergers.

▲ Apple has shops all over the world dedicated to selling its own goods – this is the entrance to the Apple store in The Galleria Mall in Abu Dhabi

Conglomerate mergers

Definition

A **conglomerate merger** occurs when two or more firms from unrelated areas of business integrate to create a new firm.

A **conglomerate merger** occurs when firms from different economic sectors and in unrelated areas of business integrate with one another. They may form a single company or be part of a large group of companies. For example, a clothing manufacturer might merge with a chocolate producer. The two firms are in the secondary sector of industry but operate in different areas of manufacturing. They can take advantage of risk-bearing economies of scale (see below) as diversification spreads risk.

An example of a conglomerate is the Tata Group, which has approximately 100 different companies in its portfolio, ranging from hotels and hospitality enterprises to mining and air conditioning. Another example is the Disney Corporation, which has four main categories of businesses: parks and resorts, media networks, studio entertainment and consumer products.

◀ Taj Mahal Palace Hotel in Mumbai is owned by the Taj Hotel group and is part of the Tata Group's portfolio of businesses

Diversification spreads risks because the conglomerate has a number of businesses in different sectors of industry. A failing business in the group may be protected by the successful businesses within the group's larger portfolio.

However, the conglomerate may become too diverse, and this may cause problems in the management of capital and human resources. If a segment of the diversified firm is under-performing, then it may drain resources from other areas of the conglomerate business.

Economies and diseconomies of scale

Economies of scale

Definition

Economies of scale are the cost-saving benefits of large-scale operations, which reduce average costs of production.

Large firms are able to take advantage of **economies of scale**, which reduce their average costs of production. This gives them a cost advantage over small firms. In many countries, small grocery stores exist alongside large supermarkets. However, supermarkets are able to provide customers with:

>> a wide choice of particular products, such as different kinds of fruit, vegetables, cheeses and canned food

>> a wide product range, so in a single store, customers can buy fresh milk, a pair of shoes, a teapot, a hairdryer, children's toys or even a television.

Modern supermarkets often have other facilities for customers, such as a café, a petrol (gas) station and cash machines. Many supermarkets also have free parking facilities and therefore provide a one-stop shopping service.

Study tip

Many of the advantages of small firms are disadvantages of large firms. Large firms can take advantage of economies of scale. Small firms cannot do this. Therefore, the advantages of large firms are disadvantages of small firms and vice versa.

The phrase economies of scale can be broken down as follows. One meaning of the word economy is reduced expenditure or saving. The word scale refers to size. Therefore, the term economies of scale means that average costs of production fall as a firm grows or increases its output.

Internal economies of scale

Internal economies of scale are cost savings that arise from within the business as it grows.

> **Definition**
>
> **Internal economies of scale** are economies of scale that arise from the internal organisation of the business, e.g. financial, bulk-buying and technical economies of scale.

» **Purchasing (bulk-buying) economies of scale** occur when the cost of raw materials, components or finished goods falls when they are bought in large quantities.

» **Technical economies of scale** occur when large firms purchase expensive pieces of machinery and automated equipment for the production process. Large firms also produce in large quantities and therefore the high initial cost of the machinery and equipment can be spread across the high quantity of output.

» **Financial economies of scale** occur as large firms are able to borrow money from banks more easily than small firms because they are perceived by financial institutions to be less risky. A large firm will also have assets of a greater value, which can act as security for loans and mortgages.

» **Managerial economies of scale** occur if large firms have the resources to employ specialist managers to undertake functions within the firm. For example, despite the high salaries paid by large firms to attract accountants, engineers and human resources specialists, the overall productivity of the firm might increase, thereby helping to cut unit costs.

» **Risk-bearing economies of scale** occur as very large firms, such as conglomerates, produce a range of products and operate in many locations. This diversity spreads risks as weak sales in one country can be supported by strong sales in another. Samsung makes a large range of products, so if one product is experiencing decreasing sales then this loss can be balanced by increased sales of other products.

» **Research and development (R&D) economies of scale** occur if large firms are able to fund R&D. This enables them to be innovative and create products that make them market leaders. For example, companies such as Amazon, Meta, Alphabet, Apple and Huawei spend large amounts on R&D.

» **Marketing economies of scale** occur as large firms tend to have large advertising budgets, so can spend large amounts of money on promoting their products. For example, a Nike or IKEA advert enables all products under the Nike brand or all products sold in IKEA stores to be promoted in a cost-effective way.

Activities

1 a Look for examples of bulk-buying economies of scale in your local supermarket. For instance, compare the cost per gram for a large bag of rice with that for a smaller bag of rice.
  b Study the labels on the supermarket shelves to find three more examples of purchasing economies of scale and be prepared to share your findings.
2 a Make a list of the names of businesses that advertise using billboards and on the television.
  b Consider what these firms have in common. Are they large or small?
  c Consider how this links to the concept of economies of scale.

External economies of scale

External economies of scale are economies that arise due to the location of the firm and are therefore external to the business. Examples of external economies of scale include the following:

» **Proximity to related firms** – Tekstilkent in Istanbul, Türkiye, is renowned for textile and garment manufacturing. A garment manufacturer will benefit from having firms which produce zippers, buttons, thread and fabrics located nearby, as this will give it easy access to its suppliers and reduce transportation costs.
» **Availability of skilled labour** – Bangalore in India is well known for being a centre of ICT. It has a pool of skilled programmers and there are over 100 ICT colleges. In addition, there tends to be an influx of suitably qualified and skilled workers moving to the area. This makes recruitment of workers with the necessary skills relatively easy, thereby cutting costs for firms in the industry.
» **Reputation of the geographical area** – this provides all firms in the industry with free publicity and exposure. For example, Silicon Valley in California has a worldwide reputation as an area for software creation and the development of information technology systems. Other businesses in the industry may also move to the area attracted by the proximity to related firms and availability of skilled labour.
» **Access to transportation networks** – manufacturing firms benefit from being located near to major road networks, ports and cargo facilities. A café or restaurant benefits from being close to other shops, public transport links and parking facilities. China has invested heavily in developing its infrastructure to facilitate efficient transportation of finished goods to ports and airports. This gives it a competitive advantage over India, which has less developed roads and rail networks.

Diseconomies of scale

Diseconomies of scale arise when a firm gets too large, so its average costs of production start to rise as output increases. At this stage, the disadvantages of growth start to outweigh the advantages.

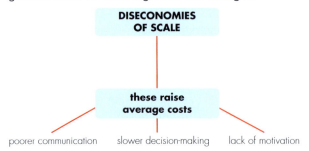

▲ **Figure 18.1** Diseconomies of scale

Reasons for the increased average costs of production include the following:

» Communication issues may arise when a firm becomes too large. There may be too many branches to control and communicate with effectively, so decision-making may be slow due to the number of people in the communication chain. This may lead to increased costs of production.
» A merger between two firms may be unsuccessful due to a clash of organisational cultures, so it may be beneficial to **demerge**.

> ### Case study: Example of a merger that achieved limited success
>
> In 2020, Walmart, the US supermarket giant and world's largest retailer, sold its stake in Asda, a European supermarket chain. Due to stricter planning rules, Walmart did not achieve the growth it predicted in Europe. It therefore decided to accept $6.8bn from the buyer. This was only slightly higher than the $6.7bn Walmart had paid for Asda 20 years earlier.

Study tip

In the real world, it can be difficult for firms to determine when they have reached their lowest average cost and therefore their ideal level of production. Many factors influence costs, and firms operate in a constantly changing environment. A firm's decision to downsize or demerge from another firm may be based on non-cost reasons, such as difficulties in control and coordination, high staff turnover or a loss of focus.

»» It may be necessary to employ more employees for all the branches of the firm, or a new factory may need to be built to accommodate the increased level of production. This will add to total costs of production and average costs of production may rise.

»» Workers within a large organisation may find it difficult to feel part of a large firm, so this may lead to a lack of motivation and reduced productivity. Average costs will tend to rise as a result.

»» The business may become too diverse and start to operate in areas in which it has less expertise. Reduced control and coordination may cause costs to increase. Again, this can lead firms to demerge.

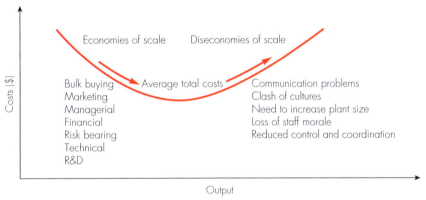

▲ **Figure 18.2** Internal economies and diseconomies of scale

Practice question: structured question

Salesforce is a cloud-based software company which provides a wide range of ICT services for businesses. Slack is a messaging app for business which brings together workforce teams and customers. In 2021, Salesforce completed its purchase of Slack for $27.7 billion. The merger of the two firms allowed them to combine their expertise and compete with Microsoft by providing businesses with a fully integrated ICT platform that covers all aspects of business. The merger brought increased sales revenue and profits. However, there has been a culture clash between Slack and Salesforce workers which has led leaders of both firms to leave their jobs.

a Explain two types of internal economies of scale which could be achieved through the takeover of Slack by Salesforce. [4]

b Explain two diseconomies of scale which may occur after the takeover. [4]

c Discuss whether or not the merger will benefit employees. [8]

Sources: 'Salesforce closes $27.7 billion acquisition of Slack' by J La Roche, 21 July 2021, Yahoo!finance website and 'Leaked Slack all-hands meeting reveals a "strong culture clash" and growing rift with parent company Salesforce' by K Robison, 6 January 2023, Fortune website

Practice question: multiple choice

Which option is an external economy of scale? [1]

A availability of skilled labour

B bulk buying

C financial

D risk bearing

? Chapter review questions

1 What are the differences between the primary, secondary and tertiary sectors?
2 How does the private sector differ from the public sector?
3 Why do so many small firms exist?
4 What are the advantages and disadvantages of small firms?
5 Give five reasons why average total costs may decrease as the firm increases in size.
6 How do horizontal, vertical and conglomerate mergers differ from each other?
7 How do internal and external economies of scale differ from each other?
8 Why might the average total costs of a firm increase as it gets bigger?

Revision checklist

✔ The primary sector of the economy contains firms that extract raw materials from the earth – for example, firms involved in fishing, mining and agricultural farming.

✔ The secondary sector of the economy contains firms that manufacture goods.

✔ The tertiary sector contains firms that provide services to the general public and other firms – for example, retail, legal, financial and accounting services.

✔ Private sector firms are owned by private individuals and owners, and their main aim is profit maximisation.

✔ Public sector firms are owned by the government, and their main aim is to provide a service to the general public.

✔ The various ways to measure the size of firms include the number of employees, market share, market capitalisation and sales revenue.

✔ Small firms are able to co-exist with larger firms due to the advantages of being small – for example, low set-up costs, profit incentives and being able to provide a personalised service.

✔ Growth of firms can occur internally (organically) or externally (inorganically).

✔ A merger occurs when two or more firms join together to create one firm.

✔ There are different types of mergers: horizontal, vertical and conglomerate mergers.

✔ Economies of scale are the cost-saving benefits of large-scale operations, which reduce average costs of production. They can be classified as internal or external economies of scale.

✔ Diseconomies of scale occur when average costs of production increase as the size of a firm increases.

19 Firms and production

This chapter will cover:

★ the determinants of the demand for factors of production
★ the advantages and disadvantages of labour-intensive and capital-intensive production
★ the difference between production and productivity
★ the influences on production and productivity
★ the effects of changes in investment on productivity.

The demand for factors of production

Factors of production (see Chapter 2) are the resources used to produce goods and to provide services. The four factors of production are land, labour, capital and enterprise.

In general, the demand for any factor of production is a derived demand. This means that the demand for factors of production depends on the demand for the goods and services which the factors will be used to produce. For example, economics lecturers at university are hired only if there is demand for economics courses from undergraduates.

On a macroeconomic scale, the demand for the factors of production in a country results from the total level of demand for goods and services in the economy. For instance, during an economic recession (see Chapter 26), firms will demand less labour.

In addition to the derived demand for land, labour and capital, the demand for factors of production also depends on their cost, availability and quality.

» The **cost** of factors of production – the higher the cost of land, labour and capital, the lower their demand tends to be. For example, Apple outsources the production of its products to factories in China and opened production facilities in India in 2017 and Vietnam in 2022, due to the relatively low costs of land and labour there. By contrast, if labour costs are relatively high compared to the cost of capital, then firms might replace workers with machinery and technology. The demand for capital depends on the cost of borrowing money – higher interest rates increase the cost of financing capital-intensive production.
» The **quantity** (or **availability**) of factors of production – the greater the availability of land, labour and capital, the lower their cost tends to be, and hence the higher their demand. For example, the relatively large size and availability of the workforce in India and China has boosted the demand for labour from multinational companies seeking to expand their operations.
» The **productivity** of factors of production – better-quality resources tend to demand a higher price due to their high productivity. For example, surgeons, pilots and barristers are in high demand due to their highly valued skills and qualifications. China, India, Vietnam and Thailand have good-quality land for growing rice, whereas Scandinavian countries, for example, do not have the natural climate to do so.

▲ Cold climates are not good for agricultural production

> ### Activity
>
> Foxconn is a Taiwanese company that makes electronics products such as the iPhone, PlayStation, and cloud and networking products including AI servers. It has operations throughout the world, including in China, Brazil, India, USA, Malaysia and Mexico.
>
> **a** Investigate the various reasons why companies such as Apple and Sony might choose to use manufacturers such as Foxconn to produce goods on their behalf.

Labour-intensive and capital-intensive production

Production of goods and services requires the four factors of production in varying proportions. For example, in a school, capital resources and labour are required in greater quantities than land (natural resources). Consider what the school could invest in to increase productivity. By contrast, production of soft drinks such as Coca-Cola and Sprite requires a large amount of machinery and therefore this process is capital intensive because it requires more machinery (a capital resource) than labour. Another example is an architectural firm. It requires workers with a range of skills, including architects and technicians, who use complex software, such as BIM (Building Information Modelling), to create the designs and produce data for each building project. Computers, software, servers, office space and enterprise are required to design high-quality, creative buildings and attract customers. The process is labour intensive because it requires more human resources compared to natural resources and capital equipment.

Labour-intensive production

In **labour-intensive** industries, the cost of labour is proportionately higher than the cost of other factors of production. Examples are traditional forms of agricultural farming, teaching, psychiatry, physiotherapy, sports coaching, management consultancy and bespoke tailors.

> **Definition**
>
> In **labour-intensive** industries, the cost of labour is proportionately higher than the cost of other factors of production, e.g. accountancy, real estate services and tourism.

▲ Fishing for scallops is labour intensive in China

Labour-intensive production can be very expensive. For example, in private fee-paying schools and health clinics, labour costs account for the largest proportion of production costs, so the price charged to customers is relatively high. Labour-intensive production processes tend to be used to produce individual or personalised products (such as a Hollywood movie or a custom-made wedding dress).

Case study: Professional football

Professional football (soccer) is highly labour intensive. The top-earning players in the world enjoy celebrity status and are rewarded generously for their services. The top ten highest-paid footballers in 2024 are listed in Table 19.1.

▶ Cristiano Ronaldo and Lionel Messi consistently feature in the highest-paid footballers list

Table 19.1 Top ten highest-paid footballers, 2024

Rank	Player	Total earnings ($m)	Club
1	Cristiano Ronaldo	260	Al Nassr
2	Lionel Messi	135	Inter Miami
3	Neymar, Jr	112	Al Hilal
4	Kylian Mbappe	110	Paris Saint-Germain
5	Karim Benzema	106	Al Ittihad
6	Erling Haaland	58	Manchester City
7	Mohammed Salah	53	Liverpool
8	Sadio Mane	52	Al Nassr
9	Kevin De Brune	39	Manchester City
10	Harry Kane	36	Bayern Munich

Note: figures rounded to the nearest million dollars

Source: 'Top ten highest-paid soccer players of 2024' by Dylan Toobey, August 2024, Progressive Soccer Training website

> **▶ Activity**
>
> Discuss whether economics is more important than ethics in deciding how much professional sports people should be paid.

Practice question: structured question

Study the hypothetical data below for two firms and answer the questions that follow. The figures show the amount of money spent by each firm on factors of production.

Firm	Labour costs ($)	Capital costs ($)	Other costs ($)
A	30,000	15,000	10,000
B	60,000	60,000	20,000

a Define 'labour-intensive production'. [2]

b Explain, using the data above, why Firm A might be considered to be more labour intensive than Firm B, despite the latter spending twice as much on labour costs. [4]

Capital-intensive production

> **Definition**
>
> In **capital-intensive** industries, the use and cost of capital is more prominent than that of any other factor of production, e.g. car manufacturing.

Capital-intensive production takes place if a firm spends more on capital costs than on any other factor of production. This includes expenditure on capital equipment such as tools, equipment, machinery and vehicles. Therefore, firms operating capital-intensive production need a lot of money to fund their activities. This can act as a barrier to entry since it proves expensive for new firms to enter such industries. Examples are aircraft and motor vehicle manufacturers, soft drinks production and oil extraction.

▲ There are significant entry barriers into the aircraft manufacturing industry

Despite the initially high costs of capital-intensive production, there are potentially huge cost savings in the form of **technical economies of scale** in the long run (see Chapter 18). Firms that become more capital intensive usually do so to increase their output and productivity levels by mass producing their products. In this way, their unit costs of production are relatively low. As countries such as India and China continue to industrialise, production also tends to become more capital intensive.

Practice question: structured question

Educational services are exploiting the use of technology in the twenty-first century. For example, long-distance learning technologies (such as e-learning and video conferencing) allow students to study courses from the comfort of their own homes without physically attending a university campus, replacing the traditional lecture-style experience. Artificial intelligence (AI) is enhancing educational resources as it can make them more inclusive and personalised for students. The speed at which changes to resources and courses can be made is increasing.

a Explain two benefits of capital-intensive technologies in the provision of educational services. [4]

b Discuss whether technology could ever replace the traditional labour-intensive nature of teaching and learning. [8]

Choosing between capital- and labour-intensive production

Whether firms choose more capital- or labour-intensive production methods depends on several related factors:

» **The cost of labour compared to the cost of capital** – firms tend to choose more capital-intensive methods of production if labour costs are relatively high (assuming that they are able to substitute factors of production in the output process), and vice versa.

» **The size of the market** – capital-intensive production tends to take place for mass-market products such as soft drinks, passenger vehicles and consumer electronics. Labour-intensive methods are often used for personalised services, such as a private tutor, counsellor, adviser, instructor or coach.

» **The firm's objectives** – profit maximisers operating in mass markets tend to opt for capital-intensive production to minimise their unit costs of production. Other firms might choose to use labour-intensive methods as they operate on a smaller scale or to safeguard jobs.

Reasons for using capital-intensive production

Firms may prefer capital-intensive production for the following reasons:

» Capital-intensive production enables firms to use mass production techniques, such as automation in car manufacturing. This enables more output to be produced in less time than using labour-intensive methods. For example, Coca-Cola produces thousands of cans of Coke per minute at its bottling plant when operating at full capacity.

» Unit costs of production are therefore relatively low.

» The use of capital-intensive technologies reduces human error in the production process – that is, machinery is more accurate than humans in the production process.

However, there are drawbacks too. Capital-intensive methods of production can involve huge set-up costs (such as purchase and installation), running costs (such as servicing and maintenance) and replacement costs (when equipment becomes outdated and in need of upgrading). The reliance on assembly lines means any breakdowns will cause major problems for the business.

Reasons for using labour-intensive production

Firms may choose labour-intensive production for the following reasons:

» It is suitable for producing products that are highly customised (individualised), such as hand-made shoes and wedding gowns.
» Similarly, labour-intensive output enables customers to receive a personalised service, so it is appropriate for firms to charge higher prices.
» As workers are highly skilled and experienced, the quality of the product will also be high.
» Labour-intensive production is more flexible than capital-intensive methods. Labour, unlike capital (such as machinery), can be used flexibly to meet changing levels of demand. For example, retail businesses tend to hire more temporary workers during peak trading seasons.

However, labour-intensive output can be expensive. Hiring highly skilled and experienced workers results in higher costs of production and hence a higher price charged to customers.

Production and productivity

Definitions

Production refers to the total output of goods and services in the production process.

Productivity is a measure of efficiency found by calculating the amount of output per unit of a factor input, e.g. output per worker or output per machine hour.

Production refers to the total output of goods and services in the production process. Production can be increased either by using more factor inputs or by raising the productivity of existing factors of production. **Productivity** is a measure of how well resources are used in the production process – that is, economic efficiency in the use of land, labour, capital and enterprise (see Figure 19.1). Productivity takes an average measure of this efficiency, such as output per worker, sales revenue per person or output per machine hour. Alternatively, productivity can be measured as a ratio, such as the value of output compared to the cost of the inputs (the factors of production).

For example, labour productivity measures the efficiency of the workforce in terms of output per worker. It can be improved by having a better-skilled workforce (through education and training) or by allowing workers to use better, more efficient technologies to increase their output.

By contrast, the use of automation, such as robotics and specialised computer equipment in car manufacturing, can help to raise capital productivity without the need to hire more workers.

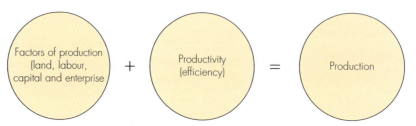

▲ **Figure 19.1** The input–output process (or production process)

Higher productivity is important for an economy for several reasons:

» **Economies of scale** – higher levels of output, whether through capital-intensive or labour-intensive methods of production, help to reduce unit costs (see Chapter 20). These cost-saving benefits can be passed on to consumers in the form of lower prices. For example, the mass production of flat screen televisions and smartphones has made these products much more affordable to many customers around the world. In addition, cost savings from higher productivity levels can help firms to earn more profit on each item sold.

» **Higher profits** – productivity gains are a source of higher profits for firms. These profits can be reinvested in the business to fund research and development or to expand the operations of the business. Either way, higher profits help to fund the long-term survival of the firm.

» **Higher wages** – highly productive firms that enjoy cost savings and higher profitability can afford to pay higher wages to their workers, especially if they become more efficient. Such firms also tend to attract the best workers as people prefer to work for firms with better prospects and profitability.

» **Improved competitiveness** – productive firms are more efficient and so can compete more effectively on a global scale.

» **Economic growth** – productivity is a source of economic growth because it increases the productive capacity of an economy, thus shifting out its production possibility curve (see Chapter 4). This helps to raise employment and standards of living in the economy. Higher wages, from improved efficiency of firms and higher labour productivity, also mean the government collects more tax revenue to fund its expenditure on the economy (see Chapter 23).

Practice question: structured question

Study the data below for two real estate firms selling residential property over a typical weekend. The number of units sold and the number of salespeople involved are also shown.

Firm	Total sales ($)	Units sold	Sales staff
Sharma Realty	3,950,000	10	8
Urvashi Realty	3,800,000	14	10

a Calculate the labour productivity as measured by sales per worker for both Sharma Realty and Urvashi Realty. [2]

b Use the information above to comment on why it might be difficult to decide whether Sharma Realty or Urvashi Realty is the more productive firm. [4]

Influences on production and productivity

The five main factors influencing production and the rate of productivity growth are as follows:

» **Investment** – this is the expenditure on physical capital such as machinery, equipment and buildings. For example, investment in the latest technologies generally helps workers to do their jobs better – that is, to produce more and better-quality output. The degree of investment in turn is determined by the level of interest rates (see Chapter 24). In general, the higher the interest rate, the more expensive capital expenditure will be, thus discouraging investment in the economy.

▲ Innovations in technology have helped business people boost productivity while working from home and on the move

»» **Innovation** – this refers to the commercialisation of new ideas and products. The invention of tablet computers, smartphones and technologies that support remote working has transformed the way many people work, as they are able to work from home rather than at the office. Such innovations have increased the speed of work, improved communications and enhanced organisation at work. Artificial intelligence (AI) is rapidly changing administrative work as it can write emails, respond to customer queries, create reports and analyse data. Thus, innovation can boost production and productivity.

»» **Skills and experience** – the productivity of labour is determined by the quantity and quality of labour. The latter can be increased by improving the skills and experience of the labour force. Education and training, for example, enhance the human capital (skills and experiences of the workforce) in the economy, thus helping to increase production and productivity.

»» **Entrepreneurial spirit** – entrepreneurs take risks in the production process in the pursuit of profit. They plan and organise the various factors of production in the production process. Productivity depends on the drive (motivation) of entrepreneurs, such as their willingness and ability to exploit new business opportunities.

»» **Competition** – rivalry creates an incentive for firms to be more productive. Without competition, firms might lack the incentive to be efficient or innovative. By contrast, competition forces firms to be more efficient, thus helping to boost the economy's overall productivity.

Case study: AI replacing jobs

AI has already replaced jobs in some industries which include journalism, law, translation, speech writing and data analysis. AI can in seconds create reports, write emails and translate them into other languages. Such activities do, however, sometimes require an experienced and skilled person to read the contents to check that it is suitable for the given circumstances.

AI can streamline procedures and therefore reduce costs and increase productivity in a business. This provides opportunities to extend the role of employees, which can be motivational and lead to further productivity gains. AI replaces jobs but also creates jobs as it is a growing industry and there are jobs in related industries such as training.

Activities

1 Find out which jobs AI has replaced and will continue to replace, and which jobs it is unlikely to replace.
2 Discuss whether AI is important for the survival of firms.

Practice question: multiple choice

Which option is **not** an indicator of productivity gains in an economy?   [1]

A greater investment in research and development
B greater number of people in the labour force
C higher wages to motivate staff to work harder
D improved education and training

> **Activity**
>
> Investigate the ways in which the level of productivity in your school might be improved. Try to make your recommendations realistic and be prepared to share your suggestions with the rest of the class.

? Chapter review questions

1 Explain how the demand for the factors of production is influenced by the demand for the product, the price, the availability and productivity of the different factors of production.
2 Why is the demand for factors of production a derived demand?
3 How does labour-intensive output differ from capital-intensive output?
4 What are the factors that determine whether firms are capital intensive or labour intensive?
5 How does production differ from productivity?
6 Why is higher productivity important for an economy?
7 What are the main influences on productivity?

Revision checklist

✔ Factors of production (land, labour, capital and enterprise) are the resources required to produce goods and provide services.
✔ The demand for factors of production is a derived demand – that is, their demand depends on the demand for the goods and services which they will be used to produce.
✔ The demand for factors of production also depends on their cost, availability and quality.
✔ In labour-intensive industries, the cost of labour is proportionately higher than the cost of other factors of production. Examples are often found in the service industries, such as accountancy, banking and tourism services.
✔ Labour-intensive production processes tend to be used to produce individual or personalised products.
✔ In capital-intensive industries, the use and cost of capital is more obvious than that of any other factor of production. Examples are often found in the manufacturing sector, such as car manufacturing.
✔ Despite the initially high costs of capital-intensive production, there are potentially huge cost savings in the form of technical economies of scale in the long run.
✔ Production refers to the total output of goods and services in the production process.
✔ Productivity is a measure of how well (efficiently) resources are used in the production process.
✔ Labour productivity measures the efficiency of the workforce in terms of output per worker.
✔ The main determinants of productivity are investment expenditure, innovation, skills and experiences of the labour force, entrepreneurial spirit and competition.

20

Firms' costs, revenue and objectives

This chapter will cover:

★ a definition and calculation of costs of production: total cost, average total cost, fixed costs, average fixed cost, variable costs and average variable cost
★ how to draw and interpret diagrams that show how changes in output affect costs of production
★ definitions and calculations of revenue: total revenue and average revenue
★ firms' objectives: survival, social welfare, profit maximisation and growth.

Defining costs of production

Costs of production are the payments that firms make in the production process. Examples of costs of production are:

>> wages and salaries paid to employees
>> rent paid to land and property owners for hiring business premises
>> advertising expenses
>> purchases of raw materials and components from suppliers
>> utility bills for telephone, gas and electricity services
>> dividend payments to shareholders
>> taxes paid to the government based on the value of company profits.

Costs of production can be categorised in several ways.

Fixed costs

Fixed costs (FC) are the costs of production that a firm has to pay irrespective of how much the firm produces or sells (see Figure 20.1). For example, salaries for senior managers, insurance payments, administrative costs, bank loan repayments and rent have to be paid regardless of the firm's output level.

▲ **Figure 20.1** Fixed costs for a firm ($4000)

Variable costs

Variable costs (VC) are costs of production that change when the level of output changes. Examples include the costs of raw materials, component parts and the payment of wages to production workers – the more goods or services the firm produces, the higher the variable costs become. The total variable cost line (see Figure 20.2) starts at the origin because when there is no output, no variable costs are incurred.

▲ **Figure 20.2** Variable costs of a firm

Total cost

Total cost (TC) refers to the sum of all fixed and variable costs of production. The total cost line, shown in Figure 20.3, starts at the same value as fixed costs because even when the firm produces nothing, it still needs to pay fixed costs.

Total cost = Fixed costs + Variable costs

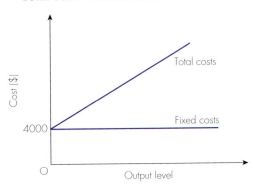

▲ **Figure 20.3** Total costs for a firm

Average fixed cost

Average fixed cost (AFC) is the fixed cost per unit. As a firm produces more output, its fixed costs are divided by a greater quantity (of output), so AFC continually declines (see Figure 20.4). It is calculated using the formula:

Average fixed cost = Fixed cost ÷ Output level

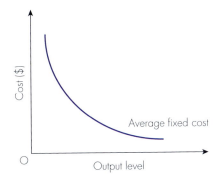

▲ **Figure 20.4** Average fixed cost

Average variable cost

Average variable cost (AVC) is the variable cost of production per unit of output. It is calculated by dividing variable cost by the number of units produced. The shape of the AVC curve is similar to that shown in Figure 20.5, where economies of scale (see Chapter 18) allow the firm to enjoy falling AVC. The onset of diseconomies of scale will increase a firm's AVC as it overproduces.

Average variable cost = Variable cost ÷ Output level

Average total cost

Average total cost (ATC), also known as the **cost per unit**, refers to the total cost of making one product – it is the unit cost of production. The diagrammatic representation of ATC is shown in Figure 20.5. The formula to calculate ATC is:

Average total cost = Total cost ÷ Output level

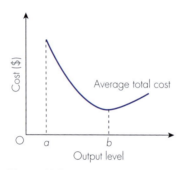

▲ **Figure 20.5** Average total cost of a firm

How changes in output affect costs of production

Firms that operate on a large scale can reduce their average cost of production (see Chapter 18). For example, Coca-Cola's bottling plants can produce many thousands of cans of soft drink per minute. This enables Coca-Cola to benefit from lower ATC (unit costs), as shown in Figure 20.5. The diagram shows that the firm can enjoy economies of scale (lower average costs) as it expands output from *a* to *b*. However, if the firm becomes too large, by operating beyond *b*, it will suffer from inefficiencies, thus leading to diseconomies of scale (see Chapter 18).

> **Activities**
>
> 1 The table below shows a firm's fixed and variable costs of production at different levels of output. Calculate the level of output where average total cost is at its lowest.
>
> | Output (units) | Fixed costs ($) | Variable costs ($) |
> |---|---|---|
> | 20 | 500 | 40 |
> | 30 | 500 | 75 |
> | 40 | 500 | 120 |
> | 50 | 500 | 250 |

2 Juke Engineering produces batteries for a major car maker. Juke's monthly cost structure is shown in the table below. Assume that the firm's average variable costs of production remain constant at all the levels of output shown.

Output level (batteries)	Total cost ($)
1,000	70,000
2,000	90,000
3,000	110,000

a Calculate the average variable cost of production for Juke Engineering.
b Calculate the value of Juke Engineering's monthly total fixed cost at each level of output.
c Calculate the average fixed costs at each level of output.
d Calculate the change in Juke Engineering's average total cost of production if it increases production from 1000 batteries per month to 3000 batteries per month.

Defining revenue

Revenue refers to the money payable to a business from the sale of its products. For example, Saudi Aramco, the world's largest oil company, received record sales revenues in 2022 due to increasing oil prices. This resulted in record annual profits in excess of $161 billion. Jollibee is a Filipino fast-food chain with 1500 stores globally. In 2023, its sales revenue from the sale of fast food grew to $4.27 billion. The higher the volume of sales, the higher the firm's revenue will be.

Sources: 'Aramco announces record full-year 2022 results', Dhahran, 12 March 2023, Aramco website

'Jollibee Group delivers solid finish to 2023', Jollibee Foods Corporation Financial Highlights 2023, Jollibee Group website

▲ A drilling rig in an oil field in Saudi Arabia

Calculation of revenue

Total revenue (TR) refers to the aggregate amount of money a firm receives from selling goods and services. It is calculated by using the formula:

Total revenue = Price × Quantity sold

For example, if a cinema charges an average price of $15 for a movie and manages to sell 5000 tickets in a week, its total revenue will be $75,000 (that is, $15 × 5000).

Average revenue (AR) refers to the typical price received from the sale of a good or service. It is calculated using the formula:

Average revenue = Total revenue ÷ Quantity sold

So, if a cinema earns $75,000 from the sale of 7500 tickets, the average revenue (or average price) will be $75,000 ÷ 7500 = $10 per ticket.

Definition

Total revenue is the amount payable to a firm from the sale of its goods and services.

Objectives of firms

Objectives are the goals or targets of an organisation, such as business survival, social welfare, growth and profit maximisation.

>> **Survival** – business survival is a vital objective for new businesses. However, even well-established firms will need to focus on this, especially during unfavourable trading times. To survive in the long run, firms need to be profitable.

>> **Social welfare** – this refers to business activity that is concerned for the quality of life of those in society. Such objectives focus on social responsibility. They include having ethical objectives and using moral principles (values and beliefs) to guide business activity. Socially responsible businesses strive to improve the treatment of workers, customers, shareholders and the natural environment. For example, since 1985, Patagonia, the outdoor clothing specialist, has pledged to donate 1 per cent of its sales revenue annually to grassroots environmental groups working to protect the planet. Pursuing social welfare as a business objective can help to improve how the general public perceives the organisation. A bad image can turn suppliers and customers against the firm's products and services.

▲ Socially responsible businesses adopt a whole-organisation approach to managing the social, environmental and economic impacts of their operations

>> **Growth** – this objective refers to increasing the size of a business. It usually means aiming to increase the firm's sales revenue and its market share (its proportion of the industry's total sales revenue). An increase in sales revenue will, other things being equal, lead to greater market share for the firm. Growth has several advantages, such as customer loyalty and economies of scale (see Chapter 18).

» **Profit and profit maximisation** – a firm earns **profit** if its total revenue exceeds its total cost of production. Profit provides an incentive for entrepreneurs to take risks. Without profit, firms will struggle to survive in the long run.
Profit is calculated by using the formula:

Profit = Total revenue −Total costs

Activities

1 Bernice's Beach Mats has fixed costs of $4000 each month. Its average variable cost is $7 per beach mat. The firm's current level of demand is 1000 mats per month. The average price of its beach mats is $15 each.
   a Using an example that might apply to Bernice's Beach Mats, explain what is meant by a fixed cost of production.
   b Calculate the firm's total cost of production each month.
   c Calculate the average total cost per month for Bernice's Beach Mats.
   d Calculate the total revenue and average revenue for Bernice's Beach Mats.
   e Draw a diagram to show fixed costs and total costs for Bernice's Beach Mats.

2 Complete the information below for a firm that sells pizzas.

Units sold (pizzas per week)	Sales revenue ($)	Total fixed costs ($)	Total variable costs ($)	Total cost ($)	Profit or loss ($)
0	0				−2,400
300			1,500	3,900	
500		2,400			
1,000	12,000				

3 The following data refer to the costs and revenues of Kurtis Cushions Ltd when operating at 400 units of output per month.

Item	Cost or revenue ($)
Price	90
Raw materials per unit	25
Advertising costs	400
Rent	4,000
Salaries	5,000

   a Explain why advertising costs are an example of a fixed cost of production for Kurtis Cushions Ltd.
   b Calculate Kurtis Cushions Ltd.'s monthly total fixed costs of production.
   c Calculate Kurtis Cushions Ltd.'s total cost of producing 300 units per month.
   d Calculate the average total costs of producing 300 units per month.

Profit maximisation is the main goal of most private sector firms. Profit is maximised when the positive difference between a firm's sales revenue and its cost of production is at its greatest.

> ### Activity
>
> The table below shows the total costs for a firm.
>
> **a** Calculate the total revenue at each level of output if the selling price is $30.
>
> | Output (units) | 40 | 60 | 80 | 100 |
> | --- | --- | --- | --- | --- |
> | Total cost ($) | 1,200 | 1,500 | 1,900 | 2,300 |
> | Total revenue ($) | | | | |
>
> **b** From the above calculations, identify the number of units that the firm should produce in order to maximise profits.

Practice question: structured question

In March 2024, The Body Shop, the well-known seller of shower gels, shampoos and cosmetics, announced that it was closing all of its US stores and many in Canada and the UK. It has struggled to survive in an increasingly competitive market. In recent years it experienced a fall in sales revenue and increasing operating costs because of higher inflation. Despite being one of the first producers of environmentally friendly products and having social objectives, such as being against animal testing and being for fair trade, the business also needed to make a profit so that it could grow and survive in an increasingly competitive market.

a Define 'revenue'.   [2]

b Discuss whether or not social welfare objectives of business create profitability.   [8]

> ### Activity
>
> Investigate the objectives of any two organisations of your choice. Compare and contrast your findings and be prepared to share them with the rest of the class.

❓ Chapter review questions

1 Label the total costs, the fixed costs and the variable costs in the diagram below.

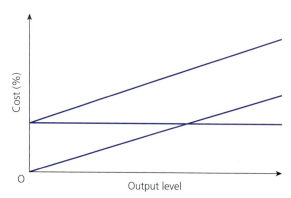

2 What is the difference between variable costs and fixed costs?
3 How might the average total cost of production change when the level of output changes?
4 What is the difference between total and average revenue?
5 What are the objectives (goals) that businesses might have?
6 What are the formulae for total cost (TC), average total cost (ATC), average fixed cost (AFC) and average variable cost (AVC)?
7 Why is survival an important goal for firms?
8 What is profit maximisation?
9 Why do most firms aim for growth?
10 Why do some firms have social welfare as a goal?

Revision checklist

✔ Costs of production are the payments made by firms in the production process, such as salaries, advertising expenditure and taxes.

✔ Fixed costs are the costs of production that a firm has to pay irrespective of its output level, such as rent and insurance costs.

✔ Variable costs are costs of production that change when the level of output changes, such as raw material costs and utility bills.

✔ Total cost is the sum of all fixed and variable costs of production: $TC = FC + VC$.

✔ Average fixed cost (AFC) is a firm's fixed cost per unit of output, which continually declines as output increases.

✔ Average variable cost (AVC) is a firm's variable cost per unit of output. It falls when the firm experiences economies of scale – for example, due to discounts for bulk purchases of raw materials.

✔ Average total cost (ATC) is the cost per unit of output – that is, the total cost of making one product.

✔ Revenue is the money payable to a business from the sale of its goods and services.

✔ Total revenue (TR) is the aggregate sum of money a firm receives from selling goods and services: $TR = P \times Q$.

✔ Average revenue (AR) refers to the typical price received from the sale of a good or service: $AR = TR \div Q$.

✔ Objectives (goals) of firms include survival, social welfare, growth and profit maximisation.

✔ Profit maximisation is the main goal of most private sector firms.

✔ As output increases the average fixed costs of production decrease.

✔ As output increases the average total costs of production decrease up to a point when diseconomies of scale may occur (see Chapter 18).

✔ As output increases the total variable costs of production increase.

Types of markets

Market structure

In economics, the term **market structure** refers to the key characteristics of a particular market. These features include:

» the number and size of firms in the market
» the degree and intensity of price and non-price competition
» the nature of **barriers to entry**.

The two extreme market structures in economics are highly competitive markets and monopoly markets.

Competitive markets

Competitive markets are those with an immense degree of competition. A real-world example are fresh food markets selling fruit, vegetables, meat and fish. These are found in most countries across the world.

Definitions

Market structure refers to the key characteristics of a particular market (or industry), such as the number and size of firms in the market, the degree and intensity of price and non-price competition, and the nature of barriers to entry. **Barriers to entry** are the obstacles that prevent firms from entering a market. Examples are the existence of intellectual property rights, large advertising budgets of existing firms and legal constraints to prevent wasteful competition.

▲ A wet market in Hong Kong — an example of a competitive market

Characteristics and effects of competitive markets

In a **competitive market** there are many firms in the industry. None of these firms has any significant market power to influence market demand or market supply (see Chapters 6 and 7). The presence of a large number of firms in the industry has an impact on price, quality, choice and profit.

» **Price** – firms in competitive markets are said to be **price takers**. This means that the price they charge is determined by the market forces of demand and supply rather than by the firms setting their own prices.

» **Quality** – in some highly competitive markets, firms produce or sell homogeneous products. This means the products being sold are identical, such as bananas or oranges being sold in fresh fruit markets. These firms do not focus on quality as a form of product differentiation.

» **Choice** – in other competitive markets, firms focus on producing differentiated products rather than homogeneous ones. For example, firms may use branding, different product designs, colours and quality to differentiate their products. Many successful and large businesses develop memorable slogans (**catchphrases**) as a form of product differentiation in order to improve their competitiveness. Some examples are Adidas ('Impossible is nothing') and BMW ('Sheer Driving Pleasure').

» **Profit** – both buyers and sellers have easy access to information about the product and the prices being charged by competitors. In addition, as there are many rivals in the industry, profits will be relatively low for each firm in the market.

Benefits and drawbacks of competitive markets

Advantages of competitive markets:

» The products tend to be of higher quality and customer service tends to be good because firms are competing using non-price competition.
» There is more choice for consumers.
» Prices are lower and output is higher as firms have an incentive to be efficient and not waste resources.
» There is innovation as firms try to keep ahead of competitors to maintain their market share.

Disadvantages of competitive markets:

» Some firms will go out of business as they will not be able to keep up with the competition.
» Some firms will not be able to innovate, as they cannot afford to invest in research and development.
» Too much choice in the market may lead consumers to waste time while making decisions about which product to buy.
» Firms may spend resources and funds on advertising to attract customers and maintain market share. These funds could have been spent on other things.
» Profits have to be shared by many firms.

Overall, a high degree of competition in a market tends to benefit consumers. This is because they get higher-quality products and good customer service. In addition, competition brings about greater choice, higher output and more competitive prices (see Figure 21.1).

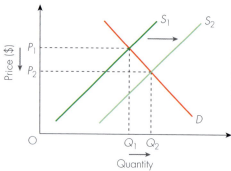

Increased competition shifts the market supply curve outwards from S_1 to S_2. This causes the market price to fall from P_1 to P_2, thereby causing the quantity demanded to increase from Q_1 to Q_2.

▲ **Figure 21.1** Impact of competition on market price and output

Practice questions: structured questions

Bubble tea is made from tea, milk, sweetener, a variety of flavourings and the boba or bubbles (tapioca), which give the drink its name. The global bubble (boba) tea market has grown in size since the turn of the century. It is most popular in Southeast Asia but many of the major bubble tea sellers have franchised their brands and expanded rapidly across the world. The bubble tea market was estimated to be worth around $2.46 billion in 2023 and is expected to grow to $4.8 billion by 2032.

Source: Bubble tea market size, share & industry, 2024–2032, 12 August 2024, Fortune Business Insights website

Bubble tea shops sell similar products and charge similar prices for their drinks. They differentiate themselves through branding, new flavours and loyalty programmes. Some brands have distinctive logos and some use organic ingredients. Others experiment with different types of tea and fruits. Others offer low sugar and dairy free versions to cater for different tastes and markets.

1 Analyse whether bubble tea shops in your area operate in a competitive market. [6]

2 Discuss whether or not consumers benefit from the competitive strategies used by bubble tea shops. Give reasons for your answer. [8]

Monopoly markets

The word monopoly comes from the Greek language, with monos meaning one and polein meaning to sell. There are different definitions of the term monopoly. In general, a **monopoly** is a market structure where one supplier dominates the market and has significant market power. Examples include Coca-Cola (carbonated soft drinks), YKK (zip fasteners) and Mabuchi (which makes most of the micro-motors used to adjust rear-view mirrors in cars).

A **pure monopoly** exists if only one firm supplies the whole market. Examples are the Indian Railway Catering and Tourism Corporation (IRCTC), which has complete control over the ticketing, catering and tourism services to Indian Railways. In the USA, the Federal Reserve is the sole supplier of US banknotes and coins.

In most industries, there are market leaders (those with a high market share). They have significant monopoly power to influence the market supply and, hence, prices. An example is the market for smartphones, which is dominated by Apple and Samsung, who in 2023 had approximately 40 per cent of the market. Hence, these firms are **price makers** (or price setters) rather than price takers.

Definitions

Monopoly is a market structure where there is only one supplier of a good or service, with the power to affect market supply and prices.

Price makers are firms that set their own prices. They have the market power to do so, and they do not have to base their price on the equilibrium price determined by the forces of demand and supply.

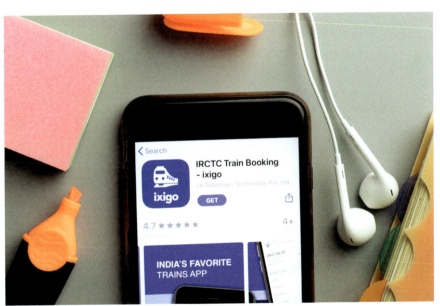

▲ Indian Railway Catering and Tourism Corporation (IRCTC) has a monopoly over selling tickets for Indian trains

Characteristics of monopoly markets

A monopoly has the following characteristics:

» **Single supplier** – as its name suggests, a monopolist is the sole supplier of a product in a given market. This is due to the lack of substitute products caused by barriers to entry into the market.
» **Price maker** – the monopolist has significant market power. It controls enough of the market supply (see Chapter 7) to enable it to charge higher prices and yet produce lower output than would be the case if it faced competition.
» **Imperfect knowledge** – a monopolist is able to protect its prestigious position, as customers and rivals have imperfect knowledge, partly as a result of the monopolist's ability to protect its trade secrets.

Study tip

It is incorrect to claim that monopolists can charge 'whatever' price they want because they are the single supplier of a good or service. While monopolists can control market supply, they cannot govern the level of market demand. Customers will switch or seek alternatives if prices are too high. Hence, monopolists must lower prices if they want to increase sales.

»» **High barriers to entry** – a monopolist can only remain so if in the long run there are very high barriers to entry. These obstacles effectively prevent other firms from entering the market. Examples are economies of scale of existing firms, ownership of essential resources, the existence of intellectual property rights (patents, trademarks and copyrights), advertising expenditure, high start-up costs and legal barriers to entry.

➡ **Case study:** EssilorLuxottica's dominance of the eyewear market

Do you or someone you know wear glasses (or spectacles) or sunglasses? Do you know which company made them? The chances are that a company named EssilorLuxottica were the manufacturers of your eyewear. You may also have bought the eyewear in a retail store owned by EssilorLuxottica.

Luxottica was founded in Italy in 1961. It produces eyewear for many well-known brands including Chanel, Coach, Dolce & Gabanna, Prada, Ralph Lauren, Tiffany & Co., Versace and many others. It owns Ray-Ban, Oakley, Persol, Oliver Peoples, Alain Mikli and several other brands. In 2018, Luxottica merged with Essilor, which was founded in 1849 in Paris, to form EssilorLuxottica. The merged company produces high-quality lenses using the latest technologies. It also produces frames and owns an extensive distribution network of physical shops around the world, such as Lenscrafters, Target Optical and Pearle Vision in North America, Sunglasses Hut, Mujosh and Laubman. In addition, it sells its eyewear online on platforms such as EyeBuyDirect, Clearly, VisionDirect, Lensstore, Ray-Ban.com and Oakley.com.

EssilorLuxottica's control of manufacturing and distribution has led to its market share in North America in 2022 being around 47 per cent. In Europe, the Middle East, Africa, Turkey and Russia its market share was approximately 35 per cent. In the Asia-Pacific region, its share was 11 per cent. Its dominance across the world, in production and distribution of eyewear, creates high barriers to entry. This means that it is difficult for new eyewear brands to establish themselves in the market. EssilorLuxottica is an unfamiliar name and the different brands and distributors within its portfolio give consumers an illusion of choice. Its influence in the industry is strong and prices can be kept high.

Source: 'Global sales share of Essilor Luxottica in 2022, by region' by Tugba Sabanoglu, 24 May 2023, Statista website

Activity

Discuss with a partner whether one firm should be allowed to dominate a market. Consider the question from the point of view of consumers, the business itself, other firms in the industry and the economy.

Practice questions: structured questions

The advertising budgets of large firms can act as a barrier to entry. America's most watched sporting event, the annual Super Bowl, is a magnet for firms with huge advertising budgets. In 2024 the average cost of a 30-second advert during the Super Bowl was $7 million! Seven years before that, in 2017, a 30-second advert cost $5 million (an increase of 40 per cent).

Source: 'Average cost of a 30-second Super Bowl TV commercial in the United States from 2002 to 2024' by Michele Majidi, 7 February 2024, Statista website

1 Define 'barriers to entry'. [2]
2 Explain, with reference to the information above, why advertising expenditure can act as a barrier to entry. [4]

Benefits and drawbacks of monopoly

A monopoly market structure has the following benefits:

» As monopolists control market supply, they operate on a very large scale. They thus benefit from huge economies of scale (see Chapter 18) – that is, lower average costs of production as output increases. This means that monopolists can supply larger quantities of output and at lower prices. Such market power can be a source of international competitiveness against foreign competitors.
» Monopolists have the financial resources to invest in innovation. Research and development expenditure can help to generate new ideas, products and production processes. Innovation can therefore act as a source of profit and improve the productive capacity of the economy. For example, Apple's innovative products, such as the iPhone and iPad, have made the company one of the most valuable businesses on the planet.
» Some natural monopolies can eliminate wasteful competition. For example, it makes economic sense to have one monopoly supplier of postal services in a town, state or country rather than allowing private sector firms to compete to provide such services. This is because profit-seeking firms may not have much of a financial incentive to provide services in remote areas of the country and a single provider can gain huge economies of scale. The same applies to suppliers of water pipes, railway tracks, telephone lines and electricity grids.

Monopoly has the following disadvantages:

» Private sector monopolies can be inefficient in terms of resource allocation. In their pursuit of profit maximisation, monopolists can restrict the output of a product and/or charge a higher price for it. This is detrimental to the welfare of consumers.
» As there are no substitutes for the products supplied by some monopolists, e.g. water suppliers and electricity providers, demand is price inelastic (see Chapter 10). As monopolists are price makers, they can charge higher prices to maximise profit from this relatively low PED.
» High barriers to entry prevent new firms from setting up in the market. This limits the degree of competition and ensures monopolists can continue to charge relatively high prices.

» Imperfect knowledge about the prices and products being charged by competitors means that consumers may not necessarily make rational choices. For example, mobile phone network providers tend to use very confusing pricing packages for their services. Similarly, banks tend to offer a variety of interest rate charges for their various types of loans. Thus, imperfect knowledge enables monopolists to maintain market power.

» Monopolists may have less incentive to innovate than firms in competitive markets. Innovation is the commercial exploitation of an invention. The lack of competitive pressures means that monopolists can become complacent (as there is no need to be worried about competition), rather than focusing on innovations to ensure their survival.

Note that if monopolies exploit their market power and act against the public interest, perhaps by deliberately charging unreasonably high prices, then the government can intervene. For example, a merger between the two largest firms in a market can be prohibited by the government if there is a strong reason to believe that the monopolist's resulting gain in market share will be against the interests of the general public.

> ### Case studies: Government intervention to prevent monopoly

In 2022, the European Union (EU) successfully passed a law which requires Apple and other manufacturers of electronic devices to make their products compatible with a USB-C type charger. This means consumers do not need to buy chargers that are not compatible with other products, thereby saving money and reducing electronic waste. The plastic covering the wires on Apple chargers (called Lightning) tended to wear out before the life of the device and users often had to purchase another expensive charger from Apple.

In April 2024, the South Korean Fair Trade Commission blocked the purchase by MegaStudy of ST Unitas. Both of these are education firms that provide exam preparation services for students and are dominant in the industry. The government organisation decided that the merger could cause tuition fees for students to increase and may limit the quality of courses. The combined firm would also have the power to cut courses and reduce the wages of teachers. The merger was therefore against the public interest.

> ### Activities

1 The top five suppliers in the sugar and tobacco industries account for about 99 per cent of the market in the UK. Use the internet to research the industries which are most dominated by monopolists in your own country.

2 In small groups, discuss whether governments should intervene in preventing mergers and acquisitions if they believe that they might be against public interest. Investigate real-world examples to support your discussions.

3 Discuss the information you would need in order to assess whether a particular monopolist benefits consumers.

Practice questions: multiple choice

1 Which option is **not** a feature of monopoly? [1]
  A Firms supply homogeneous goods.
  B Monopolists are price makers.
  C Only one firm in the industry.
  D There are major barriers to entry into and exit from the industry.

2 Which option is **not** a feature of competitive markets? [1]
  A Firms supply differentiated goods.
  B Many small firms exist in the industry.
  C There are very low barriers to entry into and exit from the industry.
  D There is perfect knowledge of prices and production information.

3 Which option is **not** a characteristic of monopoly as a market structure? [1]
  A high market share
  B imperfect knowledge
  C low entry barriers
  D price setter

4 What is an advantage of monopoly as a market structure? [1]
  A being able to charge lower prices
  B consumer sovereignty
  C having the financial resources for research and development
  D wider choice and availability of products

❓ Chapter review questions

1 What is meant by market structure?
2 What are barriers to entry?
3 What are the main characteristics of competitive markets?
4 What are the effects of competitive markets on price, quality, choice and profit?
5 What is meant by a monopoly?
6 What are the main characteristics of a monopoly?
7 What are the advantages of monopoly?
8 What are the disadvantages of monopoly?

Revision checklist

✔ Market structure refers to the key characteristics of a particular market in terms of the number and size of firms in the market, the degree and intensity of price and non-price competition, and the nature of barriers to entry.

✔ Barriers to entry are the obstacles that prevent firms from entering the market.

✔ The two extreme market structures in economics are highly competitive markets and monopoly.

✔ Competitive markets are those with an immense degree of competition.

✔ In general, a high degree of competition tends to benefit consumers in terms of higher-quality products, better customer service, greater choice and more competitive prices.

✔ Monopoly is a market structure where there is only one supplier of a good or service, with the power to affect market supply and prices.

✔ Characteristics of monopoly include a single supplier in the market, being a price maker, imperfect knowledge and high barriers to entry.

✔ The effects of having only one firm in a market (a single seller) is that prices may be very high, quality may be poor (as there is no incentive for the firm to provide good-quality products), consumers have no choice, and the monopolist may make excessively high profits.

✔ Advantages of monopoly include the potential to supply larger quantities and at lower prices, having the financial resources for research and development, and the elimination of wasteful competition.

✔ Disadvantages of monopoly include the potential to exploit customers through higher prices and limited supply, high entry barriers to limit competition, imperfect knowledge which can lead to irrational decision-making, and a lack of innovation due to the absence of competition.

SECTION 4

Government and the macroeconomy

Chapters

Government macroeconomic intervention

This chapter will cover:

★ the six macroeconomic aims of government
★ the reasons behind the choice of aims and the criteria that governments may set for meeting each aim
★ the possible conflicts between macroeconomic aims.

The six macroeconomic aims of government

The general role of the government is to improve the welfare of its people. The government collects tax revenues in order to fund its expenditure on essential services, such as healthcare, infrastructure and national security.

The central government makes decisions about how to achieve its six macroeconomic aims: economic growth, full employment (low unemployment), stable prices (low inflation), balance of payments stability, redistribution of income and environmental sustainability. It does this by seeking to use appropriate macroeconomic policies (see Chapters 23–25).

Economic growth

Definition
Economic growth is the annual increase in the level of national output, i.e. the annual percentage change in gross domestic product.

Economic growth refers to an increase in a country's real gross domestic product (GDP) over time. Economists believe that sustained economic growth is an important macroeconomic aim because it is the most practical measure of standards of living in a country. Economic growth represents a long-term expansion in the productive capacity of the economy.

Diagrammatically, economic growth can be shown by an outward shift of the production possibility curve (PPC). In Figure 22.1, a combination of an increase in the quantity and quality of factors of production shifts the PPC outwards from PPC_1 to PPC_2, creating more producer and consumer goods, shown by the movement from A to B. By contrast, negative economic growth results in a recession in the business cycle (see Chapter 26).

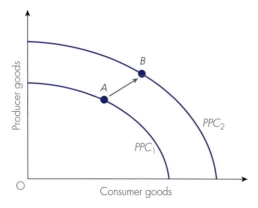

▲ **Figure 22.1** Economic growth and the PPC

Full employment/low unemployment

Definition

Unemployment occurs when people are willing and able to work, and actively seeking employment, but are unable to find work. Low unemployment is a key macroeconomic aim.

Unemployment occurs when people are willing and able to work, and actively seeking employment, but are unable to find work. Low unemployment is a key macroeconomic aim because it complements economic growth – higher employment tends to lead to greater GDP. Hence, low unemployment tends to increase the standards of living in an economy. In addition, full employment or low unemployment represents greater efficiency in the use of the economy's scarce resources.

▲ Governments aim to reduce unemployment

The **unemployment rate** calculates the percentage of the labour force that is unemployed. It is measured using the formula:

$$\frac{\text{Number of unemployed people}}{\text{Number in the labour force}} \times 100$$

For example, in a country with a workforce of 50 million people, of which 5 million are of working age and actively seeking employment but cannot find work, the unemployment rate equals (5m ÷ 50m) × 100 = 10%.

Practice question: structured question

Calculate, using the data below, the total number of people unemployed in the economy. [2]

Labour force	30 million
Population of working age	35 million
Unemployment rate	8%

Stable prices/low inflation

Inflation is the sustained rise in the general price level in an economy. This does not mean that the price of every good and service is increasing, but that on average prices are rising. Governments set a target inflation rate as a key macroeconomic aim in order to control economic activity. Inflation is typically measured by using a Consumer Price Index (CPI). This weighted index measures the change in prices of a representative basket of goods and services consumed by the average household in the economy (see Chapter 28).

Practice question: structured question

The data below show the inflation rates for a country over three years.

Year	1	2	3
Inflation rate (%)	2.5	1.7	2.3

a Define 'inflation rate'. [2]
b Explain, using the data above, why inflation was at its highest level in the third year. [2]

Balance of payments stability

Definition

The **balance of payments** is a financial record of a country's transactions with the rest of the world for a given time period, usually one year.

The **balance of payments** is a financial record of a country's transactions with the rest of the world for a given time period, usually one year. This includes the country's trade in goods and services with other countries. The government records **credit** items (all payments received from other countries) and **debit** items (all payments made to other nations) in its balance of payments. For example, the expenditure by Canadian tourists visiting the USA would be recorded as a credit item on the USA's balance of payments. In theory, the balance of payments must always balance over time. This is because a country, like an individual, can only spend what it earns.

In general, a large and persistent balance of payments deficit (see Chapter 36) suggests that the country is uncompetitive in international markets. This can have detrimental consequences for the domestic economy, such as job losses. Thus, a deficit on the balance of payments will have a negative impact on economic growth and standards of living.

Redistribution of income

Definition

Redistribution of income refers to the macroeconomic aim of achieving greater equality in the distribution of income in an economy.

Governments aim to achieve greater equality through the **redistribution of income**. A report by Oxfam International in 2023 suggested that the world's richest 1 per cent had nearly twice as much wealth as the rest of the world put together.

Source: 'Richest 1% bag nearly twice as much wealth as the rest of the world put together' by Annie Theriault, 16 January 2023, Oxfam International website

According to the World Bank, in 2022 712 million people in the world had to live on less than $2.15 per day.

Source: 'March 2024 global poverty update from the World Bank' by R. Andres Castaneda Aguila et al, 26 March 2024, World Bank Blogs website

The world's ten richest people had a combined wealth of more than half of the world's population (see Table 22.1).

Table 22.1 The world's richest billionaires, March 2024

Ranking	Billionaire	Wealth (US$bn)
1	Bernard Arnault & family	233
2	Elon Musk	195
3	Jeff Bezos	194
4	Mark Zuckerberg	177
5	Larry Ellison	141

Source: 'Forbes World's Billionaires List 2024: the top 200' by Rob LaFranco, Grace Chung and Chase Petersen-Withorn, 4 April 2024, Forbes website

Economies face unequitable distribution of income due to the naturally unequal ownership of factors of production in a free market economy. For example, consider the wage differentials between professional footballers, doctors and pilots, on the one hand, and those earning the national minimum wage on the other.

A major role of taxation is to redistribute income to help the relatively less well-off in society. For example, **progressive taxation** charges a higher percentage tax as an individual's income rises – in other words, those who earn more pay a greater proportion of their income in tax (see Chapter 23). Other ways to redistribute income include the use of subsidies and social welfare benefits, such as old age pensions and unemployment benefits.

Practice questions: multiple choice

1 What is inflation? [1]
   A a fall in the general price level, over a given period of time
   B a sustained increase in the general price level, over a given period of time
   C a sustained increase in the level of national income
   D an increase in the rate of interest

2 Which option is the least likely economic consequence of high unemployment? [1]
   A a fall in the level of consumption due to lower earnings
   B a fall in the level of national income
   C an increase in the rate of inflation
   D higher government expenditure on welfare benefits

3 Which option is least likely to cause economic growth? [1]
   A an increase in wages
   B greater investment expenditure
   C higher general price level
   D higher level of consumption

Environmental sustainability

Definition

Environmental sustainability is the management of an economy's resources to meet current needs without jeopardising the needs of future generations.

Environmental sustainability refers to the management of an economy's resources in order to meet current needs without harming the needs of future generations. Environmental sustainability is becoming a common macroeconomic aim of governments across the world due to the growing recognition of the long-term economic impacts of environmental degradation. Climate change, for example, caused by excessive greenhouse gas emissions, leads to costly natural disasters, disrupts agricultural productivity and affects public health, all of which can hinder economic growth and standards of living. In addition, resource depletion, such as deforestation and overfishing, threatens the sustainability of industries reliant on these resources. Governments are now prioritising policies that promote renewable energy, reduce carbon emissions and encourage sustainable practices to ensure economic stability and sustainable growth.

> **Activity**
>
> Discuss the extent to which international agreements such as the Paris Agreement can actually achieve a common goal such as environmental protection.

 Case study: The Paris Agreement

In 2016, a total of 197 countries signed the Paris Agreement, which is designed to limit climate change. All the countries involved agreed to the aim of limiting global warming to 1.5 degrees Celsius. International decisions like this will have an impact on the actions of domestic firms and consumers in order to achieve environmental sustainability.

Source: United Nations Framework Convention on Climate Change, 2016, United Nations Climate Action website

Case study: Sustainable Development Goals

Another international agreement among governments concerns the Sustainable Development Goals (SDGs) created by the United Nations in 2015. These are 17 goals designed to 'end poverty, protect the planet, and ensure prosperity for all'. Each goal has specific targets which are to be met by 2030.

Source: The 17 Goals, United Nations Department of Economic and Social Affairs Sustainable Development, July 2024, United Nations website

> **Activity**
>
> Go to the United Nations Development Programme (UNDP) website and research the SDGs. Choose a single goal that you feel is the most important in terms of environmental sustainability. With a partner (who has preferably chosen a different top goal), discuss the reasons for your choice.

Possible conflicts between macroeconomic aims

It is not usually possible for a government to achieve all six macroeconomic aims at once. This is because there are a number of possible conflicts between these macroeconomic aims, which leave governments with a trade-off. Ultimately, the government has to decide which macroeconomic aim is the most important to the economy at a particular time.

Examples of the potential conflicts between macroeconomic aims are described below.

Full employment and stable prices

When the economy expands and more people are in employment, it is likely that inflationary pressures will occur. People will have more money to spend as the economy reaches full employment. Demand-pull inflation (see Chapter 28) may occur because demand in the economy increases faster than supply. Cost-push inflation can also occur because full employment makes it harder for firms to attract skilled labour, and this can lead to wage inflation (and hence higher prices in general).

Economic growth and environmental sustainability

You will recall that environmental sustainability is the management of resources to meet current needs without jeopardising the needs of future generations. Economic growth often conflicts with environmental sustainability due to the increased exploitation of natural resources and higher pollution levels. For instance, growth often leads to the loss of biodiversity and the depletion of non-renewable resources. Balancing the pursuit of economic growth with environmental sustainability requires policies that promote green technologies and sustainable practices to mitigate the negative environmental impacts.

Full employment versus balance of payments stability

As the employment level increases, people become wealthier. They then tend to buy more imported products. This can lead to balance of payments problems. In addition, as an economy reaches the level of national income at which there is full employment, wages tend to rise. This contributes to cost-push inflation, making the country's exports less competitive. Therefore, full employment can worsen the country's balance of payments.

Economic growth versus stable prices

A cut in interest rates or an increase in the money supply in order to stimulate economic growth can conflict with other macroeconomic objectives, such as inflation (price stability). A cut in interest rates enables those with existing loans and mortgages to have more income at their disposal to spend. It also means that borrowing is cheaper, so firms can raise their investment expenditure. However, the combination of higher consumption and investment in the economy can cause demand-pull inflation.

Activity

During the global COVID-19 pandemic, governments across the world were conflicted with their macroeconomic priorities. For a country of your choice, investigate how the government tackled the problems of higher price levels, higher unemployment, reduced international trade and negative economic growth. Use real-world examples and data to support your analysis.

Be prepared to share your findings with your teacher and the rest of the class.

? Chapter review questions

1. What is the general role of a government?
2. What are the six macroeconomic aims of government?
3. What is meant by economic growth and how is it measured?
4. What is meant by unemployment and how is it measured?
5. What is meant by inflation and how is it measured?
6. What is the balance of payments?
7. How do credit and debit items differ on the balance of payments?
8. Why do countries try to avoid a persistent deficit on their balance of payments?
9. Why do governments aim to redistribute income?
10. Why do governments care about environmental sustainability?
11. How might there be conflicts between macroeconomic aims?

Revision checklist

✔ The principal role of the government is to improve the general welfare of its people.

✔ The government collects taxes in order to fund its expenditure on essential services.

✔ Governments try to achieve six macroeconomic aims: economic growth, full employment or low unemployment, stable prices or low inflation, balance of payments stability, redistribution of income and environmental sustainability.

✔ Economic growth refers to an increase in a country's real gross domestic product (GDP) over time. It is shown by an outwards shift of the production possibility curve. The government aims to achieve economic growth as it tends to raise standards of living for the majority of the population.

✔ Unemployment occurs when people are willing and able to work and actively seeking employment, but are unable to find work.

✔ Inflation is the sustained rise in the general price level in an economy. It is calculated using a weighted price index, which measures the change in prices of a representative basket of goods and services consumed by the average household.

✔ The balance of payments is a financial record of a country's transactions with the rest of the world for a given time period.

✔ Governments aim to achieve greater equality in the distribution of income.

✔ Governments are also increasingly aiming for environmental sustainability.

✔ It is not usually possible for a government to achieve all of its macroeconomic aims at once because there are a number of conflicts between these goals.

Fiscal policy

This chapter will cover:

★ a definition of the government budget, government budget deficit and government budget surplus
★ how to calculate the size of a government budget, including its deficit or surplus
★ main areas of government spending and the reasons for these
★ the reasons for taxation
★ the various classifications of taxes
★ the impact of taxation on various stakeholders
★ a definition of fiscal policy
★ fiscal policy measures
★ the effects of fiscal policy on macroeconomic aims.

Government budget

A **government budget** refers to a government's financial plans in terms of planned revenues and expenditure (see Figure 23.1). Tax revenues are by far the most significant source of government revenue. Other sources of government revenue include government borrowing or privatisation proceeds from the selling of state assets.

Tax revenues
Income tax
Corporation tax
Inheritance tax
Sales tax
Import taxes

Non-tax revenues
Fines, tolls, fees and penalties
Foreign aid
Loans from banks
Revenue from state-owned enterprises
Donations

Government spending
Communications
Debt interest
Defence
Education
Environment
Healthcare
Housing
Law and order
Postal services
Roads and motorways
Sewage systems
Transport
Welfare benefits

▲ **Figure 23.1** Tax revenues and government spending

If the government manages to balance its revenues and its spending, then the budget is **balanced**. However, if the government spends more than it collects from its revenues per time period (usually one year), then a **budget deficit** exists. This often happens during a recession (see Chapter 26). As the government is spending more than it is earning, it may need to borrow, and this contributes to the national debt of the country.

Finally, if there is more government revenue than is spent per time period, the government has a **budget surplus**. This can happen when the economy is in a boom. Having a budget surplus enables the government to pay off some of its national debt.

In the long run, governments strive to balance their budgets. This is partly because increasing government revenues by raising taxes is highly unpopular. On the other hand, government borrowing to fund a budget deficit is hugely expensive due to the amount of interest owed on such loans.

Definitions

The **government budget** refers to a government's financial plans in terms of planned revenues (mainly tax revenues) and expenditure (such as healthcare, education and welfare payments).

A **budget deficit** exists when the government spends more than its sources of revenue per time period. The deficit contributes to the national debt of the country.

A **budget surplus** exists when the government collects more revenue than it spends, per time period. Any surplus can be used to pay off parts of the national debt.

Practice question: structured question

Suppose the government's revenues total $865 billion and its expenditure is $897 billion.

a Define 'budget deficit'.   [2]
b Calculate the value of the country's budget deficit in this case. [2]

Practice question: multiple choice

A government wants to reduce its budget deficit. Which fiscal policy measure is **most** likely to achieve this?   [1]

A Cutting the highest rate of progressive income tax
B Increasing government spending on welfare benefits
C Increasing the highest rate of progressive income tax
D Raising interest rates

Reasons for government spending

Essential services, such as state education, housing, healthcare and postal services, are provided by the public sector (see Figure 23.1). The government also exists to redistribute income, such as by providing welfare benefits and state pensions. The government may also intervene to correct market failures (see Chapter 13), such as by providing subsidies to create incentives for firms to invest in green technologies and environmentally sustainable production processes.

The central or federal government collects taxes which it uses to fund local services such as rubbish collection (public refuse collection), street lighting, libraries, schools, hospitals and public parks. Central government gives local government funding to spend on these public and merit goods (see Chapter 13) in the local area.

▲ Refuse collection is a service funded by government at the local level

> ### ▶ Activities
>
> Investigate the latest government budget in your country or a country of your choice.
>
> 1 Identify the main areas of government spending.
> 2 Evaluate the strengths and weaknesses of the budget and the effects of spending in different areas on various economic agents, such as:
>   * consumers
>   * workers on fixed incomes
>   * the elderly
>   * families
>   * businesses (firms/producers)
>   * home-owners
>   * the economy as a whole.

Reasons for taxation

To fund government expenditure, the government tends to rely on tax revenues (see Figure 23.1). A **tax** is a government levy on income or expenditure.

Before the government can spend money on the economy, it must first raise the revenue from taxpayers (both individuals and firms). The reasons why the government imposes taxes are:

» **Raising revenue** – taxes on salaries and profits raise government revenue to help fund its public services, such as healthcare, education, infrastructure and national defence. For example, the USA collects federal income taxes to fund programmes such as Social Security and Medicare (federal health insurance for those aged 65 or older and people with disabilities).

» **Discouraging consumption of demerit goods** – the government may impose taxes on demerit products (see Chapter 13), such as tobacco and alcohol, in order to reduce their consumption. For example, Australia imposes high excise taxes on cigarettes to deter smoking and improve public health.

» **Reducing imports** – import tariffs (see Chapter 34) are used to make foreign goods and services more expensive and also to protect domestic industries. For example, Indonesia imposes tariffs ranging from 100 per cent to 200 per cent on imported footwear and ceramics from Vietnam and Bangladesh to promote local manufacturing and reduce the reliance on foreign products.

» **Redistributing income** – progressive taxes, where higher earners pay a larger percentage of their income, help to reduce income inequalities. The UK, for example, uses a progressive tax system, with the highest rate being 45 per cent for those with a taxable income of over £125,140 per year (about $158,500). The government uses this revenue to fund extensive social welfare programmes and to support lower-income citizens.

» **Influencing total demand** – governments may adjust taxes to manage economic activity, either by stimulating the economy or by cooling it down. For example, during the 2008 financial crisis and again during the COVID-19 pandemic, governments across the world reduced taxes to encourage consumer spending and stimulate economic recovery.

» **Encouraging environmental sustainability** – environmental taxes, such as carbon taxes, aim to reduce pollution and promote the use of green (renewable) energy. For example, the Canadian government charges carbon taxes on greenhouse gas emissions, including propane and natural gas. The aim is to incentivise firms and individuals to reduce their carbon emissions.

The **tax burden** refers to the amount of tax that households and firms have to pay. This can be measured in three ways. For a country, the tax burden is measured by calculating total tax revenues as a proportion of gross domestic product (GDP). For individuals and firms, the tax burden can be measured by the absolute value of tax paid or by the amount of tax paid as a proportion of their income or profits.

> ### Activity
> During the COVID-19 pandemic, economists referred to the term furlough schemes being used by governments in many parts of the world. Investigate what this term means. What is the potential impact of furlough schemes on the economy (in terms of influencing total demand in the economy) in the short run and the long run? Be prepared to show your findings to others in the class.

Classification of taxes

Some of the main taxes are explained in Table 23.1.

Table 23.1 Examples of taxes

Tax	Definition
Income tax	A direct tax levied on personal incomes – wages, interest, rent and dividends. In most countries, this is the main source of tax revenues
Corporation tax	A direct tax on the profits of businesses
Sales tax	An indirect tax, such as value added tax (VAT), charged on an individual's spending
Excise duties	Indirect inland taxes imposed on certain goods and services such as alcohol, tobacco, petrol, soft drinks and gambling
Customs duties	Indirect cross-border taxes on foreign imports
Capital gains tax	A direct tax on the earnings made from investments such as buying shares and private property
Inheritance tax	A direct tax on the transfer of income and wealth such as property when passed on to another person
Stamp duty	A progressive tax paid on the sale of commercial or residential property
Carbon tax	A tax imposed on vehicle manufacturers or firms that produce excessive carbon emissions
Windfall tax	A tax charged on individuals and firms that gain an unexpected one-off amount of money, such as a person winning the lottery or a firm gaining from a takeover bid

Direct and indirect taxation

Taxes can be classified into direct and indirect taxation:

» **Direct taxation** – this type of tax is paid from the income, wealth or profit of individuals and firms. Examples are taxes on salaries, inheritance and company profits.
» **Indirect taxation** – these are expenditure taxes imposed on spending on goods and services. For example, countries such as Australia and Singapore use a goods and services tax (GST), whereas the European Union and South Africa, for example, use value added tax (VAT). Other examples are taxes on petrol, alcohol and cigarettes.

Practice question: structured question

Countries such as Saudi Arabia, Gibraltar and Qatar do not have a sales tax (a type of indirect tax). In other countries, sales taxes can be quite high (such as 20 per cent in the UK and 25 per cent in Denmark).

a Define 'indirect tax'. [2]

b Analyse the advantages and disadvantages for countries that do not impose sales taxes. [6]

> ### Activity
>
> Copy the table below. Place a tick (check) in the correct section of the table to identify whether the tax is direct or indirect. The first one has been completed as an example.
>
> **Table 23.2** Direct and indirect taxes
>
> | Tax | Direct | Indirect |
> |---|---|---|
> | Airport tax | | √ |
> | Capital gains tax | | |
> | Carbon tax | | |
> | Corporation tax | | |
> | Customs duties | | |
> | Excise duties | | |
> | Income tax | | |
> | Inheritance tax | | |
> | Stamp duty | | |
> | Tariffs | | |
> | VAT or GST | | |
> | Windfall tax | | |

Progressive, regressive and proportional taxation

Taxes can also be classified as progressive, regressive or proportional.

Progressive taxation

Under this tax system, those with a higher ability to pay are charged a higher rate of tax. This means that as the income, wealth or profit of the taxpayer rises, a higher rate of tax is imposed (see Figure 23.2). Examples of progressive taxes are income tax, capital gains tax and stamp duty (see Table 23.1).

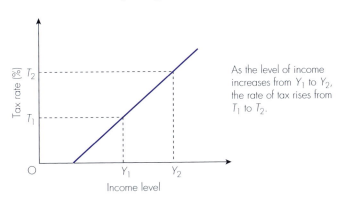

As the level of income increases from Y_1 to Y_2, the rate of tax rises from T_1 to T_2.

▲ **Figure 23.2** Progressive taxes

> ### Activity
>
> In Country A, the progressive tax rates are 10 per cent on incomes between $10,001 and $40,000 per year and 15 per cent on incomes over $40,000 per year.
>
> **a** Copy the table below. By completing the table, calculate the total amount of tax paid by an individual who earns $75,000 per year.
>
> | Income level ($) | Tax rate (%) | Amount of tax paid ($) |
> |---|---|---|
> | 10,000 | 0 | |
> | 10,001–40,000 | 10 | |
> | 40,001+ | 15 | |
> | | Total tax: | |
>
> **b** Show how the average rate of income tax paid by the individual is 11 per cent.

Regressive taxation

Under this tax system, those with a higher ability to pay are actually charged a lower rate of tax – in other words, the wealthier the individual, the lower the tax they pay as a percentage of their income level (see Figure 23.3). For example, although a high-income earner pays the same amount of airport tax or vehicle excise duty as a less wealthy person, the amount of tax paid is a smaller proportion of the wealthier person's income.

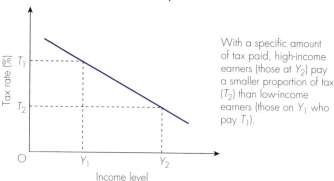

With a specific amount of tax paid, high-income earners (those at Y_2) pay a smaller proportion of tax (T_2) than low-income earners (those on Y_1 who pay T_1).

▲ **Figure 23.3** Regressive taxes

Proportional taxation

Under this tax system, the percentage paid stays the same, irrespective of the taxpayer's level of income, wealth or profits (see Figure 23.4). An example is a sales tax, such as VAT or GST. For example, Sweden has a 25 per cent GST whereas sales taxes in Vietnam, Malaysia and Paraguay are set at 10 per cent.

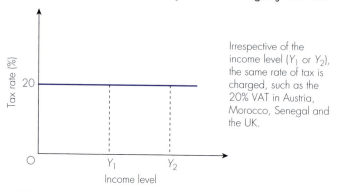

Irrespective of the income level (Y_1 or Y_2), the same rate of tax is charged, such as the 20% VAT in Austria, Morocco, Senegal and the UK.

▲ **Figure 23.4** Proportional taxes

Activities

1 Study the data below and answer the questions that follow.

Income ($ per year)	Tax paid per year ($)		
	Tax A	Tax B	Tax C
10,000	1,000	1,000	1,000
15,000	1,000	1,800	1,500
20,000	1,000	3,000	2,000
25,000	1,000	4,500	2,500

a Identify the tax (A, B or C) that is progressive.
b Identify the tax (A, B or C) that is proportional.
c Explain the difference between a regressive and a proportional tax.

2 Study the three tax systems below. Calculate the percentage of tax paid on each level of income in order to determine whether the tax systems are progressive, regressive or proportional.

Tax system A		Tax system B		Tax system C	
Annual income ($)	Amount of tax paid ($)	Annual income ($)	Amount of tax paid ($)	Annual income ($)	Amount of tax paid ($)
4,500	900	10,000	1,500	8,000	800
10,000	1,800	20,000	3,000	20,000	3,000
20,000	2,800	30,000	4,500	45,000	11,250

Impact of taxation

Taxation directly impacts consumers, workers, producers (firms), the government and the economy as a whole. However, taxation has varying impacts depending on the type of tax in question.

Impact on price and quantity for consumers

The imposition of a sales tax will shift the supply curve of a product to the left (see Chapter 7) due to the higher costs of production. This will increase the price charged to consumers and reduce the quantity produced and sold. Depending on the price elasticity of demand for the product (see Chapter 10), this could reduce the amount of tax revenue for the government.

Impact on economic growth

Taxation tends to reduce incentives to work and to produce. This has a negative impact on the economy as a whole. By contrast, tax cuts can boost domestic spending, thus benefiting individual consumers, producers (firms) and the economy as a whole (through job creation). Nevertheless, tax revenues are essential to fund government spending (such as the construction of schools, hospitals, railways, airports and roads), which increases economic growth.

Case study: Income tax and incentives

In 2023, the Kenyan government tried to introduce a range of tax hikes, which included a proposal to double the fuel tax in order to pay off some of the country's escalating national debt. Protestors claimed the tax hikes would worsen the cost of living for Kenyans at a time when many were already struggling with high food prices such as maize flour. Some economists argue that the government would actually receive more revenue by cutting tax rates. This is because lower rates of tax can create incentives to work and also help to reduce tax avoidance and tax evasion.

Impact on inflation

As taxation tends to reduce the spending ability of individuals (consumers and workers) and the profits of producers/firms, it helps to reduce the likelihood of inflation (see Chapter 28). By contrast, a cut in taxes will boost the disposable income of workers and firms, and thus fuels inflationary pressures in the economy.

Impact on business location

The rates of corporation tax and income tax will affect where multinational companies choose to locate (see Chapter 34). For example, high corporation tax rates in Puerto Rico (37.5 per cent), Argentina (35 per cent), Venezuela (34 per cent) and Cameroon (33 per cent) can discourage some companies from locating in these countries. As a result, foreign direct investment (FDI) in these economies might be lower than otherwise. By contrast, it might be easier to attract workers in economies with low income tax rates, such as Bulgaria (10 per cent), Macedonia (10 per cent), Moldova (12 per cent) and Mauritius (15 per cent).

Impact on social behaviour

Governments can use taxation to alter the social behaviour of consumers by reducing the consumption of demerit goods (see Chapter 13). For example, taxing tobacco and alcohol should, in theory, reduce the demand for such products. Governments also use taxes to protect the natural environment by charging those who pollute or damage it. For example, the UK and China tax cars based on their engine size because vehicles with larger engines tend to cause more pollution.

Impact on tax avoidance and tax evasion

It is possible for people to avoid paying some taxes. **Tax avoidance** is the legal act of not paying taxes – for example, non-smokers do not pay tobacco tax and non-overseas travellers do not pay air passenger departure taxes. On the other hand, **tax evasion** is illegal. This refers to non-payment of taxes due, perhaps by a business under-declaring its level of profits. High levels of taxation will tend to encourage both tax avoidance and tax evasion from consumers, workers and firms. By contrast, low rates of taxation create far fewer incentives for consumers and firms to avoid taxes or defraud the government.

Impact on the distribution of wealth

Governments can use taxes to help redistribute income and wealth from the relatively rich to the poorer members of society. For example, wealthier individuals will pay more income tax, sales taxes and stamp duty when they buy private properties. The government can use these funds to support education, healthcare and social benefits for less affluent consumers and workers.

Definitions

Tax avoidance is the legal act of minimising payment of taxes, such as by avoiding spending on items with a large sales tax.

Tax evasion is the illegal act of not paying the correct amount of tax, perhaps due to a firm under-declaring its corporate profits.

Case study: Hong Kong's plastic shopping bag charging scheme

Up until July 2009, people in Hong Kong used an average of 30 million plastic carrier bags every day! For a relatively small population of 7 million people, this meant the average person was using more than four plastic carrier bags per day, often on a single-use basis. This staggering figure meant that the country's landfills would soon be unable to cope with the bags when they were thrown away.

Hong Kong's introduction of a HK$0.50 (5 US cents) tax on the use of carrier bags has encouraged people to use recycled shopping bags. In fact, demand for plastic carrier bags fell by 85 per cent within the first 2 days of the tax being introduced. In December 2022, the government doubled the levy to $1 per plastic carrier bag.

This follows similar moves made by other countries such as China (in 2009) and Ireland (in 2002).

Activity

List ten uses of plastics in everyday life. Apart from the use of fines (taxes), discuss how an economy should be encouraged to use less plastic.

Practice questions: structured questions

1 In October 2019, inflation in Japan slowed to 0.2 per cent, partly due to the reduced spending in the economy caused by an increase in the country's sales tax from 8 per cent to 10 per cent. (Source: 'Japan inflation rate stays at 7-month low in October' by Rida Husna, 22 November 2019, Trading Economics website)

a Explain how taxes can be used to reduce the rate of inflation. [4]

b Analyse how an increase in taxation might conflict with any two macroeconomic objectives of the Japanese government. [6]

2 In November 2008, following the recession caused by the global financial crisis, the UK government reduced the rate of value added tax (VAT) from 17.5 per cent to 15 per cent. However, by January 2011 the government's escalating debt problems had forced it to increase VAT to 20 per cent. Today, this rate applies to most goods and services in the UK.

a Explain how a reduction in VAT from 17.5 to 15 per cent might help to reduce the effects of a recession. [4]

b Analyse three impacts of the increase in VAT to 20 per cent. [6]

Activity

Some countries, such as Brunei, Monaco, Oman and Saudi Arabia, have a zero rate of income tax. Other countries such as The Bahamas and the Cayman Islands have a zero rate of corporation tax.

a Which other countries have a zero rate of income tax?
b Investigate the reasons behind such government decisions. Be prepared to share your findings with the rest of the class.

Fiscal policy

Fiscal policy is the use of taxation and government expenditure strategies to influence the level of economic activity and achieve macroeconomic aims such as high employment, economic growth and the control of inflation. For example, a government can use taxation to redistribute income and wealth to benefit less wealthy members of society. Government spending can be used to improve standards of living, such as building schools, hospitals and transportation networks.

Fiscal policy measures

Fiscal policy can be used either to expand or to contract economic activity in order to achieve macroeconomic aims (see Chapter 22) and promote economic stability.

Expansionary fiscal policy is used to stimulate the economy, by increasing government spending and/or lowering taxes. For example, if a government increases social security payments (such as unemployment benefits and state pensions), domestic consumption should increase. This type of fiscal policy is used to reduce the effects of an economic recession (see Chapter 26), by boosting gross domestic product (GDP) and reducing unemployment.

By contrast, **contractionary fiscal policy** is used to reduce the level of economic activity by decreasing government spending and/or raising taxes. For example, countries such as China and the USA have used property taxes to slow down escalating house prices. Contractionary fiscal policies are used to reduce inflationary pressures during an economic boom (see Chapter 26).

In the short term, expansionary fiscal policy has a negative impact on the government's budget as revenues fall (because of lower taxes) and government spending increases. As the economy improves in the long run, people earn and spend more money (helping to raise tax revenues) and there is less need for the government to boost its own expenditure to stimulate the economy. The opposite case is true for the use of contractionary fiscal policy (with a probable positive impact on the budget in the short term, but a negative impact in the long term).

Case study: Sweden's housing bubble

Prior to the COVID-19 pandemic, Sweden saw substantial increases in property prices between 2010 and 2020, particularly in its major cities such as Stockholm and Gothenburg. The increase was driven by low interest rates and housing shortages. The housing market has shown signs of cooling due to contractionary fiscal measures and rising interest rates in the post-pandemic period. The government has also discussed adjustments to property taxes to further discourage speculation in the housing market.

▲ A residential housing development in Stockholm, Sweden

Fiscal policy is also used to redistribute income and wealth in the economy. Some countries have quite high rates of income tax to reallocate resources from wealthier individuals to the poorer members of society. Austria, Belgium, Cuba and Senegal, for example, all have a top tax band of 50 per cent or more. However, this can cause severe distortions to the labour market due to potential disincentives to work.

Effects of fiscal policy on government macroeconomic aims

A government can use fiscal policy to achieve its macroeconomic aims (see Chapter 22). Examples are provided below.

» **Economic growth** – government capital expenditure on infrastructure (such as railways, motorways, schools and hospitals) helps to boost investment in the economy. Lower rates of corporation tax can help to attract foreign direct investment (FDI) into the country, thereby boosting the economy's potential output.

» **Low inflation** (stable prices) – lower taxes, and hence higher FDI, can boost the productive capacity of the economy in the long run, which helps to keep the general price level relatively low. Contractionary fiscal policy measures also help prevent price levels from soaring.

» **Employment** (low unemployment) – cuts in income tax can be used to create incentives for people to seek employment and to work harder. Government support for business start-ups, through subsidies or tax concessions, can also create incentives for entrepreneurs, thus helping to lower unemployment.

» **Healthy balance of payments** – relatively low rates of taxation help to keep domestic firms competitive, thereby benefiting exporters. The government might also choose to subsidise domestic industries to improve their international competitiveness. These fiscal measures should benefit the country's balance of payments.

» **Redistribution of income** – the use of both progressive taxes and government spending (on welfare benefits, education and healthcare) helps to redistribute income and wealth in the economy.

» **Environmental sustainability** – implementing taxes on carbon emissions and pollutants, offering subsidies and tax incentives for renewable energy and green technologies, as well as funding environmental conservation projects are fiscal measures that encourage producers/firms and consumers to adopt more sustainable practices and reduce their environmental footprint.

Practice questions: structured questions

1 Explain why expansionary fiscal policy can cause a budget deficit for the government. [4]
2 Analyse how fiscal policy can be used to promote long-term economic growth. [6]

Chapter review questions

1 What is meant by the government budget?
2 What is the difference between a budget deficit and a budget surplus?
3 What are the various reasons for government spending?
4 What are the various reasons for taxation?
5 How can taxes be classified?
6 What is the difference between direct and indirect taxes?
7 What is the difference between progressive, proportional and regressive taxes?
8 How does tax avoidance differ from tax evasion?
9 What is meant by fiscal policy?
10 What are the differences between expansionary and contractionary fiscal policy?
11 How might a government use fiscal policy to achieve its macroeconomic aims?

Revision checklist

✔ The government budget refers to the government's financial plans in terms of planned revenue and expenditure. The budget can be in balance, deficit or surplus.
✔ Areas of government spending might include healthcare, education, infrastructure, and so forth. Reasons for government spending include to provide essential goods and services, to redistribute income and wealth, and to correct market failures.
✔ The main reason for taxation is to raise funds for government expenditure.
✔ A tax is a government levy on income or expenditure.
✔ Taxation has direct impacts on consumers, workers, producers/firms, the government and the economy as a whole.
✔ The tax burden refers to the amount of tax that households and firms have to pay.
✔ Classifications of tax include direct and indirect; and progressive, proportional and regressive.
✔ Fiscal policy is the use of taxation and government expenditure strategies to influence the level of economic activity and the government's macroeconomic aims.
✔ Taxation and government spending have a direct impact on all six macroeconomic aims.

24 Monetary policy

This chapter will cover:

★ a definition of money supply
★ a definition of monetary policy
★ different monetary policy measures
★ the effects of monetary policy measures on macroeconomic aims.

Defining money supply

> **Definition**
>
> **Money supply** refers to the amount of money in the economy at a particular point in time, e.g. coins, banknotes, bank deposits and central bank reserves.

Money is any commodity that can be used as a medium of exchange for the purchase of goods and services. The **money supply** refers to the amount of money in the economy at a particular point in time. This consists of coins, banknotes, bank deposits and central bank reserves (see Chapter 15).

▲ The money supply includes banknotes in circulation

Defining monetary policy

> **Definition**
>
> **Monetary policy** refers to the use of interest rates, exchange rates and the money supply to control macroeconomic objectives and to affect the level of economic activity.

Monetary policy is when the government manipulates interest rates, exchange rates and the money supply to control the amount of spending and investment in an economy. Interest rates can refer to the price of borrowing money or the yield from saving money at a financial institution. The money supply refers to the entire quantity of money circulating in an economy, including notes and coins, bank loans and bank deposits (see Chapter 15).

Direct control of the **money supply** is relatively difficult, as the definition of money is quite loose and banks can create credit fairly easily (see Chapter 15). Manipulation of **exchange rates** (see Chapter 35) is also rather difficult for many countries, as they rely on international trade and have to comply with the regulations of the World Trade Organization. Hence, most governments rely on **interest rate policy** to achieve economic stability. In most countries, the central bank or monetary authority (see Chapter 15) is responsible for making exchange rate changes.

▲ The European Central Bank uses monetary policy to control spending and investment in the European Union

Monetary policy measures

There are three main monetary policy measures:

» **Changes in interest rates** – the main monetary policy measure is using interest rates to influence the level of economic activity. For example, higher interest rates will make borrowing more expensive and create more of an incentive to save. This tends to reduce overall spending in the economy.

» **Changes in money supply** – the government can control the money supply in order to influence the level of economic activity. For example, allowing commercial banks to lend more money (rather than leaving a higher proportion of their deposits at the central bank) will tend to boost consumption and investment expenditure in the economy.

» **Changes in foreign exchange rates** – the foreign exchange market has a direct impact on the domestic money supply. For example, domestic customers need to purchase foreign currency in order to buy imports. The buying and selling of foreign currencies (see Chapter 35) will therefore affect the money supply in an economy.

Like fiscal policy, monetary policy can be used either to expand or to contract economic activity in the economy.

» **Expansionary monetary policy** is also known as **loose monetary policy**. It aims to boost economic activity by expanding the money supply. This is done mainly by lowering interest rates. This makes borrowing more attractive to households and firms because they are charged lower interest repayments on their loans. Those with existing loans and mortgages have more disposable income, so they have more money available to spend.

» **Contractionary monetary policy** is also known as **tight monetary policy**. Here, an increase in interest rates tends to reduce overspending and limit investment in the economy. This slows down economic activity. Tight monetary policy is used to reduce the threat of inflation. However, it can harm economic growth and therefore cause job losses in the long run.

The effects of monetary policy measures on macroeconomic aims

Monetary policy measures can enable the government to achieve its macroeconomic aims (see Chapter 22):

» **Economic growth** – the government can use the monetary policy measure of lower interest rates to achieve economic growth. This will tend to reduce the cost of borrowing for households and firms, thus boosting their consumption and investment respectively. Savers will receive a lower rate of return, discouraging savings and encouraging more spending. Finally, those with existing loans and mortgages will have lower repayments costs, and so will have more money to spend. The combination of lower savings, more consumption and more investment will lead to economic growth.

» **Full employment/low unemployment** – lower interest rates, as described above, tend to cause economic growth. More spending and investment in the economy tend to create more jobs.

» **Stable prices/low inflation** – economic growth (stimulated by lower interest rates) will result in higher consumption and investment expenditure. This will increase the productive capacity of the economy, so more can be produced without having to incur higher prices. By contrast, higher interest rates are used to limit consumption and investment in order to control the rate of inflation.

» **Balance of payments stability** – a lower exchange rate, through government intervention in the foreign exchange market (see Chapter 35), tends to improve the international competitiveness of the country. Hence, this should help to improve the current account of the balance of payments (see Chapter 36).

Study tip

There is no single interest rate in an economy. Rather, there is a structure of different interest rates. This is because there is no single market for loans, such as bank overdrafts, credit cards and mortgages. Different rates of interest are charged for all of these different kinds of loan. Borrowers also have different levels of risk. For example, lending money to governments and large multinational companies tends to be less risky than lending money to sole traders or partnerships.

Case study: Quantitative easing

During the COVID-19 pandemic in 2020 to 2022, the UK and US central banks made significant cuts in interest rates to encourage people to spend money, rather than to save it. However, with interest rates at their lowest levels in history, near zero per cent, they could not go any lower.

The Bank of England and the Federal Reserve had one other option: quantitative easing (QE). This form of monetary policy injects money directly into the economy. The central bank purchases bonds, which are a debt security or a promise to pay a lender at a later date. The institutions selling these bonds to the government, such as commercial banks or insurance companies, then have 'new' money in their accounts, thus helping to boost the money supply and to promote lending (and hence spending).

> **Activity**
>
> In May 2024, the Bank of Japan (Japan's central bank) increased interest rates to between 0 and 0.1 per cent. This was the first time interest rates had been positive in Japan since 2016. Use the internet to investigate the reasons behind Japan's policy of extremely low or negative interest rates.
>
> Source: 'Japan raises interest rates for first time in 17 years' by Peter Hoskins and Mariko Oi, 19 March 2024, BBC News website

Limitations of monetary policy

As with fiscal policy, there are time lags in the reaction to interest rate changes in the economy. This can make the effectiveness of monetary policy less certain or even destabilising for the economy.

Furthermore, economic activity is not only dependent on interest rates. Other factors, such as consumer and business confidence levels, have an impact on GDP. During the global COVID-19 pandemic from 2020 to 2022, despite interest rates being close to or equal to zero per cent in countries such as Japan, the UK and the USA, the lack of business and consumer confidence led to very low levels of economic growth.

Some economists argue that the use of monetary policy can be counterproductive, because it restricts economic activity and discourages foreign direct investment in the country. For example, higher interest rates raise the costs of production for firms, as existing and new loans become more expensive. This has a negative impact on profits, job creation, research and development expenditure, and innovation. Hence, higher interest rates (used to combat inflation) can conflict with other macroeconomic objectives, especially with economic growth and employment.

Practice question: multiple choice

Which option is **not** an example of monetary policy?   [1]

A bank credit control
B capital investment in research and development
C interest rate policy
D the money supply

Practice questions: structured questions

1 Explain how monetary policy can be used to influence the level of economic activity.   [4]
2 Explain how the use of interest rate policy can help a country to control its inflation rate.   [4]

> **? Chapter review questions**
>
> 1 What is meant by the money supply?
> 2 What is monetary policy, and what are the three categories of monetary policy measures?
> 3 How does loose monetary policy differ from contractionary monetary policy?
> 4 How can monetary policy be used to achieve an economy's macroeconomic aims?

Revision checklist

✔ The money supply refers to the amount of money in the economy at a particular point in time, such as coins, banknotes, bank deposits and central bank reserves.

✔ Monetary policy refers to the use of interest rates, exchange rates and the money supply to control macroeconomic objectives and to affect the level of economic activity.

✔ Monetary policy measures include controlling the money supply, the manipulation of exchange rates and the use of interest rate policy.

✔ Expansionary monetary policy is used to boost economic activity by expanding the money supply or lowering interest rates.

✔ Tight monetary policy involves an increase in interest rates in order to reduce overspending and limit investment in the economy.

✔ Governments can use monetary policy measures to achieve their macroeconomic aims, such as economic growth, full employment/ low unemployment, stable prices/low inflation and balance of payment stability.

25 Supply-side policy

This chapter will cover:

★ a definition of supply-side policy
★ various supply-side policy measures
★ the effects of supply-side policy measures on government macroeconomic aims.

Defining supply-side policies

Supply-side policies are long-term strategies aimed at increasing the productive capacity of the economy by improving the quality and/or quantity of factors of production (see Chapter 2). Examples of supply-side policies are education and training, infrastructure spending, labour market reforms, lower direct taxes, deregulation, improving incentives to work and invest, and privatisation.

▲ Education is a supply-side policy

With more and improved factors of production, the economy can produce more goods and services. This results in an outward shift of the country's production possibility curve (PPC) from PPC_1 to PPC_2, as shown in Figure 25.1.

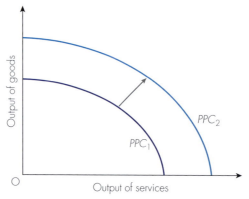

▲ **Figure 25.1** Supply-side policies and the PPC

Supply-side policy measures

Education and training

Improved education and training in the economy result in a workforce with better skills, productivity, flexibility and mobility. Hence, increased spending on education and training is likely eventually to improve the productive capacity of the economy.

However, in a market economic system (see Chapter 12) there is often under-provision of educational services, so there is often a need for government intervention. The government may choose to spend money directly on providing education and training, or it may prefer to provide incentives for private firms to supply these services. For example, government-funded retraining schemes can help the unemployed to improve their chances of finding paid employment. Increased government spending on education is another example. The government is likely to set and monitor quality standards of teaching in schools. However, such supply-side policies will cost the government a lot of money, which typically requires higher taxes.

Labour market reforms

Supply-side economists argue that there are benefits of making labour markets more flexible, as this results in greater productivity. Such labour market reforms include reducing or removing:

» the power of trade unions (see Chapter 17)
» unemployment benefits (see Chapter 27)
» minimum wages (see Chapter 17).

Labour market reforms help to promote greater competition through the removal of rigidities in labour markets. Such barriers include excessive and complex employment legislation and the threat of strike action from trade unions, which hinder efficiency in labour markets. In the long run, such supply-side policies should reduce unemployment as labour markets become more internationally competitive.

Lower direct taxes

Lower direct taxes (see Table 25.1) can create incentives for work, especially for people on low wage rates, because they get to keep a greater proportion of what they earn. Over time, higher disposable income provides a boost to consumption expenditure and hence an increase in GDP.

Table 25.1 Various tax rates, selected countries 2021–2023

Country	Highest income tax rate (%)	Lowest income tax rate (%)	Corporate tax rate (%)	Sales tax (VAT / GST) (%)
Qatar	0	0	10	0
Kuwait	0	0	16	0
Russia	13	13	20	20
Isle of Man	20	10	0	20
Singapore	22	0	17	8
Nigeria	24	7	30	7.5
New Zealand	39	10.5	28	15
Vietnam	35	5	20	10
Taiwan	40	5	20	5
Sweden	52	32	20.6	25

Source: adapted from Highest taxed countries 2024, World Population Review website

Deregulation

Deregulation refers to the reduction or removal of barriers to entry in order to make markets more competitive. Increased competition in an industry tends to lead to lower prices and better-quality output of goods and services. An example of deregulation is allowing new firms to enter an industry previously dominated by a monopolist, such as a single provider of telecommunications services in a country. The aim of this is to make the market more competitive and increase efficiency. However, the expected benefits of deregulation only materialise (if at all) after new firms have entered and competed in the market, which could take a long time to happen.

Incentives to work

Direct tax cuts encourage people to find work or to work harder. In general, countries that impose lower rates of income tax will tend to create greater incentives to work. In Qatar and Kuwait, no income tax is charged (see Table 25.1). Lower rates of indirect taxes, such as value added tax (VAT) and goods and services tax (GST), can create incentives for households and individuals to spend.

Incentives to invest

Tax incentives can also stimulate firms to invest in the economy in order to maximise their profits in the long run. In general, countries that impose lower rates of corporate tax (see Table 25.1) will tend to create greater incentives for firms to invest so they can maximise their returns. By contrast, high corporate tax rates in countries such as Nigeria and New Zealand (see Table 25.1) can reduce incentives to invest in these nations.

Alternatively, governments may provide firms with subsidies to give them an incentive to invest in **enterprise zones**. These are special areas designated by the government, typically locations with relatively high rates of unemployment. The government thus creates financial incentives for firms to relocate to these areas in order to create employment. Such incentives include tax rebates and reduced regulations in order to attract private sector investments. Enterprise zones are common in the UK, USA, China and India.

▲ Investment in new technology can help the economy grow

Supply-side policies focus on the importance of investment in research and development (R&D), new product development, new technologies and infrastructure, thus contributing to growth of the economy. As with all forms of supply-side policies, capital increases the productive capacity and productivity of the economy in the long run. For example, the USA's investment expenditure has generated new products for consumption, such as Apple's iPhone (smartphones) and iPad (tablet computers), and Tesla's environmentally friendly electric cars. Such investments have created huge competitive advantages at an international level for the USA.

Privatisation

This is the policy of selling off state-owned assets (such as government properties or public sector businesses) to the private sector so they can be run more efficiently. Private sector firms are motivated by profit, so they can, in theory, develop better products and deliver better services. Competition, productivity and efficiency are essential components of the private sector, thus helping to boost the productive potential of the economy.

Privatisation of state industry was a fundamental part of India's supply-side policy in the 2000s, which helped to raise a lot of government revenue, cut public sector expenditure and foster an entrepreneurial culture. Delhi and Mumbai airports were privatised in 2006 and the Bharat Aluminium Company in 2005. In 2021, the Indian government sold the government-owned Air India to the Tata Group. Chapter 14 provides more information about privatisation.

Spending on infrastructure

Spending on infrastructure includes spending on roads, railways, telecommunications systems, high speed internet connections, drainage and sanitation, all of which support economic activity. Spending on infrastructure can be provided by the public sector, the private sector or a combination of both. Infrastructure systems increase efficiency within an economy, which leads to increases in productivity and output. For example, in the short term, the building of an airport creates jobs. In the long term, an airport will improve transport links in the country and may improve trade and attract foreign investment.

> **Case study:** Infrastructure spending in the United Arab Emirates
>
> The United Arab Emirates (UAE) is investing in its railway system. There are three phases. The first, operational since 2016, is based on transport of freight. It aims to reduce carbon emissions and provide efficient and cost-effective transport for goods and raw materials. The second phase is focused on passenger transport and will connect cities within the UAE. The third phase consists of an integrated transport system that connects local light rail with intercity services. The railway system will create cheaper, faster and more efficient transport, for freight and passengers. It will reduce road transport and will therefore reduce carbon emissions. As of 2024, phases 2 and 3 were already in progress.
>
> Source: The UAE railway programme, 7 February 2024, UAE website

Activities

1 Investigate the supply-side policies in your home country, or a country of your choice.
2 How have these policies helped or hindered the productive capacity of the economy?

The effects of supply-side policy measures on macroeconomic aims

Supply-side policy measures can enable the government to achieve its six macroeconomic aims (see Chapter 22):

» **Economic growth** – supply-side policy measures can increase the productive capacity of the economy, leading to sustainable economic growth. For example, investment in education and cuts in corporate taxes can help to boost economic growth in the long term.

» **Full employment/low unemployment** – an increase in the economy's productive capacity tends to increase national output, thereby creating jobs in the economy in the long term. Also, supply-side policies such as investment in training can help to reduce both frictional and structural unemployment (see Chapter 27).

» **Stable prices/low inflation** – as supply-side policies increase the productive potential of the economy, they help to prevent the general price level from rising beyond control. A limitation of using demand-side policies such as fiscal and monetary policies (see Chapters 23 and 24) to achieve economic growth is that they stimulate demand-pull inflation. Supply-side policy measures increase the productive capacity of the economy, resulting in economic growth, without higher prices.

» **Balance of payments stability** – since supply-side policies can improve productivity and national output without putting upward pressure on the general price level, the international competitiveness of the country should improve. This helps to boost the economy's export earnings. Therefore, supply-side policies tend to improve a country's current account of the balance of payments (see Chapter 36).

» **Redistribution of income** – supply-side policies, such as greater investment in education and training, along with greater incentives to work, tend to benefit low-income earners more than high-income earners. For example, a cut in the basic rate of income tax means that low-income earners have a proportionately higher disposable income. They are more likely to spend any extra income they have due to the lower rate of direct tax.

» **Environmental sustainability** – government investment into renewable energy, such as wind and hydro power, may contribute to improved environmental sustainability. Research and development grants and tax breaks for firms that use production methods and materials that contribute to environmental sustainability are examples of how supply-side policies can contribute to environmental sustainability.

The main criticism (or limitation) of supply-side policies is the time that it takes to reap the benefits. For example, it might take decades for a nation to enjoy the benefits of an improved education system or better infrastructure in the country.

Practice question: multiple choice

Which option is **not** a supply-side policy? [1]

A deregulation of markets
B human capital investment
C progressive income tax policies
D tax reforms to create incentives to work

Practice questions: structured questions

1 Define 'supply-side policies'. [2]
2 State two examples of supply-side policies. [2]
3 Analyse how supply-side policies can help to achieve any two macroeconomic objectives. [6]

> ### Activity
>
> Use the internet to research the number of years of compulsory schooling in five countries of your choice. Try to choose a combination of low-, middle- and high-income countries.
>
> a Present your findings based on the mean average years of compulsory schooling.
> b How do your figures differ for boys and girls?
> c How close is the relationship between a country's mean average years of compulsory schooling and its gross domestic product (GDP)?

❓ Chapter review questions

1 What is meant by supply-side policy?
2 What are the main supply-side policy measures?
3 How does investment in education and training create productive capacity in the economy?
4 How do labour market reforms create greater flexibility in the economy?
5 How do lower taxes create incentives to work and invest?
6 What is deregulation?
7 What are enterprise zones?
8 How does privatisation create greater productive capacity in the economy?
9 Give one example of how a supply-side policy can affect each of the macroeconomic aims of a government.
10 What is the main criticism (or limitation) of supply-side policies?

Revision checklist

✔ Supply-side policies are long-term measures to increase the productive capacity of the economy, leading to an outward shift of the production possibility curve.

✔ Examples of supply-side policy measures are education and training, labour market reforms, lower direct taxes, deregulation, incentives to work, incentives to invest, privatisation and spending on infrastructure.

✔ Supply-side policies focus on the importance of investment in research and development (R&D), new product development, new technologies and infrastructure.

✔ Improved education and training will result in a workforce with better skills, productivity, flexibility and mobility, which will eventually improve the productive capacity of the economy.

✔ Labour market reforms can help to promote greater competition through the removal of rigidities in labour markets.

✔ Lower direct taxes tend to create incentives for work, especially for those on low wages.

✔ Deregulation involves the reduction or removal of barriers to competitive markets.

✔ Lower direct taxes can create incentives for firms to invest in their pursuit of profit maximisation.

✔ Privatisation is the act of selling state-owned assets in order to increase competition, productivity and efficiency.

✔ Supply-side policy measures can be used to achieve sustainable economic growth, full employment/low unemployment, stable prices/low inflation, balance of payments stability, a redistribution of income in the economy and environmental sustainability.

Economic growth

Defining economic growth

Definitions

Economic growth is the annual increase in the level of national output, i.e. the annual percentage change in gross domestic product.

Gross domestic product measures the monetary value of goods and services produced within a country for a given period of time, usually one year.

Economic growth is the annual increase in the level of national output – that is, the annual percentage change in the country's **gross domestic product** (GDP). Hence, in theory, an increase in any of the components of GDP (consumption, investment, government spending and net exports) can cause economic growth.

Economic growth increases the long-term productive capacity of the economy. This is shown by the outward shift of the production possibility curve in Figure 26.1.

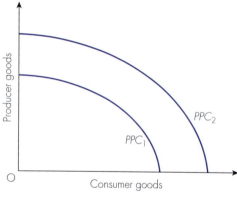

Economic growth can be shown diagrammatically by an outward shift of the production possibility curve (PPC) for an economy. In this case, a combination of an increase in the quantity and quality of factors of production shifts the PPC outwards from PPC_1 to PPC_2, creating more producer and consumer goods in the economy.

▲ **Figure 26.1** Economic growth

Measurement of economic growth

We can measure economic growth using real gross domestic product (real GDP) and GDP per head (or GDP per capita). We arrive at these from a calculation of nominal GDP, as follows. Economic growth is measured by the increase in real GDP over a given period of time, usually one year.

Nominal gross domestic product (nominal GDP) measures the monetary value of goods and services produced within a country during a given period of time, usually one year. The components of nominal GDP are:

Definition

Consumption expenditure is the value of all private household consumption within a country.

» **Consumption expenditure** (C) – this refers to the total spending on goods and services by individuals and households in an economy. Examples are spending on housing, transport, food, clothing and domestic holidays.

» **Investment expenditure** (I) – this refers to the capital spending of firms, which is used to increase production and to expand the economy's productive capacity. Examples are spending on new machinery and technologies and on the construction of new factories.

» **Government spending** (G) – this is the total consumption and investment expenditure of the government. Examples are spending on infrastructure (such as rail and road networks) and spending on education and healthcare. The calculation of government spending excludes payments made to others without any corresponding output, such as unemployment benefits.

» **Export earnings** (X) – this measures the monetary value of all exports sold to foreign buyers. For example, France exports a huge amount of wine, dairy products and fruit, so the earnings from these exports are included in the measure of its GDP.

» **Import expenditure** (M) – this measures the monetary value of all payments for imports. France imports a lot of cars, oil and smartphones. The spending on these items means that money leaves the French economy, so this must be deducted in the calculation of its GDP. The difference between the values of a country's exports and imports (X − M) is called **net exports**.

Therefore a country's GDP is calculated using the formula:

$$GDP = C + I + G + (X − M)$$

From this, two measures can be used to gauge the level of economic growth:

» **Real GDP** refers to the value of national income (GDP) that is adjusted for inflation. It reflects the true value of goods and services produced in a given year because inflation artificially raises the value of a country's output.

» Economists also use **GDP per head** (or GDP per capita) to measure the GDP of a country divided by its population size. This is a key measure of a country's economic growth and standards of living, as GDP per head indicates the mean average national income per person. All things being equal, the larger the population size, the lower the GDP per head for a certain level of GDP (see Table 26.1).

Table 26.1 GDP per capita and nominal GDP: selected countries, 2022

Country	GDP per capita (US$)	Nominal GDP (US$bn)
USA	62,789	25,440
China	11,560	17,963
India	2,090	3,417
Indonesia	4,074	1,319
Netherlands	50,547	1,009
Kenya	1,755	113
Luxembourg	109,705	82
Malaysia	11,399	407
Pakistan	1,696	375
Mauritius	10,570	13

Source: GDP per capita and Nominal GDP, December 2022, Trading Economics website

Practice question: structured question

Calculate the GDP per capita (per head) of the population in Australia and Cambodia in 2022.

[2]

	Australia	Cambodia
GDP (USD billion)	1724	31.77
Total GDP as a percentage of world GDP (%)	1.64	0.03
Population (million)	26.97	16.94

Source: Trading Economics

Causes and consequences of economic growth

Economic growth occurs when there is an increase in the level of economic activity in a country over time. The **business cycle** (also known as the **trade cycle**) describes the fluctuations in economic activity in a country over time. These fluctuations create a long-term trend of growth in the economy (see Figure 26.2).

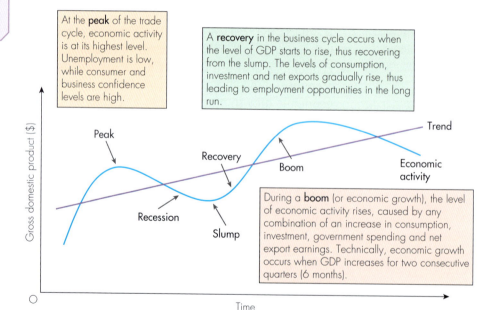

At the **peak** of the trade cycle, economic activity is at its highest level. Unemployment is low, while consumer and business confidence levels are high.

A **recovery** in the business cycle occurs when the level of GDP starts to rise, thus recovering from the slump. The levels of consumption, investment and net exports gradually rise, thus leading to employment opportunities in the long run.

During a **boom** (or economic growth), the level of economic activity rises, caused by any combination of an increase in consumption, investment, government spending and net export earnings. Technically, economic growth occurs when GDP increases for two consecutive quarters (6 months).

There is a fall in GDP during an economic recession. Technically, a **recession** occurs when a country's GDP falls for two consecutive quarters. During a recession, there is a decline in consumption, investment and net exports (due to falling export earnings).

At the bottom of a recession in the trade cycle, a **slump** (or **trough**) is said to exist. There will be high unemployment while consumption, investment and net export earnings will be low. Many businesses will have collapsed and consumers have little confidence in the economy. Hence, government spending may be needed to help the economy to recover from the recession.

▲ **Figure 26.2** The business cycle

Causes of economic growth

An increase in any of the components of GDP (consumption, investment, government spending or net exports) can cause economic growth. In addition, an increase in the quantity and/or the quality of factors of production can also create economic growth, such as an increase in the labour supply or improvements in the state of technology.

Consumption expenditure is related to purchases of goods and services by individuals and households. An increase in expenditure may increase economic growth.

Total demand in an economy is the sum of consumption, investment, government spending, value of exports minus value of imports. An increase in total demand in an economy may cause an increase in economic growth.

The factors that cause economic growth and lead to differences in the economic growth rates of different countries include variations in the following:

» **Factor endowments** – this refers to the quantity and quality of a country's factors of production. For example, Chile is well endowed in the supply of lithium, which is used in batteries for electric vehicles. France has plenty of arable land for its agricultural output and Australia has many natural resources such as lithium, coal, gold and iron ore. These countries can therefore specialise production on a large scale and benefit from economies of scale (see Chapter 18) and export their lower-price products to overseas markets. By contrast, countries that lack natural resources, land and productive labour will tend to struggle to achieve economic growth.

» **The labour force** – the size, skills and mobility of the economy's workforce has an impact on the country's economic growth. For example, India's large labour force and Germany's highly skilled workers have contributed to the economic growth of these countries. The mobility of labour refers to the extent to which workers can change between jobs (known as **occupational mobility**) and the extent to which they are willing and able to move to different locations for employment (known as **geographical mobility**). Generally, the more occupationally and geographically mobile workers are in a country, the greater its economic growth is likely to be.

» **Labour productivity** – this refers to the amount of goods and services that workers produce in a given time period. It is often referred to as **output per worker**, expressed as a monetary value (real GDP divided by the country's labour force). Labour productivity (the productive use of labour) is a key determinant of economic growth. It depends on several interrelated factors such as the qualifications, experience, training and motivation of the labour force. Technological advances can also enhance labour productivity, such as the use of internet technologies in e-commerce (online trading) and artificial intelligence (AI). An increase in the labour productivity of a country helps to improve its international competitiveness and hence its prospects for economic growth.

» **Investment expenditure** – investment is a component of overall demand in the economy, so any increase in investment should help to boost the country's GDP. Investment helps to boost the country's productive capacity in the long run. Investment expenditure on physical capital, such as the use of robotics in production (see Chapter 19), can also help to improve labour productivity. To remain competitive in the long run, countries must invest in capital resources.

▲ Japan's Nissan and Toyota production plants in the UK help to create jobs in the UK and therefore boost its GDP

Activity

Discuss in pairs the reasons for the following:

a Why government spending on infrastructure (such as road and rail networks) and training programmes for the unemployed are examples of investment expenditure.
b Why the spending by foreign tourists in Mauritius represents export earnings for the country.
c Why investment is important for a country's economic growth.

Positive consequences of economic growth

In general, economic growth is desirable due to its positive consequences for members of society. The advantages of economic growth include the following:

» **Improved standards of living** – economic growth tends to lead to higher standards of living for the average person. Higher income levels in a country enable people to spend more money to meet their needs and wants (see Chapter 1). This helps to eliminate absolute poverty in the country.
» **Employment** – economic growth leads to higher levels of employment in the economy. This helps to raise consumption and encourages further investment in capital, helping to sustain economic growth.
» **Tax revenues** – economic growth is associated with higher levels of spending in the economy. This generates more tax revenues for the government. For example, the government can collect more from sales taxes (on consumption), corporate tax (on the profits of firms) and import taxes. Hence, there are more funds for the government to use to further sustain the growth of the economy.

Practice question: structured question

In the third quarter of 2023, India was among the fastest growing economies in the world. The reasons for India's growth in this period included an increase in foreign direct investment, manufacturing, government spending on capital formation and infrastructure.

a Define 'economic growth'. [2]

b Explain how investment in India helps to boost its economic growth. [4]

Negative consequences of economic growth

Despite the advantages of economic growth, there are also potential drawbacks:

» **Environmental consequences** – high rates of economic growth can create negative externalities such as pollution, congestion, climate change and land erosion (see Chapter 13). Such environmental impacts can damage people's well-being and quality of life in the long run. In many cases, there is a correlation between the share of the world's GDP and carbon dioxide emissions per capita.

» **Risk of inflation** – if the economy grows due to excessive demand, there is the danger of demand-pull inflation (see Chapter 28). This can lead to prices of goods and services rising to unstable levels, with negative consequences for the economy, such as a decline in the country's international competitiveness.

» **Inequalities in income and wealth** – although the country as a whole might experience economic growth, not everyone will benefit in the same way. Economic growth often creates greater disparities in the distribution of income and wealth: the rich get richer, and the poor get relatively poorer, creating a widening gap between the rich and poor. For example, in 2024 South Africa had the world's most unequal distribution of income and wealth. Economic growth in South Africa up to that point had not lessened the wealth gap between rich and poor in the economy.

» **Resource depletion** – economic growth often involves using up the world's scarce resources at rates that are not sustainable. For example, deforestation and overfishing have led to problems in the ecosystem.

Hence, economic growth does not necessarily resolve a country's socioeconomic problems, such as resource depletion, market failures (see Chapter 13) and income inequality.

Activity

Research whether there is a correlation between an economy's share of the world's GDP and its carbon dioxide emissions.

▲ Pollution is a negative consequence of rapid economic growth

> ### Activity
>
> In small groups, research the economic problems of overfishing. Searching for 'overfishing' in a search engine or looking at the National Geographic website will help. Be prepared to present your findings to the rest of the class.

Recession

Definition

Recession occurs in the business cycle when there is a fall in GDP for two consecutive quarters.

A **recession** occurs in a business cycle when there is a fall in GDP for two successive quarters of a year.

Causes of recession

There are several interrelated reasons why a recession may come about:

» a higher level of unemployment which causes a reduction in demand for goods and services
» higher interest rates, which discourage investment but raise demand for savings
» lower investment by firms and lower productivity in the economy
» a falling population, for example due to increased emigration, which leads to lower consumer spending and fewer workers
» lower rates of disposable income, causing a fall in consumer spending
» lower levels of government expenditure causing a decrease in real GDP
» a decline in demand for exports
» an increase in demand for imports, which may lead to less demand for domestically produced goods
» lower levels of consumer and business confidence, leading to less spending and investment
» wars and natural disasters causing a destruction of factors of production

» higher income tax rates leading to less disposable income and therefore less consumer spending
» higher corporate tax rates leading to lower after-tax profits and therefore less investment by firms
» a collapse in financial markets, such as a stock market crash or banking crisis, erodes investor and consumer confidence, potentially triggering a recession
» a decline in the quality of resources may lead to a decrease in demand for the goods and therefore a decrease in demand for exports and/or an increase in demand for imports.

During the global COVID-19 pandemic, most economies around the world faced an increase in unemployment and a decrease in economic growth. Tax revenue decreased because of falling incomes and profits. Many governments increased spending to support the economy, and some gave sums of money to individuals and businesses to help them to keep spending. Others chose to reschedule debts (e.g. increase the repayment period or allow people a break in making repayments).

➡️ **Case study:** Hong Kong's strategies to deal with recession

The economy of Hong Kong, Special Administrative Region of China, entered a recession during the COVID-19 pandemic. This was due to business closures, as lockdown measures reduced business hours and prevented people from shopping and eating out. Labour productivity fell because of illness and mandatory COVID-19 testing. To encourage consumer spending and stimulate economic growth during the pandemic in 2022, Hong Kong's Financial Secretary, Paul Chan, announced that residents would receive vouchers to spend on goods and services to increase consumption. The government also reduced profits and income tax for firms and individuals, and provided workers who were temporarily unemployed because of business closure due to the COVID-19 pandemic a one-off subsidy payment.

Consequences of recession

A recession has consequences for consumers, workers, producers and the government:

» **Consumers** – shops may close. A lack of earnings and confidence will lead to saving rather than spending. Some people might have to dissave (spend their savings).
» **Workers** – wages are unlikely to increase and there will be a lack of job security. Unemployment rates will rise.
» **Producers/firms** – a lack of demand for goods/services may lead to the closure of businesses. Due to falling revenue, some firms may decide to make workers redundant, downsize or defer investment spending.
» **Government** – decreased tax revenue from firms and workers may lead to or worsen a budget deficit and increase spending on welfare benefits for the unemployed and low-income families. Lower confidence in the economy may lead to a lack of investment from local and international firms.

Policies to promote economic growth

A government can promote economic growth by using macroeconomic policies to increase demand in the economy and/or boost the productive capacity of the economy. These policies include demand-side policies (namely fiscal and monetary policies) and supply-side policies:

» **Fiscal policy** involves the use of taxation and/or government spending to control the level of economic activity in the economy. If demand in the economy is too low, the government may choose to stimulate economic growth by cutting taxes and/or increasing its own expenditure in order to boost the level of economic activity. This should also have a positive impact on employment in the economy. See Chapter 23 for more about fiscal policy.

» **Monetary policy** involves the central bank changing interest rates in order to control the level of demand and hence economic activity. To promote economic growth, lower interest rates can be used to cut the costs of borrowing to consumers and firms. This should help to fund consumer expenditure and business investments, thereby boosting economic growth. See Chapter 24 for more about monetary policy.

» While both fiscal and monetary policies target demand in order to achieve economic growth, **supply-side policies** are used to increase the economy's productive capacity. These policies seek to increase competition, productivity and innovation in order to promote economic growth. One example is government funding to encourage education and training. Another example is a reduction in corporate taxes, which can encourage risk taking and foreign direct investment in the economy. In the long run, supply-side policies increase the productive capacity of the economy, thereby promoting economic growth. See Chapter 25 for more about supply-side policy.

> **Study tip**
>
> While economic growth is generally seen as a desirable macroeconomic objective, remember that individuals do not benefit equally from economic growth.

> **Activity**
>
> Explain how fiscal, monetary and supply-side policies can be used to deal with the problem of mass unemployment. Discuss the limitations of each policy.

Practice question: structured question

Cambodia's economy grew by an average of 6.91 per cent from 1994 to 2024. As a result, the poverty rate decreased to 17.8 per cent of the population in 2019/2020 from 33.8 per cent in 2009/2010. However, in 2021 approximately 75 per cent of the population still lived in rural areas where the standards of living remained low.

Foreign direct investment (FDI), increases in tourism and investment in infrastructure are some of the reasons behind Cambodia's growth. However, economic growth in Cambodia has also brought about loss of mangroves due to construction work, and overfishing has depleted fish stocks.

a Identify the social costs and benefits of economic growth in Cambodia. [4]
b Discuss the potential long-term impacts of economic growth in Cambodia and whether the benefits outweigh the costs. [8]

Sources: Pandemic checks Cambodia's progress on poverty, 28 November 2022, World Bank Group website; Cambodia – Country summary, *The World Factbook*, 28 August 2024, CIA website

? Chapter review questions

1 What is meant by real gross domestic product (GDP)?
2 What is economic growth and how is it calculated?
3 What are the causes of economic growth?
4 What are the consequences, both positive and negative, of economic growth?
5 What is meant by a recession?
6 What is the business cycle?
7 How do calculations of real GDP help to measure economic growth?
8 What are the main policies used to promote economic growth?

Revision checklist

✔ Economic growth is the annual increase in the level of national output, that is, the annual percentage change in the country's gross domestic product (GDP). It can be represented in a diagram by an outward shift of the PPC.

✔ Real GDP, a measure of economic growth, refers to the value of national income (GDP) that is adjusted for inflation.

✔ An improved measure of economic growth is GDP per head (GDP per capita), which measures the GDP of a country divided by the population size.

✔ The business cycle (also known as the trade cycle) describes the fluctuations in economic activity in a country over time: boom, recession, slump and recovery.

✔ Causes of economic growth depend on the quality and quantity of a country's factors of production, such as factor endowments, the labour force, labour productivity and investment expenditure. Economic growth can also be caused by an increase in total demand in an economy which is made up of consumption, investment, government spending and net exports.

✔ There are both positive and negative consequences of economic growth. Economic growth tends to improve standards of living (although not equally), but it tends to have negative environmental consequences such as depletion of natural resources and damage to the environment.

✔ A recession occurs in a business cycle when there is a fall in GDP for two successive quarters of a year.

✔ A recession may be caused by a decrease in total demand, a decrease in the quantity of resources or a decrease in the quality of resources. A recession has negative consequences for consumers, workers, producers/firms and the government.

✔ Policies to promote economic growth include expansionary fiscal policy, expansionary monetary policy and supply-side policies.

27 Employment and unemployment

This chapter will cover:

★ a definition of employment, unemployment and full employment
★ how to measure unemployment
★ the causes/types of unemployment
★ the consequences of unemployment
★ the policies to reduce unemployment.

Defining employment, unemployment and full employment

Employment refers to the economic use of labour as a factor of production. For example, people may work in the primary, secondary or tertiary sectors of the economy (see Chapter 18). Employment also includes those who are self-employed.

Unemployment occurs when people of working age are both willing and able to work but cannot find employment.

What do we mean by working age? The United Nations International Labour Organization (ILO) states the lower limit of the working age to be 15 years old. While there is no official upper limit, many countries use an age limit of between 65 and 70. For example, the official retirement age for females in the UK is 66 years and 5 months, while the retirement age is 67 years for all workers in Norway and Iceland. In Saudi Arabia, workers can officially retire with full state benefits aged 47. In general, men and women retire at similar ages but in Estonia, Argentina, Finland and France, women currently tend to retire later than men.

Source: Charted: 'Retirement age by country' by Rida Khan, 2 October 2023, Visual Capitalist website

Figure 27.1 shows the unemployment rates in Portugal from 2014 to 2024.

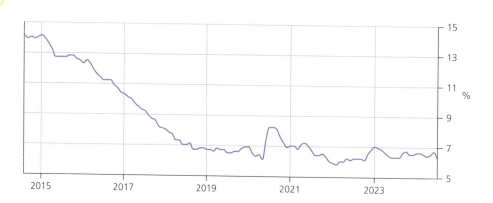

▲ **Figure 27.1** Unemployment rates: Portugal 2014–2024

Source: Portugal unemployment rate, Statistics Portugal, 2024, Trading Economics website

Full employment refers to the ideal situation when everyone in a country who is willing and able to work has a job. Governments strive to ensure that everyone who is able and willing to work finds employment. This helps the economy to make the most of its human resources.

Measuring unemployment

The main way of measuring (or defining) unemployment is the **labour force survey**.

The **labour force survey** (LFS) is a measure of unemployment produced by the ILO. It uses a standardised household-based survey to collect work-related statistics, such as employment status, education and training opportunities. The LFS is used by all member states of the European Union as well as other countries. Questionnaires are collected face-to-face or completed over the telephone.

The ILO measures a country's unemployment based on the number of people who are:

» willing to work, but unable to find employment
» actively looking for work – that is, they have looked for a job in the last 4 weeks, and
» able to start work within the next 2 weeks, or
» waiting to start a new job within the next 2 weeks.

▲ Job seekers look at employment advertisements in China

To measure unemployment, economists calculate the **unemployment rate**, which shows the proportion of the country's workforce (those of working age) that is unemployed. It is calculated by the formula:

$$\frac{\text{Number of unemployed}}{\text{Workforce}} \times 100$$

Alternatively, this can be expressed as:

$$\frac{\text{Number of unemployed}}{(\text{Number of unemployed} + \text{employed} + \text{self-employed})} \times 100$$

Practice questions: structured questions

1 Calculate the unemployment rate for a population of 75 million people, of whom 40 million are employed and 5 million are unemployed. [2]

2 Calculate the number of unemployed people in a country with the following population data and an unemployment rate of 7.5 per cent:
- Population = 56 million
- Age 0–14 = 21 million
- Age 15–64 = 26 million
- Age ≥ 65 = 9 million [2]

3 With a population of over 236 million, Nigeria is one of the most populated countries in Africa. With over 40 per cent of the population aged below 15 in 2020, the country had a large dependency ratio of almost 86 per cent. Gender inequalities meant that only approximately 52 per cent of working-age females were in employment in 2023. Most people are employed in primary industries. Nigeria is a large producer of crude oil. In 2023, 92 per cent of its export earnings came from the sale of oil and related products. Figure 27.2 shows the unemployment rates in Nigeria between 2013 and 2023. Youth unemployment in the third quarter of 2023 stood at 8.6 per cent.

Sources: Nigeria population and Nigeria exports by category, Trading Economics website; Nigeria – Country summary, *The World Factbook*, 28 August 2024, CIA website

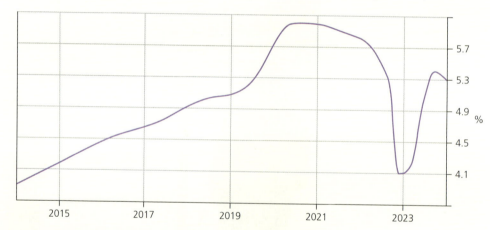

▲ **Figure 27.2** Unemployment rates for Nigeria, 2013–2024

Source: Nigeria unemployment rate, National Bureau of Statistics Nigeria, 2024, Trading Economics website

a Nigeria's working population was around 75.7 million in 2023. With an unemployment rate of 5 per cent, calculate the number of unemployed people in the country in that year. [2]

b Explain two possible reasons why Nigeria's youth unemployment of 8.6 per cent in 2023 was higher than its average unemployment rate of 5 per cent. [4]

4 Bangladesh's annual unemployment rate between 2013 and 2023 was about 4.4 per cent with the exception of 2020 and 2021 when it rose to 5.3 and 5.2 per cent during the COVID-19 pandemic. At the same time, Bangladesh's

GDP grew on average 5.88 per cent from 1994 to 2022. These changes have helped to reduce some of the poverty in Bangladesh.

a Explain why it might be difficult at times to know the exact rate of unemployment in a country. [4]

b Analyse the possible consequences of low unemployment for the Bangladeshi economy. [6]

Sources: Bangladesh unemployment rate and Bangladesh GDP annual growth rate, World Bank, 2024, Trading Economics website

Causes and types of unemployment

There are several causes of unemployment. These causes can be explained by examining the various types of unemployment:

>> **Frictional unemployment** is transitional unemployment. It occurs when people change jobs due to the time delay between leaving a job and finding or starting a new one. Therefore, frictional unemployment always exists in the economy, because it takes time for the labour market to match available jobs with the people looking for jobs.

>> **Seasonal unemployment** is unemployment that arises when jobs are seasonal. Examples include life guards at beaches in regions where beaches close in winter, ski instructors, hospitality workers where demand for their services is seasonal and agricultural workers who work during the harvest season.

>> **Structural unemployment** occurs when the demand for products produced in a particular industry continually falls, often due to foreign competition. The industry therefore suffers from structural and long-term changes in demand for its products. The UK, for example, has suffered from structural unemployment in shipping, textiles, steel production, coal mining and car manufacturing. Those who have become unemployed after working in such industries usually find it quite difficult to find a new job and often need retraining for other types of work.

>> **Cyclical unemployment**, also known as **demand-deficient unemployment**, is the most severe type of unemployment, as it can affect every industry in the economy. It is caused by a lack of total demand in the economy, which causes a fall in national income. In Figure 27.3, the fall in total demand (or aggregate demand) in the economy from AD_1 to AD_2 causes national income to fall from Y_1 to Y_2, therefore creating mass unemployment and causing the general price level to fall from P_1 to P_2. Demand-deficient unemployment is experienced during an economic downturn – that is, during recessions and slumps.

Definitions

Frictional unemployment is transitional unemployment which occurs when people change jobs or are in between jobs.

Seasonal unemployment is unemployment that arises when jobs are seasonal.

Structural unemployment occurs when the demand for products produced in a particular industry continually falls, often due to foreign competition.

Cyclical unemployment is unemployment caused by a lack of demand, which causes a fall in national income. It is a severe type of unemployment as it can affect every industry in the economy.

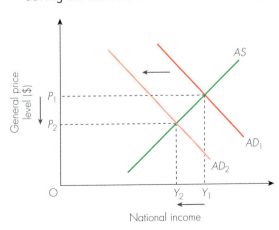

▲ **Figure 27.3** Cyclical unemployment

> ## Activity
>
> Find real-world examples of frictional, seasonal, structural and cyclical unemployment, with an image or picture to represent each type of unemployment.

While Spain and Greece saw unemployment rates of 11.8 per cent and 10.8 per cent respectively in 2023, these are relatively modest compared to the countries with the world's highest unemployment rates (see Table 27.1).

Source: Greece and Spain unemployment rate, March 2024, Trading Economics website

Table 27.1 The world's highest unemployment rates

Ranking	Country	Unemployment rate (%)	Date
1	South Africa	32.9	Mar 24
2	Angola	31.9	Dec 23
3	Djibouti	27.9	Dec 22
4	Botswana	25.9	Sept 23
5	Senegal	22.3	Dec 23

Source: Unemployment rate – World, dates as shown, Trading Economics website

> ## Activities
>
> Find out the current unemployment rate in your country or a country of your choice. Compare this with the rates for the previous five years. A good starting point is the Trading Economics or the International Labour Organization website.
>
> 1 What trends can you identify?
> 2 Investigate the possible causes of these unemployment trends.

Consequences of unemployment

Unemployment affects a range of stakeholders: the individuals who are unemployed themselves, producers/firms (employers), the government and the economy as a whole. The consequences of unemployment include the following:

Personal costs

» The individuals who are unemployed may suffer from stress, depression, other health problems, low self-esteem, a lack of dignity and homelessness. In extreme cases, unemployment can even lead to suicide.
» Family and friends may also suffer from lower incomes as a result of unemployment. This could lead to family discord, or separation or divorce.

Social costs

» The local community may suffer if there is mass unemployment, as it may lead to poverty, falling house prices (and hence asset values) and increased crime rates.
» Businesses in areas of high unemployment may face lower demand for goods and services and therefore close down. This causes more unemployment and increases the lack of resources in the area.

Economic costs

» Firms suffer as unemployment leads to lower levels of consumer spending, investment and profits. Business failures and bankruptcies are therefore more likely to occur during periods of high unemployment.

» The government may face higher expenditure on welfare benefits and healthcare for the unemployed. Hence, prolonged periods of high unemployment can lead to increased government debt.

» Taxpayers stand to lose due to the opportunity costs of unemployment – namely, increased reliance on taxpayers' money to finance unemployment and welfare benefits.

» The economy as a whole suffers from being less internationally competitive due to reduced levels of spending and national output.

Policies to reduce unemployment

High employment, or low unemployment, is a key macroeconomic objective of all governments. There are several reasons for this:

» High employment raises standards of living for the average person in the country (see Chapter 29).

» It promotes economic growth – another key macroeconomic objective (see Chapter 26).

» It increases tax revenues (due to higher levels of income and spending in the economy), which are used to finance government spending.

» It reduces the financial burden and opportunity cost to the government as spending on welfare benefits falls.

» It prevents brain drain from the economy. This can occur during periods of high unemployment when highly skilled workers leave the country in search of job opportunities elsewhere.

» It reduces income and wealth inequalities – poorer people are more affected by unemployment as they lack savings and wealth.

Governments can try to deal with the problems of unemployment in a number of ways. These will partly depend on the causes of unemployment in the economy. There are four general policies for reducing unemployment: fiscal policy (see Chapter 23), monetary policy (see Chapter 24), supply-side policy (see Chapter 25) and protectionist policies (see Chapter 34):

» **Fiscal policy** is the use of taxation and government spending policies to influence the level of economic activity. It can be used to tackle unemployment caused by demand-side issues, such as cyclical and structural unemployment. Expansionary fiscal policy (such as tax cuts and increased government spending) boosts the level of consumption and investment in the economy. This causes an increase in real GDP, which brings about more employment opportunities.

» **Monetary policy** is the use of interest rates to affect the level of economic activity. When interest rates are lowered, the cost of borrowing falls. This encourages households and firms to spend and invest. In Figure 27.4, higher spending in the economy shifts the demand for labour curve from DL_1 to DL_2. This results in employment in the economy increasing from N_1 to N_2. The resulting rise in real wage rates from W_1 to W_2 also helps to attract more labour, causing an expansion along the supply of labour (*SL*) curve. Like fiscal policy, monetary policy tackles demand-side causes of unemployment.

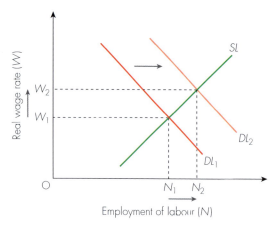

▲ **Figure 27.4** Monetary policy and the labour market

» **Protectionist measures** include tariffs and quotas (see Chapter 34). Governments can use them to safeguard domestic jobs from the threat of international competition. For example, in 2024, the US government proposed to impose 100 per cent tariffs on the imports of Chinese electric vehicles in order to protect jobs in the US electric vehicle industry.

Source: White House Fact Sheet, 14 May 2024

» **Supply-side policies** are strategies that governments use to deal with imperfections in the labour market and to reduce unemployment caused by supply-side factors. Thus, these policies are aimed at addressing frictional and voluntary unemployment, although they can also be used to help reduce structural and cyclical unemployment. Examples of supply-side policies are as follows:
  – **Investment in education and training** helps unemployed people to gain new skills so they can find employment. An example is retraining structurally unemployed manufacturing workers to help them find work in the tertiary sector. Education and training expenditure should also help future generations to become more skilled and employable.
  – **Labour market reform** – reducing the powers of trade unions will mean that labour unions are not in such a strong bargaining position to obtain higher wages (see Chapter 17). Strong trade unions have been able to demand annual pay rises in excess of inflation. Hence, government intervention to reduce the influence and power of trade unions can help to reduce unemployment.
  – **Incentives** can be offered to firms for training and hiring the long-term unemployed. For example, the government can offer tax allowances and/ or subsidies to reduce the costs of training and hiring workers. Similarly, special economic zones can be set up in areas of high unemployment to create jobs.
  – **Reducing welfare benefits** may give some unemployed people an incentive to find a job rather than to rely on state welfare benefits. If it is made more difficult for people to claim unemployment benefits, some may become more proactive in searching for jobs. This could significantly help to reduce unemployment. A drawback to this approach is that some people who have to rely on benefits may have their standard of living reduced.

While supply-side policies tend to have more permanent impacts on employment, these effects take longer to achieve when compared to demand-side policies aimed at reducing unemployment in the economy.

Practice question: structured question

Artificial intelligence and technology have reduced the demand for labour and caused unemployment in some industries. For example, supermarkets have introduced self-service checkouts. Internet banking has taken over from physical banking. Amazon uses robots in its distribution centres to increase productivity. The increase in online shopping has reduced the demand for retail shops in some parts of the world. In the future there is likely to be a decrease in demand for data entry clerks, ticket sellers, cashiers, accounting and payroll clerks. According to the World Economic Forum, there will be an increase in demand for data analysts, AI and machine learning specialists, digital marketers, e-commerce specialists, renewable energy engineers and sustainability experts.

a Define 'unemployment'.   [2]
b Analyse the ways in which the UK government could reduce
   unemployment caused by technological advances such as AI
   and machine learning.   [6]

Practice question: multiple choice

Which option is **least** likely to suggest why it is difficult to compare the unemployment rates of different countries?

A Different countries calculate unemployment in different ways.
B The minimum age to work differs in different countries.
C The retirement age varies between countries.
D There is no agreement on the measurement of unemployment.

? Chapter review questions

1 What is meant by unemployment?
2 How does the International Labour Organization measure unemployment?
3 How is the unemployment rate calculated?
4 Why is employment a macroeconomic objective of all governments?
5 Outline the main types (and hence the causes) of unemployment.
6 Name any four consequences of high unemployment in an economy.
7 What are the four main government policies that can be used to reduce domestic unemployment?
8 Give three examples of supply-side policies that can be used to reduce unemployment.

Revision checklist

✔ Employment refers to the economic use of labour as a factor of production, with people working in the primary, secondary and tertiary sectors of the economy.

✔ Unemployment occurs when people of working age are both willing and able to work but cannot find employment.

✔ Full employment refers to the ideal situation when everyone in a country who is willing and able to work has a job.

✔ Unemployment can be calculated using the labour force survey. The formula for calculating unemployment is Number of unemployed/ Workforce × 100

✔ Types of unemployment include frictional, structural, seasonal and cyclical unemployment.

✔ Unemployment affects a range of stakeholders: the individuals who are unemployed, producers/firms (employers), the government and the economy as a whole.

✔ Policies to tackle the problems of unemployment include fiscal policy, monetary policy, protectionist measures and supply-side policies (for example, investment in education and training, a reduction in trade union power, creating incentives for firms to train and employ people, and reducing welfare benefits).

28 Inflation

This chapter will cover:

★ a definition of inflation and deflation
★ how to measure inflation using the Consumer Price Index (CPI)
★ the causes of inflation
★ the consequences of inflation
★ the policies to control inflation.

Defining inflation

Inflation is the sustained rise in the general price level in an economy over time. This does not mean the price of every good and service increases – rather, it means that on average prices are rising in the economy.

Governments aim to control inflation because it reduces the value of money and the spending power of individuals, producers (firms) and governments. For example, the inflation rate in Syria was around 140 per cent in December 2023.

Source: Syria inflation rate, Central Bureau of Statistics, Syrian Arab Republic, January 2024, Trading Economics website

This meant that the general price level in Syria increased by an average of about 140 per cent (more than double) within a year. Hence, a product priced at 100 Syrian pounds would increase to 240 Syrian pounds by the end of the year. This makes conditions far less predictable for economic stability in Syria than in other countries with low and stable rates of inflation such as Macau, Canada, the UK and the USA (see Table 28.1 and Figure 28.1).

Table 28.1 Inflation rates around the world, selected countries, 2024

Country	Inflation rate (%)
Argentina	289.0
Syria	140.0
Turkey	69.8
Venezuela	67.8
Sierra Leone	41.7
Egypt	32.5
Ghana	25.0
Pakistan	17.3
Bangladesh	9.7
USA	3.4
Canada	2.7
UK	2.3
Armenia	−0.7
Afghanistan	−9.0

Source: Inflation rate World, March 2024, Trading Economics website

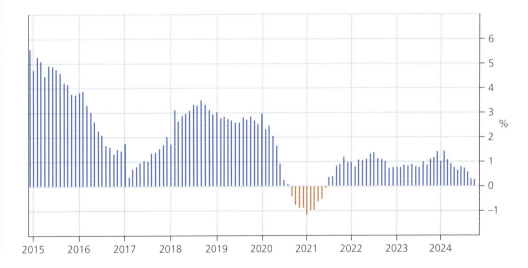

▲ **Figure 28.1** Macau's relatively stable inflation rates (2014–2024)

Source: Macau inflation rate, Statistics and Census Service, Government of Macao SA, 2024, Trading Economics website

Case study: Hyperinflation in Zimbabwe

Major economic problems in Zimbabwe caused the country to suffer from extreme rates of inflation (**hyperinflation**) between 2003 and 2009. In June 2006, the Central Bank introduced a new 100,000 Zimbabwean dollar banknote (less than $1 back then). However, by July 2008, inflation had reached 231,000,000 per cent. Several months later in January 2009, the Zimbabwean government launched the 100 trillion Zimbabwean dollar banknote (ZWD100,000,000,000,000). This meant the currency became worthless and was eventually abandoned. Today, the southern African country still does not have its own official currency, with the US dollar being its main transacting currency. In June 2024, Zimbabwe's inflation rate stood at 49.7 per cent. With GDP per capita at $1345 (around $3.68 per day), an estimated 6.6 million people in the country were living in extreme poverty in 2024.

Source: Inflation rate (World), July 2024, Trading Economics website

Practice question: structured question

The data below show the inflation rates for a country over three years.

Year	1	2	3
Inflation rate (%)	2.5	1.7	2.3

a Define 'inflation rate'. [2]
b Explain, using the data above, why the rate of inflation was at its highest in the third year. [4]

Defining deflation

While the price of goods and services tends to rise, the price of some products actually falls over time. This could be due to technological progress or a fall in demand for the product, both of which can cause prices to fall. **Deflation** is defined as the persistent fall in the general price level of goods and services in the economy over time, i.e. the inflation rate is negative. Some of the countries that experienced deflation in 2024 are shown in Table 28.2.

The causes of deflation can be categorised as either demand or supply factors. Deflation is a concern if it is caused by falling demand for goods and services (often associated with an economic recession and rising levels of unemployment).

Table 28.2 Deflation rates around the world, 2024

Country	Deflation rate (%)
Afghanistan	−9.0
Comoros	−2.0
Central African Republic	−1.12
Armenia	−0.7
Costa Rica	−0.52
Rwanda	−0.5
Brunei	−0.5
Seychelles	−0.14

Source: Inflation rate (World), March 2024, Trading Economics website

Case study: The global COVID-19 pandemic

In late 2019, the world experienced the outbreak of a novel coronavirus, SARS-CoV-2, which causes the disease COVID-19. This highly contagious respiratory illness spread rapidly, leading to a global pandemic by early 2020. The pandemic had profound impacts on health, society and economies worldwide. Governments implemented unprecedented social, political and economic measures to control the spread of the virus and mitigate its effects. Malaysia experienced malign deflation during the COVID-19 pandemic (see Figure 28.2).

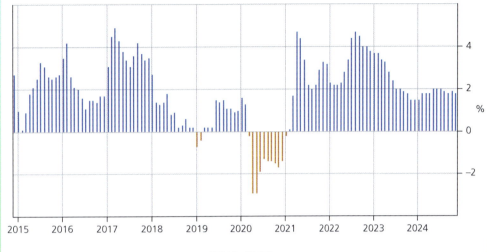

▲ **Figure 28.2** Malaysia's inflation rate (2014–2024)

Source: Malaysia inflation rate, Department of Statistics, Malaysia, 2024, Trading Economics website

Measuring inflation

The **Consumer Price Index (CPI)** is a common method used to calculate the inflation rate. It measures price changes of a representative basket of goods and services (those consumed by an average household) in the country. Items such as staple food products, clothing, petrol (gasoline) and transportation are likely to be included. However, different statistical weights are applied to reflect the relative importance of the average household's expenditure. For example, a 10 per cent increase in the price of electricity will affect the average household far more than a 50 per cent increase in the price of light bulbs, batteries or bananas. Changes in the CPI thus represent changes in the cost of living for the average household in the economy.

The statistical weights in the CPI are therefore based on the proportion of an average household's spending on the items in the representative basket of goods and services. For example, if food items account for 15 per cent of the typical household's total spending during a given time period, then 15 per cent of the weights in the index would be assigned to food items. Therefore, items of expenditure that take a greater proportion of the typical household's spending are assigned a larger weighting. Changing fashions and trends, such as greater household expenditure on smartphones, online apps and air fryers, require a review (or update) of the weights in the CPI.

The CPI is also used for international comparisons of inflation rates, partly because it uses a wide sample of the population when calculating and assigning statistical weights to the index. The CPI, as the key measure of inflation for most countries, is also important as a benchmark when central banks set interest rates (see Chapter 24).

Calculating the CPI

We use a price index to indicate the average percentage change in prices compared to a starting period. The starting period is called the **base year**. The CPI compares the price index of buying a representative basket of goods and services with the base year, which is assigned a value of 100. Hence, a price index of 115.2 means that prices have in general increased by 15.2 per cent since the base year. If prices were to rise by another 5 per cent in the subsequent year, the price index number would become 120.96 (i.e. 115.2 × 1.05), or 20.96 per cent higher since the base year. Price changes in the CPI are measured on a monthly basis but reported for a twelve-month period.

Calculating changes in the CPI will give the rate of inflation. To do so, two main steps are involved:

» collection of the price data for a representative basket of goods and services, collected on a monthly basis
» assigning the statistical weights, representing different patterns of spending over time.

The simplified example below, with three products in the representative basket, shows how a CPI is calculated. Assume 2020 is the base year when the total basket price was $20.

Table 28.3 Calculating the total basket price

Product	Price in 2024 ($)	Price in 2025 ($)
Pizza	9	10
Cinema ticket	10	11
Petrol	3	3.5
Total basket price	22	24.5

To calculate the inflation rate between 2024 and 2025, first calculate the price indices for the two years in question:

» 2024: $22/$20 × 100 = 110 (prices in 2024 were 10 per cent higher on average than in 2020).
» 2025: $24.5/$20 × 100 = 122.5 (prices in 2025 were 22.5 per cent higher on average than in 2020).

The inflation rate between 2024 and 2025 is the percentage change in the price indices during these two periods:

$$\frac{(122.5 - 110)}{110} \times 100 = 11.36\%$$

However, the products measured in the CPI are of different degrees of importance to the typical household, so statistical weights are applied to reflect this. Suppose, for example, in a particular country, food consumption accounts for 40 per cent of the average household spending, whereas entertainment represents

20 per cent, transport represents 25 per cent and all other items of expenditure represent the remaining 15 per cent. To create a weighted price index, economists multiply the price index for each item of expenditure (in the representative basket of goods and services) by the statistical weight for each item. Applying these weights gives the results shown in Table 28.4.

Table 28.4 Creating a weighted price index

Product	Price index	Weight	Weighted index
Food	110.0	0.40	110 × 0.4 = 44.0
Entertainment	115.0	0.20	115 × 0.2 = 23.0
Transport	116.4	0.25	116.4 × 0.25 = 29.1
Others	123.3	0.15	123.3 × 0.15 = 18.5
Weighted index			114.6

While the price of food has increased the least since the base year (by only 10 per cent), food accounts for 40 per cent of the typical household's spending. So, this 10 per cent price increase has a much larger impact on the cost of living than the 15 per cent increase in the price of entertainment, which accounts for only 20 per cent of the average household's expenditure. Without using weights, the average price index would be 116.18, i.e. (110 + 115 + 116.4 + 123.3) / 4. However, the statistical weights reduce the price index to 114.6 because the relatively higher prices of non-food items account for a smaller proportion of spending by the typical household. This shows that prices have, on average, increased by 14.6 per cent since the base year. Therefore, a weighted price index is more accurate in measuring changes in the cost of living, and hence inflation.

> **Study tip**
>
> Although the CPI is the most widely used price index for measuring inflation, it only takes an average measure. Thus, the CPI hides the fact that the price of some products increases more rapidly than others, while the price of other products might have actually fallen.

Practice questions: structured questions

1 a Calculate the inflation rate if the Consumer Price Index changes from 123.0 to 129.15. [2]

 b Calculate the price index if there is 3.0 per cent inflation during the year if the index was previously at 130. [2]

 c Calculate how much a basket of goods and services which is currently priced at $1,200 would cost if the CPI increased from 125 to 135. [2]

2 The data below is for Country Y.

Item	Consumer Price Index	Weight
Clothing	110	10
Food	120	20
Housing	130	30
Others	140	40

 a Define 'Consumer Price Index (CPI)'. [2]

 b 'The typical household in Country Y spends more money on housing than on food or clothing.' Explain this statement. [4]

Causes of inflation

There are two main causes of inflation: demand-pull inflation and cost-push inflation.

Cost-push inflation is caused by higher costs of production. These higher costs make firms raise their prices in order to maintain their profit margins. For example, higher raw material costs, increased wages and soaring rents cause economic activity to fall. This is shown in Figure 28.3 by the leftward shift of the total supply or aggregate supply (AS) curve from AS_1 to AS_2. Hence, cost-push inflation reduces the economy's national income from Y_1 to Y_2.

Definitions

Cost-push inflation is a cause of inflation, triggered by higher costs of production which forces up prices.

Demand-pull inflation is a cause of inflation. It is triggered by higher levels of total demand in the economy, which drive up the general price level.

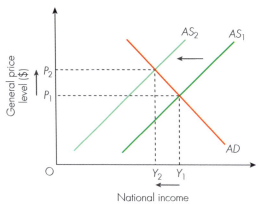

▲ **Figure 28.3** Cost-push inflation

▲ Higher rents in popular locations can cause cost-push inflation

Demand-pull inflation is caused by higher levels of total demand or aggregate demand (AD) in the economy, shown by the shift from AD_1 to AD_2 in Figure 28.4. This drives up the general price level of goods and services. For example, during an economic boom, household consumption of goods and services increases due to higher GDP per capita and higher levels of employment. This causes an increase in real national income from Y_1 to Y_2 but forces up the general price level in the economy from P_1 to P_2, ceteris paribus.

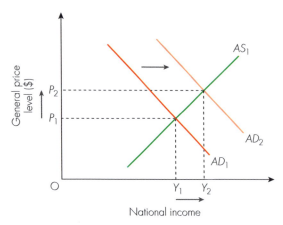

▲ **Figure 28.4** Demand-pull inflation

Practice questions: multiple choice

1 Which option would not cause demand-pull inflation? [1]
   A higher interest rates to make borrowing more difficult
   B higher level of consumer and producer confidence in the economy
   C increase in government spending
   D reduction in direct taxes

2 What is unlikely to cause cost-push inflation? [1]
   A a reduction in indirect taxes
   B an increase in demand for exports
   C higher interest rates
   D increase in raw material costs

Definition

Imported inflation is a cause of inflation. It is triggered by higher import prices, which force up costs of production and thus cause domestic inflation.

Other possible causes of inflation are as follows:

» Monetary causes of inflation are related to increases in the money supply (see case study on Zimbabwe) and easier access to credit, such as loans and credit cards.
» **Imported inflation** occurs due to higher prices of important imported products, forcing up costs of production and therefore causing domestic inflation.

Practice question: structured question

Study the graph below which shows the inflation rates in India between 2014 and 2024, and answer the questions that follow.

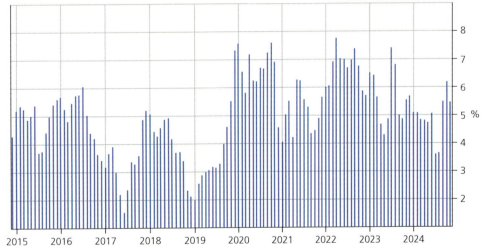

▲ Inflation rates in India (2014–2024)

Source: India inflation rate, Ministry of Statistics and Programme Implementation (MOSPI), 2024, Trading Economics website

Activity

Discuss in small groups the economic strategies you would use to control demand-pull inflation and cost-push inflation. You may want to refer to Chapters 23 to 25 to help with this activity.

a Identify when the rate of inflation was at its highest and lowest in India. [2]
b Explain the difference between cost-push inflation and demand-pull inflation. [4]
c Analyse why the COVID-19 pandemic might have caused India's inflation rate to rise. [6]

Consequences of inflation

Inflation can complicate planning and decision-making for consumers, workers, savers, lenders, borrowers, producers (firms) and the economy as a whole.

Consequences of inflation for consumers

The purchasing power of consumers goes down when there is inflation. In other words, there is a fall in their real income because money is worth less than before. Inflation also causes **shoe leather costs**. This is because inflation causes fluctuations in price levels, so consumers spend more time searching for the best deals. They might do this by physically visiting different businesses to find the cheapest supplier or by searching online. Shoe leather costs therefore represent an opportunity cost for consumers (see Chapter 3).

Consequences of inflation for workers

As inflation causes the cost of living to increase, workers see a decline in the real value of their wages and salaries. Therefore, workers will demand higher pay in order to purchase the same amount of goods and services as before. Inflation affects fixed-income earners the most. During periods of inflation, workers on fixed incomes (such as salaried workers) and the elderly on fixed pension payments are worse off than before, as the purchasing power of their fixed income declines with higher prices. Even if employees receive a pay rise, the rate of inflation reduces the real value of this. For example, if workers get a 4 per cent pay rise but inflation is 3 per cent, then the real pay increase is only 1 per cent.

Inflation harms the poorest members of society far more than those on high incomes. Low-income workers tend to have a high price elasticity of demand (see Chapter 10) for goods and services. By contrast, those on high incomes and those who have accumulated wealth (for example, Taylor Swift) are not so affected by higher prices. Furthermore, those in highly skilled professions such as surgeons, pilots and barristers are in a strong bargaining position because their skills are in short supply and in high demand. This can create a **wage-price spiral** where demand for higher wages to keep in line with inflation simply causes more inflation.

Consequences of inflation for producers/firms

Inflation causes **menu costs** for firms – that is, inflation affects the prices charged by firms. Catalogues, price lists and menus have to be updated regularly and this is costly to businesses. Of course, workers also have to be paid for their time to reprice goods and services. As workers are likely to demand a pay rise during times of inflation in order to maintain their level of real income, labour costs of production rise and, other things being equal, the profit margins of firms will fall.

Exporters and importers are also affected by inflation. The international competitiveness of a country will tend to fall when there is domestic inflation. In the long run, higher prices make exporters less price-competitive, thus causing a decrease in profits. This leads to a fall in export earnings, lower economic growth and higher unemployment. By contrast, imports become more expensive for individuals, firms and the government due to the decline in the purchasing power of money. Essential imports such as petroleum and food products can cause imported inflation (higher import prices, forcing up costs of production and thus causing domestic inflation). Hence, inflation can cause major problems for countries that lack natural resources.

Definition

A **wage-price spiral** occurs when trade unions and workers negotiate higher wages to keep income in line with inflation but this simply causes more inflation as firms raise prices to maintain their profit margins.

Table 28.5 The world's most expensive cities, 2023

Rank	City
1	Singapore
2	Zurich, Switzerland
3	New York, USA
4	Geneva, Switzerland
5	Hong Kong
6	Los Angeles, USA
7	Paris, France
8	Copenhagen, Denmark
9	Tel Aviv, Israel
10	San Francisco, USA

Source: Worldwide cost of living: Singapore and Zurich top the ranking of the world's most expensive cities, 30 November 2023, EIU website

Inflation also harms employers located in expensive areas, because these employers have to pay relatively high wages to attract workers. For example, Singapore, Zurich and New York were the top three most expensive cities in 2023 (see Table 28.5). Singapore has repeatedly been the most expensive city in the annual Economics Intelligence Unit (EIU) Worldwide Cost of Living Index.

Inflation also causes uncertainty for producers/firms. The combination of uncertainty and the lower-than-expected real rates of return on investment (due to higher costs of production) tends to lower the amount of planned investment in the economy.

▲ Singapore tops the most expensive cities index

Consequences of inflation for savers

Savers, be they individuals, firms or governments, will lose out because of inflation, assuming there is no change in interest rates for savings. This is because the money they have saved is worth less than before. For example, if interest rates average 2 per cent for savings accounts in a country, but the inflation rate is 3 per cent, then the real interest rate on savings is actually minus 1 per cent. Hence, inflation can act as a disincentive to save. In turn, this leads to fewer funds being made available for investment expenditure in the economy.

Consequences of inflation for lenders and borrowers

Lenders, be they individuals, firms or governments, will also lose from inflation. This is because the money lent out to borrowers becomes worth less than before due to inflation.

By contrast, borrowers tend to gain from inflation as the money they need to repay is worth less than when they initially borrowed it, i.e. the real value of their debt declines due to inflation. For example, if a borrower took out a mortgage at 5 per cent interest, but inflation was 3.5 per cent, this means the real interest rate is only 1.5 per cent.

Consequences of inflation for the economy as a whole

As discussed, most economic agents tend to lose out because of inflation (namely, the consumers, workers, savers, lenders and producers). Only borrowers of money gain from inflation. Therefore, the economy as a whole will tend to lose out because of inflationary pressures.

Practice question: structured question

Study the following data and answer the questions that follow.

Year	Inflation rate (%)	Wage increase (%)
1	2.5	3.0
2	3.1	3.5
3	2.9	3.1

a Describe which year saw the largest increase in real wages. [2]
b Explain why average wages were higher in Year 3 than Year 2. [2]

Practice questions: structured questions

1 Over the past decade, Japan has suffered from periods of deflation (see graph).

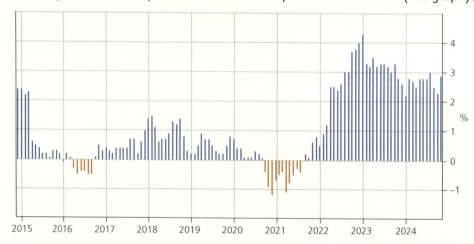

▲ Inflation rates in Japan (2014–2024)

Source: Japan inflation rate, Ministry of Internal Affairs & Communications, Japan, 2024, Trading Economics website

a Define 'deflation'. [2]
b Explain what evidence there is in the graph to suggest that Japan has suffered periods of deflation during the past 10 years. [4]

2 Iran's inflation rate fell from 54.6 per cent in May 2023 to 30.9 per cent in May 2024. The country, with a population of around 89 million, experienced double-digit inflation rates for most of the past decade. The country's non-oil trade deficit, alongside the removal of government subsidies for food and fuel, have driven prices upwards. In addition, international sanctions due to Iran's disputed nuclear programme have forced down the value of the Iranian rial, the country's official currency. This added pressure on higher prices in the economy.

Period	Inflation (%)
April 2022	32.9
April 2023	55.5
April 2024	30.9

Sources: Inflation rate (World), May 2024, Trading Economics website; 'What are the economic challenges facing the government in Iran?' by Mohammad Reza Farzanegan, 6 March 2023, Economics Observatory website

  a With reference to the data above, explain why prices in Iran were generally higher in April 2024 than in April 2023. [4]

  b Explain two reasons why the Iranian government might aim to control the level of inflation in its economy. [4]

  c Analyse how some Iranians are likely to have been more affected than others by the double-digit inflation rates. [6]

> ### Activity
> Discuss the impact of an increase in oil prices on the rate of inflation in your country or a country of your choice. Which stakeholders are affected the most? Why?

Policies to control inflation

Inflation can be controlled by using macroeconomic policies. The government can use these to slow down the growth of demand in the economy and/or boost the rate of growth of the economy's overall supply of goods and services. In the short run, fiscal and monetary policies are used to control inflation. In the long run, supply-side policies boost the productive capacity of the economy, thereby giving it flexibility to grow without suffering from the costs of inflation.

Fiscal policy

Fiscal policy involves the use of taxation and/or government spending to control the level of economic activity in the economy. If the general level of demand in the economy is too high (causing demand-pull inflation), the government may choose to 'tighten fiscal policy' by raising taxes and/or reducing its own expenditure. This will reduce the level of economic activity.

See Chapter 23 to read more about fiscal policy.

Monetary policy

Monetary policy involves the central bank changing interest rates in order to control the level of economic activity. For example, higher interest rates may reduce consumer and investment expenditure as the cost of borrowing (to fund household spending and business investments) soars. This can help control inflation.

See Chapter 24 to read more about monetary policy.

Supply-side policies

While both fiscal and monetary policies target the demand side of the economy in order to tackle the issue of inflation, supply-side policies are used to increase the economy's productive capacity. These policies seek to increase competition, productivity and innovation in order to maintain lower prices. Some countries, such as Iran and France, have used subsidies for food and fuel to reduce prices in the economy.

A reduction in corporate tax rates can also encourage risk-taking and greater investment. Countries that do not charge any corporate tax include Bahrain, the Bahamas, the Cayman Islands, the Isle of Man and the United Arab Emirates.

See Chapter 25 to read more about supply-side policy.

? Chapter review questions

1 What is meant by inflation?
2 What is the Consumer Price Index (CPI)?
3 Why are weights used in the calculation of the CPI?
4 What is a base year?
5 What are the two key causes of inflation?
6 Outline the main consequences of inflation.
7 What is deflation?
8 What macroeconomic policies can be used to deal with inflation?

Revision checklist

✔ Inflation is the sustained rise in the general price level in an economy over time.
✔ Deflation is the persistent fall in the general price level of goods and services in the economy, i.e. the inflation rate is negative.
✔ The Consumer Price Index (CPI) is used to calculate the inflation rate by measuring price changes of a representative basket of goods and services.
✔ Cost-push inflation is caused by higher costs of production, which makes firms raise their prices in order to maintain their profit margins.
✔ Demand-pull inflation is caused by higher levels of total demand in the economy, which drives up the general price level of goods and services.
✔ Costs of inflation include menu costs, shoe leather costs, lower consumer and business confidence (thereby reducing consumption and investment respectively), and reduced international competitiveness (as exports become more expensive).
✔ Losers of inflation include consumers, lenders, savers, fixed-income earners, low-income earners, exporters and employers.
✔ Winners of inflation include borrowers.
✔ Policies to tackle inflation include deflationary fiscal policies, tight monetary policies and supply-side policies.

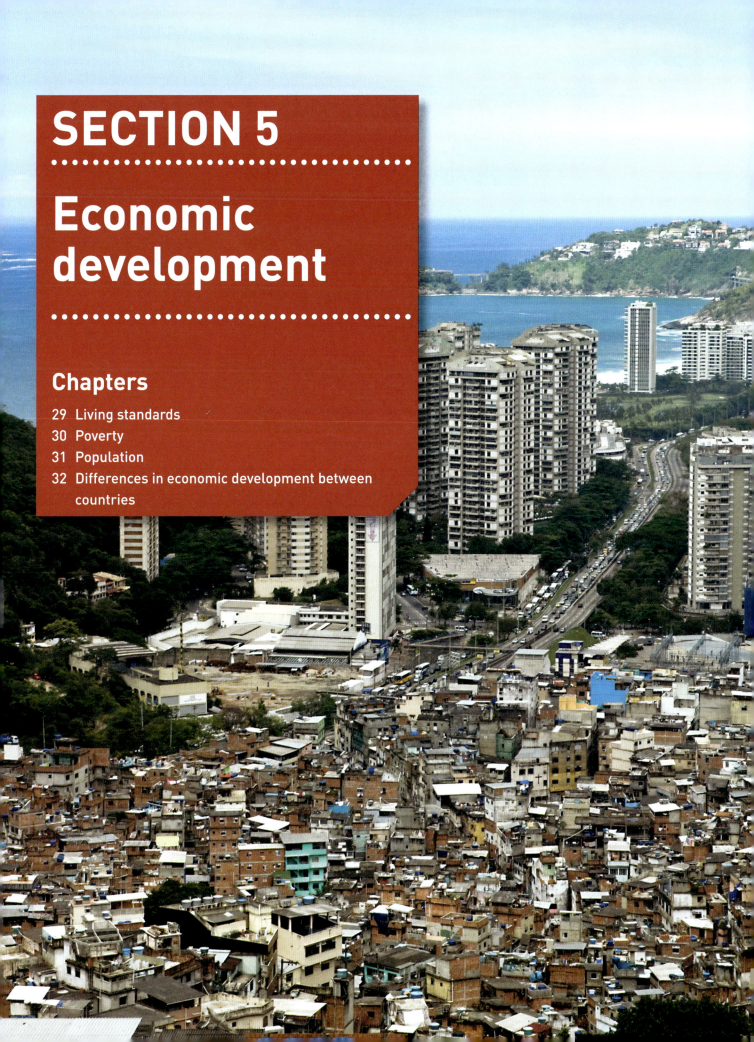

SECTION 5

Economic development

Chapters

Living standards

This chapter will cover:

★ indicators of living standards
★ the components of real GDP per head and the Human Development Index (HDI)
★ the advantages and disadvantages of real GDP and HDI as indicators of living standards
★ a comparison of living standards and income distribution
★ reasons for differences in living standards and income distribution within and between countries.

Defining indicators of living standards

Definition

Standard of living refers to the social and economic well-being of individuals in a country at a particular point in time.

Economists believe that sustained economic growth is an important macroeconomic aim (see Chapter 26) because it is the most practical measure of the **standard of living** in a country. Living standards can be described as the social and economic well-being of individuals in a country at a particular point in time. For example, China's phenomenal economic growth for more than three decades (see Figure 29.1), apart from the COVID-19 era, has led to an increase in living standards for the majority of its population. With an average growth rate of around 10 per cent per year, the income of the average Chinese citizen would have doubled every seventh year.

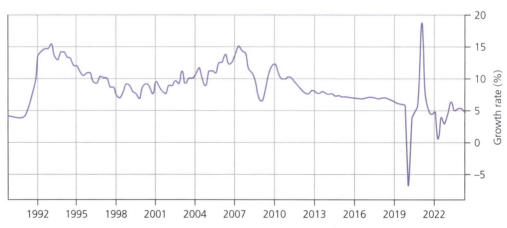

Source: China GDP annual growth rate, National Bureau of Statistics of China, 2024, Trading Economics website

▲ **Figure 29.1** China's economic growth rate, 1990–2024

The two main measures or indicators of living standards are **GDP per head** (also referred to as GDP per capita or GDP per person) and the **Human Development Index** (HDI).

Components of real GDP per head

As a single measure of standards of living, real GDP is perhaps the best indicator. Higher real GDP means that people have more to spend on goods and services. Real GDP is also relatively easy for economists to calculate.

One problem in using GDP figures (see Chapter 26) to measure standards of living is that the size of the population is ignored. For example, China's GDP is significantly larger than that of Luxembourg or Sweden. However, China's much larger population means that Sweden and Luxembourg's GDP per head of the population is greater (see Table 29.1). Hence, GDP per head is a better indicator of standards of living.

Table 29.1 GDP per capita: selected countries, 2023

Country	GDP ($bn)	GDP per capita ($)	Population (millions)
China	31,227	22,100	1,416
Sweden	676.4	64,200	10.59
Luxembourg	88.5	132,400	0.671

Source: *The World Factbook*, Country summaries, 2024, CIA gov website

Another consideration is inflation – the persistent increase in the general level of prices over time (see Chapter 28). Inflation erodes the value of GDP because the value of money falls if there is inflation.

For example, if a country's GDP increases by 5 per cent in a year but inflation also increases by 5 per cent, then the real value of its GDP has not changed. Hence, for a more accurate measure of GDP as an indicator of living standards, the monetary value of GDP must be adjusted for price changes. This adjusted measure is known as **real GDP**. Hence, **real GDP per capita** is an even better indicator of living standards than GDP per capita.

Components of the Human Development Index (HDI)

An alternative measure of living standards that looks at factors beyond real GDP is called the **Human Development Index** (HDI). This is a composite indicator of living standards in a country, combining three dimensions of human development:

Definition

The **Human Development Index** (HDI) is the United Nations' composite indicator of living standards in a country. It comprises three dimensions of human development: education, healthcare and income.

» **Healthcare** – this indicator measures life expectancy at birth. The better the healthcare in a country, the greater its social and economic well-being tends to be.
» **Education** – this indicator measures the mean years of schooling and the expected years of schooling in the country. In general, the higher the average years of schooling, the greater the degree of human development.
» **Income levels** – the higher the national income (or GDP) of a country, the greater human development tends to be. Hence, countries with a lower national income, such as Mozambique, Afghanistan, Sudan and Rwanda, tend to have a low HDI. Countries with a higher national income such as Norway, New Zealand, South Korea, Singapore, Japan, the UAE and Canada have a high HDI.

The main advantage of using the HDI rather than real GDP is that the former is a composite index. This means HDI considers several key indicators of standards of living, rather than a single one. In addition, improvements in education and healthcare are more likely than real GDP to indicate a country's level of social well-being, especially if income is not distributed very evenly in the economy.

However, there are limitations in using the HDI to measure living standards. These include the following:

» **Qualitative factors** – the HDI ignores qualitative factors affecting living standards, such as gender inequalities and human rights.
» **Income distribution** – the HDI does not take account of the inequitable distribution of income in the economy. It lacks accuracy as an indicator of living standards for the 'average' person.
» **Environmental issues** – the HDI ignores environmental and resource depletion resulting from economic growth.
» **Cultural differences** – although the HDI is a composite indicator, it ignores cultural variations and different interpretations of the meaning of standards of living.

> ### Activity
>
> Study the information below about the HDI of four countries. Use the internet to research Australia, Ethiopia, Russia and Vietnam. (You could start by searching on the UNDP's website.) Then identify which of these countries could be represented by A, B, C and D in the table. Explain the reasoning behind your answers.
>
> **Table 29.2** The HDI of four countries
>
> | Country | HDI | Country | HDI |
> |---------|---------|---------|---------|
> | A | ± 0.946 | C | ± 0.726 |
> | B | ± 0.821 | D | ± 0.492 |

> ### Activities
>
> 1 Use the internet to research the top ten countries as measured by the HDI. You could start by searching on the UNDP's website.
> 2 Discuss whether the HDI is a good measure of living standards in these countries.

Comparing living standards and income distribution

There are many factors that cause differences in living standards and income distribution within and between countries. These factors include, but are not limited to, the following:

» **Productivity levels** – differences in productivity levels cause differences in wages and earnings. Highly skilled and experienced workers (see Chapter 17) earn higher salaries, so will tend to enjoy a higher standard of living.
» **Role of governments** – governments can use direct taxes (imposed on income, wealth or profits) to redistribute income in the economy. A mixed economy is more likely to do this than a market economy (see Chapter 14). A fairer distribution of income and wealth can help to raise living standards for the majority of a population.
» **Size of population** – the size and demographics of a population (see Chapter 31) have a direct impact on living standards. Densely populated cities tend to have higher rents due to limited space and high demand. They also generally have more congestion, pollution and higher living costs (see Table 28.5).

» **Distribution of national income** – although national income may be high, it may not be distributed in a socially desirable way. For example, there are huge wealth gaps in most societies (hence the need to redistribute national income). In addition, the composition of GDP is important to consider. For example, if it increases because of higher government spending on the military, this does not translate to better living standards for the majority of the population.

» **Regional differences** – there are regional income and wealth disparities within countries. For example, data from Statista show that the mean annual income in London is higher than in other parts of the UK. In 2023 the median annual earnings for full-time employees was £44,370 ($56,905) for Londoners but only £32,371 ($41,516) for those in Wales, £32,879 ($42,168) for those in Northern Ireland and £35,518 ($45,552) for those in Scotland.

Source: 'Median annual earnings for full-time employees in the United Kingdom in 2023, by region' by D Clark, 3 July 2023, Statista website

» **General price level** – inflation (see Chapter 28) increases the cost of living, so an increase in the general price level tends to have a negative impact on standards of living. For example, economic instability in Venezuela caused the inflation rate to average 83.7 per cent in the first quarter of 2024. This means that something priced at 100 Venezuelan bolívar fuerte (VEF) at the beginning of the year would have increased in price to VEF183.70 by the end of the year.

Source: Venezuela inflation rate, Banco Central de Venezuela, May 2024, Trading Economics website

» **Level of education** – there is a positive correlation between educational attainment and earnings (see Table 17.3 and Table 29.3). In general, the more educated and well qualified a person is, the higher their earning potential tends to be. This has a direct impact on their living standards.

» **Level of freedom** – various measures of living standards include consideration of civil liberties, political rights, religious freedom and economic rights. The Human Freedom Index measures 79 indicators of personal, civil and economic freedom. It is the most comprehensive index on freedom for countries around the world (see Table 29.4).

Table 29.3 The world's ten best school systems

Rank	Country
1	Finland
2	Australia
3	Sweden
4	Estonia
5	Slovenia
6	Poland
7	Denmark
8	Belgium
9	Czechia
10	Canada

Source: Education, Organisation for Economic Cooperation and Development (OECD) Better Life index website

Table 29.4 Human Freedom Index, 2024

Rank	Country	Rank	Country
1	Singapore	184	North Korea
2	Switzerland	183	Cuba
3	Ireland	182	Venezuela
4	Taiwan	181	Sudan
5	Luxembourg	180	Zimbabwe
6	New Zealand	179	Burundi
7	Estonia	178	Eritrea
8	Denmark	177	Iran
9	Sweden	176	Central African Republic
10	Norway	175	Burma

Source: Index of economic freedom, All country scores, October 2023, Heritage Foundation website

Practice questions: multiple choice

1 Which option is **not** a measure of a country's standard of living? [1]
  A education indicators
  B healthcare indicators
  C population size
  D real GDP per head

2 Which statement best explains why a country's real GDP per capita is likely to affect its citizens' standard of living? [1]
  A Higher real GDP per head means the average citizen can buy more goods and services.
  B Inflation must be accounted for when considering living standards.
  C Real GDP per head always falls when the population size increases.
  D Real GDP per head is the only measure of living standards in a country.

? Chapter review questions

1 What is meant by living standards?
2 How does real GDP per head differ from GDP per head?
3 What is the HDI?
4 What are the limitations of using the HDI as a measure of living standards?
5 What are the main reasons for differences in living standards and income distribution within and between countries?

Revision checklist

✔ Standard of living refers to the social and economic well-being of individuals in a country at a particular point in time.
✔ The two main indicators of living standards are real GDP per head and the Human Development Index (HDI).
✔ Real GDP per head is a measure of living standards that involves dividing a country's GDP by the size of the country's population.
✔ Higher real GDP means that people have more to spend on goods and services. Real GDP is also relatively easy for economists to calculate. However, it does not take into account the size of the population.
✔ The Human Development Index (HDI) is the United Nations' composite indicator of living standards in a country. It measures three dimensions of human development: healthcare, education and income levels.
✔ The main advantage of using the HDI rather than real GDP is that the former is a composite index. However, the HDI has several drawbacks, including that it does not take account of qualitative factors, income distribution, environmental issues or cultural differences.
✔ Factors that cause differences in living standards and income distribution within and between countries include different productivity levels, population size, the role of governments, the distribution of national income, regional differences in incomes, the general price level, the overall level of educational attainment and the level of freedom.

30 Poverty

This chapter will cover:

★ definitions of absolute and relative poverty
★ the causes of poverty
★ policies to alleviate poverty and redistribute income.

Defining poverty

Poverty is a condition that exists when people lack adequate income and wealth to sustain a basic standard of living (see Chapter 29). The eradication of poverty is a fundamental macroeconomic aim for many governments around the world. This is because poverty creates numerous social and economic problems, including poor health (such as malnutrition and famine), deaths, crime, high unemployment, the need for welfare provision and lower national output.

The United Nations defines poverty as 'a lack of income and productive resources to ensure sustainable livelihoods'. This includes:

» hunger and malnutrition
» ill health and mortality from illness
» limited or lack of access to education and other basic services
» homelessness and inadequate housing
» unsafe environments
» social discrimination and exclusion.

Table 30.1 shows the countries with the highest and the lowest GDP per capita. According to *The CIA World Factbook*, in 2023 Liechtenstein (located between Austria and Switzerland) had the highest GDP per capita at around $382 per day, while Burundi (located in Eastern Africa) had only approximately $1.92 per day.

Table 30.1 The world's richest and poorest countries, 2023

Richest countries			Poorest countries		
Rank	Country	GDP per capita ($)	Rank	Country	GDP per capita ($)
1	Liechtenstein	139,100	1	Burundi	700
2	Luxembourg	117,700	2	Central African Republic	800
3	Monaco	115,700	3	Congo, Democratic Republic of the	1,100
4	Ireland	112,400	4	Niger	1,300
5	Singapore	108,000	5	Mozambique	1,300
6	Qatar	96,600	6	Chad	1,400
7	Isle of Man	84,600	7	Somalia	1,400
8	Bermuda	81,200	8	Madagascar	1,500
9	United Arab Emirates	74,900	9	Malawi	1,500
10	Switzerland	72,300	10	Afghanistan	1,500

Source: Compiled from *The World Factbook*, Country summaries, 2024, CIA gov website

Practice question: structured question

According to the US Census Bureau, in 2022 11.5 per cent of individuals in the USA were living below the poverty line (the minimum level of income judged to be adequate in a particular country). The aftershock of the global financial crisis of 2008 meant rising unemployment and related problems for the economy. This resulted in over 46 million people living in poverty in the USA – more than at any point in the nation's history.

Source: Data on poverty in the United States, US Census Bureau, 2023, Center for American progress website

a Define 'poverty'. [2]
b Explain why poverty is a concern for the US government. [4]
c Discuss whether the standard of living is always higher in developed than in developing countries. [8]

There are two categories of poverty: absolute poverty and relative poverty.

Absolute poverty

> **Definition**
>
> **Absolute poverty** exists when there is extreme outright poverty, i.e. income equal to or less than $2.15 per day.

Absolute poverty exists when there is extreme outright poverty. People in absolute poverty are undeniably poor. Their income, if any, is entirely spent on minimal amounts of food, clothing and shelter – that is, the basic human needs essential for survival. For many, absolute poverty can mean hunger, malnutrition and homelessness.

There is more than one way to measure absolute poverty. The most common method is to calculate the number of individuals living below a certain level of income (called the **income threshold** or the **poverty line**). The most common income threshold, set by the World Bank, is $2.15 a day (the international poverty line). Many people around the world still live below this amount, so such extreme poverty means they are unable to buy enough food to survive.

Since 1995, the United Nations has adopted the following definition of absolute poverty:

A condition characterised by severe deprivation of basic human needs, including food, safe drinking water, sanitation facilities, health, shelter, education and information. It depends not only on income but also on access to services.

Source: The definition of poverty around the world, United Nations, 1995, World Vision website

Case study: Burundi

Burundi is one of the poorest countries on the planet, with around 65 per cent of its population of 12.9 million people living below the international poverty line in 2023. In that same year GDP per head in the East African country was a meagre $700 (or $1.92 per day) and 32.9 per cent of the country's GDP came from agriculture. Burundi has a staggering infant mortality rate of 37.877 deaths per 1000 live births in 2023 – one of the highest rates in the world. The median age in the same year was just 16.1 years and life expectancy was 61.66 years.

Source: *The World Factbook*, Country summaries, Burundi, 2023, CIA gov website

Relative poverty

> **Definition**
>
> **Relative poverty** is a comparative measure of poverty, referring to those who have a lower standard of living in comparison to the average member of society.

Relative poverty is a comparative measure of poverty, rather than an absolute measure. People in absolute poverty are undeniably impoverished, whereas those in relative poverty have a lower standard of living in comparison to the average member of society. For example, it is rather pointless to compare what is meant by poverty for the average person living in Singapore or Luxembourg with the situation of someone living in poverty in Sierra Leone or Niger. Relative poverty measures the extent to which a person's financial resources fall below the average income for the country's population. Although real GDP (see Chapter 26) and standards of living (see Chapter 29) have grown over time across the world, these gains are not evenly distributed across populations and countries.

Case study: The United Nations Sustainable Development Goals

On 25 September 2015, the United Nations devised the anti-poverty Sustainable Development Goals (SDGs). These consist of 17 international development goals to be achieved by 2030 to end poverty, protect the planet and ensure prosperity for all (see Figure 30.1).

Source: United Nations

▲ **Figure 30.1** The Sustainable Development Goals

Causes of poverty

Poor countries, with a high degree of poverty, have common characteristics. The causes (and consequences) of poverty include the following interrelated factors:

» **Unemployment** – people in poverty are likely to be unemployed, perhaps due to the combination of low literacy, lack of skills and poor health. Hence, labour productivity in less economically developed countries also tends to be low. This, in turn, makes it difficult for people to break out of poverty. Labour productivity is a measure of the efficiency of labour in the production process, such as output per worker (see Chapter 19).

>> **Low wages** – GDP per head is calculated by dividing the gross domestic product (GDP) of a country by its population to find the income level of the average person. The lower the GDP per person, the poorer the country tends to be due to the low wages in the economy. This tends to be the case in countries with a high proportion of unskilled workers. This limits consumption and investment in the economy, and so can cause poverty. According to data from the World Bank, in 2024 Monaco had the highest GDP per head at $240,862 (about $660 per day), whereas Sierra Leone had the lowest at $433 (just $1.18 per day).

>> **Illness** – illnesses (possibly caused by malnutrition and a lack of healthcare) reduce life expectancy in a country. Life expectancy measures the number of years that the average person in a country is anticipated to live for, based on statistical trends. The lower the life expectancy, the poorer the country tends to be and so the greater the degree of poverty in the country. Data from the World Bank support this, with the likes of Chad, Nigeria, Lesotho, South Sudan and Somalia all having life expectancy of between 53 and 56 years in 2022. By contrast, wealthy economies such as Hong Kong, Japan, Singapore, Italy, Iceland and Switzerland all have good healthcare provision, so life expectancy is between 82 and 85 years in these countries.

Source: Life expectancy at birth, total (years), United Nations Population Division, 2022, World Bank Group website

>> **Age** – age is a key factor causing poverty. For example, the root cause of child labour in many parts of the world is extreme poverty, which forces parents to allow their children to work. Poverty also exists among the elderly – a growing proportion of people are living longer, yet many elderly people have no income to sustain their standard of living.

➡ Case study: Tony's Chocolonely

Child labour is a significant issue in the chocolate industry, particularly in West Africa, where many cocoa farms rely on children who work under poor conditions. Tony's Chocolonely, a Dutch chocolate manufacturer, is actively combatting this problem by sourcing cocoa directly from farms that follow fair labour practices. The company ensures that farmers are paid a living wage so as to alleviate the reliance on child labour, and invests in community development to prevent the exploitation of labour and modern slavery.

Source: Together we'll end exploitation in cocoa, Tony's Chocolonely UK website

>> **Poor healthcare** (illness) – insufficient investment in health services hinders the ability of a country to develop and lift people out of poverty. Healthcare expenditure per capita is low in less economically developed countries. Their governments are unable to provide preventive and curative healthcare services for the mass population. According to the World Bank, in 2021 the USA spent 16.57 per cent of its GDP on healthcare services, whereas this figure was only 5.19 per cent in Chad, 4.15 per cent in Ghana, 2.91 per cent in Pakistan and just 2.36 per cent in Bangladesh.

Source: Current healthcare expenditure (% GDP), World Health Organization global health expenditure database, 15 April 2024, World Bank Group website

>> **Environmental factors** – events such as natural disasters, climate change and resource depletion are significant causes of poverty. For instance, prolonged droughts in East Africa in 2024 have devastated crops and livestock, leading to food shortages and economic instability. Similarly, frequent hurricanes and flooding in countries

like Bangladesh destroy homes and infrastructure, displacing communities and hindering growth and development. Deforestation in the Amazon affects indigenous populations, stripping them of their livelihoods and accelerating poverty. These environmental challenges disrupt economies, widen income inequalities and increase the vulnerability of the poor, trapping communities in a poverty cycle.

» **Low literacy rates** – literacy rates measure the proportion of the population aged 15 and above who can read and write. Low-income countries have insufficient investment in education and training, so their literacy rates tend to be low. This has major consequences for employment, production and productivity, thus negatively impacting on GDP and making it extremely difficult to eradicate poverty. The vast majority of high-income countries will have 100 per cent adult literacy rates whereas low-income countries have very low literacy rates – for example, Niger (38 per cent), South Sudan (35 per cent), Afghanistan (37 per cent), Mali (31 per cent) and Chad (27 per cent), based on data from the World Bank from 2018–2022.

Source: Literacy rate adult total (% people ages 15 and above), UNESCO Institute for Statistics, 24 April 2024, World Bank Group website

» **High population growth** – population growth measures the annual percentage change in the population of a country (see Chapter 31). Poorer countries tend to have high population growth rates for several reasons: limited availability and knowledge of contraception and family planning, poor access to contraception and cultural norms (it is common and widely accepted to have a large number of children in some countries and cultures). Sharing a limited amount of resources among a growing population hinders the country's ability to lift itself out of poverty.

» **Poor infrastructure** – infrastructure refers to the transportation and communications networks necessary for the efficient functioning of an economy, such as buildings, railways, roads, airports, water systems, ICT systems including the internet, and power supplies. Countries with very poor infrastructure include Bosnia and Herzegovina, Angola, Mongolia, Nepal, Lebanon and Chad. Table 30.2 shows internet users by percentage of population in some of the most and the least connected countries in 2022 and 2023.

Table 30.2 Internet users by percentage of population, 2022 and 2023

Most connected countries		Least connected countries	
Country	**Internet users (% of population)**	**Country**	**Internet users (% of population)**
Iceland	100	Burundi	11
Bahrain	100	Eritrea	27
Monaco	98	Somalia	28
Finland	94	Guinea-Bissau	32

Source: Adapted from Individuals using the internet (% of population), World Bank Group

» **Low foreign direct investment** (FDI) – the lack of capital resources also limits the ability of a country to create income and wealth. FDI refers to cross-border investment made by multinational companies and other investors. Low-income countries, with their lack of economic growth and poor infrastructure, do not tend to attract FDI due to the expected high risks and low financial returns, so these countries remain in poverty.

227

» **High public debt** – public debt refers to the money owed by the government (public sector). In general, low-income countries are far more likely to borrow money to finance their public sector expenditure, and the higher the public debt, the lower a country's standard of living tends to be. This is because the government will need to repay its loans, along with interest payments, rather than using the funds for investment in the economy. It is common for less economically developed countries to pay more for financing their public debts, partly due to the high interest rates imposed and partly due to a fall in the value of their currency. This makes repayment of public debt increasingly unsustainable for many of these countries, leading to further borrowing, ever-increasing debts and widespread poverty.

➡ **Case study:** Japan

The huge impact of the COVID-19 pandemic harmed high-income as well as low-income countries (see Table 30.3). In fact, Japan tops the chart of government debt, partly because of its exposure to the global financial crisis in 2008, the devastating earthquake and tsunami of March 2011 (the worst natural disaster in the country's history), followed by extreme lockdown measures due to COVID-19.

Table 30.3 Government debts around the world, 2024

Most indebted countries		Least indebted countries	
Country	Public debt as % of GDP	Country	Public debt as % of GDP
Japan	214.27	Brunei Darussalam	2.06
Greece	192.41	Kuwait	2.92
Eritrea	163.77	Turkmenistan	5.19
Italy	140.57	Tuvalu	7.59
Singapore	135.86	Norway	13.17
Laos	128.51	Switzerland	14.4
Sudan	127.55	Kiribati	15.21
Cabo Verde	127.41	Timor-Leste	16.27
Barbados	126.83	Solomon Islands	16.85
Bhutan	124.79	Estonia	18.83

Source: Central government debt, percent of GDP, 2024, International Monetary Fund website

» **Reliance on primary sector output** – low-income countries tend to over-rely on the production and export of primary sector output, such as agricultural products. These tend to have low prices and profit margins in comparison to manufactured products and tertiary sector services. Table 30.4 compares the output from the three sectors of the economy for selected countries.

» **Corruption and instability** – a final cause of poverty is the high degree of corruption and instability (economic, social and political) that can exist in a country. There are huge opportunity costs of civil war, dishonest government officials, fraudulent behaviour, and the purchase of arms and weapons. Corruption and instability therefore hinder economic development. This results in greater inequalities in income distribution and creates poverty.

Table 30.4 Output of the economy by sector: selected countries

Country	Sector of the economy (%)			Real GDP per capita ($)
	Primary	**Secondary**	**Tertiary**	
Sierra Leone	60.7	6.5	32.9	1,600
Chad	52.3	14.7	33.1	1,400
Guinea-Bissau	50.0	13.1	36.9	1,900
Central African Republic	43.2	16.0	40.8	800
Ethiopia	34.8	21.6	43.6	2,400
Denmark	1.3	22.9	75.8	59,900
United Kingdom	0.7	20.2	79.2	47,600
Germany	0.7	30.7	68.6	54,000
Luxembourg	0.3	12.8	86.9	117,700
Monaco	0.0	14.0	86.0	115,700

Source: GDP – composition, by sector of origin, 2024, *The World Factbook*, CIA gov website

Policies to alleviate poverty and redistribute income

Policies to help alleviate poverty and to redistribute income include the following:

» **Promoting economic growth** – any expansionary policy, such as lower taxes (see Chapter 23) or lower interest rates (see Chapter 24), can encourage consumer spending and investment expenditure in the economy. In the long run, this can help to create more jobs and alleviate the problems of poverty. Similarly, lower exchange rates (see Chapter 35) can encourage export sales, as the price for foreign buyers is lower. As higher export earnings help to boost GDP, this can also help to create more jobs and wealth in the economy over time. Sustained economic growth helps to create more income and wealth for the country (see Chapter 26). This can then be redistributed to the deprived and underprivileged members of society.

» **Improving education** – government provision of education can help to alleviate poverty. Improving access to education for everyone helps to eventually narrow the gap between the rich and the poor. In most cases, a person's level of education tends to affect their earnings and earning potential (see Table 17.5). Over time, policies to increase the quantity and quality of education in the economy will help to improve the human capital and productive capacity of the country, as they will create economic growth and lower poverty. Similarly, the provision of or increased access to other essential services, such as healthcare and housing, will also help.

» **Improved healthcare provision** – improved healthcare provision can help to alleviate poverty and redistribute income by reducing the financial burden of healthcare and medical expenses on low-income households. Access to affordable and quality healthcare allows individuals to spend their income on other essential wants and needs (see Chapter 1). Healthy populations are more productive, leading to higher earnings and economic growth. In addition, government-funded healthcare reduces income inequalities by providing essential services to all, regardless of income. In this way, it ensures equitable access to healthcare and fosters a more sustainable economy.

» **Providing more generous state benefits** – government provision of welfare benefits gives financial assistance to enable the unemployed and disadvantaged to meet their basic needs. Examples of such payments include unemployment welfare benefits, state pension funds for the elderly and child benefit (to reduce child poverty). State benefits help to redistribute income and alleviate poverty by ensuring every citizen has access to basic necessities. Macroeconomic policies aimed at reducing unemployment (see Chapter 27) also help, because unemployment is a major cause of poverty and inequality. Examples are government incentives to attract foreign direct investment (FDI) and government-funded job creation and retraining schemes.

» **Using progressive taxation** – a progressive tax system (see Chapter 23) reduces the gap between the rich and poor members of a country. Higher-income groups pay a higher percentage of their incomes in tax, with the tax revenues being used by the government to support lower-income groups or those without any income. This is a common method used to alleviate poverty and redistribute income and wealth in society.

» **Introducing (or increasing) a national minimum wage (NMW)** – the introduction of a national minimum wage, or imposing a higher minimum wage rate (see Chapter 17), can improve the standard of living for low-income households. Hence, NMW policies help to alleviate poverty in the economy.

> ## Activity
>
> - Produce a short piece of writing of 500–750 words that outlines a day in the life of a teenager living in a low-income country of your choice.
> - You need to gather the necessary data and information before you begin your writing.
> - Your work must reflect the macroeconomic indicators, without actually mentioning the indicators by name.
> - This can be in the format of an essay, diary entry, magazine article or letter.
>
> Be prepared to share your findings with your teacher and classmates.

? Chapter review questions

1 What is meant by poverty and what are the signs that there is poverty in the economy?
2 How does absolute poverty differ from relative poverty?
3 What are the main causes of poverty?
4 Why does an overreliance on primary sector output hinder the growth of low-income countries?
5 What are the main policies that can be used to alleviate poverty and redistribute income in the economy?

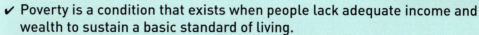

Revision checklist

✔ Poverty is a condition that exists when people lack adequate income and wealth to sustain a basic standard of living.

✔ Poverty creates problems for society and the economy because it causes poor health (such as malnutrition and famine), deaths, crime, high unemployment, the need for welfare provision and lower national output.

✔ Absolute poverty exists when there is extreme outright poverty – that is, income equal to or less than $2.15 per day (according to the World Bank). Such extreme poverty means people are unable to buy enough food to survive.

✔ Relative poverty is a comparative measure of poverty, referring to those who have a lower standard of living than the average member of society.

✔ Causes (and consequences) of poverty include unemployment, low wages, poor healthcare and illness, age, environmental factors, low GDP per capita, low life expectancy, low literacy rates, high population growth, poor infrastructure, low foreign direct investment, low productivity, high public debt, overreliance on primary sector output, and corruption and instability in the economy.

✔ Policies to alleviate poverty and redistribute income include policies to promote economic growth, improve education, improve healthcare provision, provide more generous state benefits, use progressive taxation and introduce (or increase) a national minimum wage.

Population

> This chapter will cover:
>
> ★ the factors that affect population growth
> ★ reasons for the different rates of population growth in different countries
> ★ the effects of changes in the size and structure of populations on different countries.

Factors that affect population growth

Population refers to the total number of inhabitants of a particular country. Economists are interested in population size as people are essential for the economic prosperity of a country and also responsible for the depletion of the Earth's scarce resources. **Population growth** refers to the rate of change in the size of a country's population. Change in population size can have huge and long-lasting effects on the world's economy and the natural environment.

▲ The higher a country's birth rate, the greater its population growth tends to be

Changes in three key factors affect the rate of population growth: birth rate, death rate and migration.

Birth rate

The **birth rate** measures the number of live births per thousand of the population in a year. It is measured by dividing the total number of births in a country by the population size, expressed per thousand of the population. The higher a country's birth rate, the greater its population growth will tend to be. According to *The CIA World Factbook*, in 2024 Niger had the highest birth rate at 46.6 per thousand of the population. Other countries with high birth rates include Angola (41.1), Benin (40.3) and Mali (40). The country with the lowest birth rate (per 1000 people) is Saint Pierre and Miquelon (6.54). Other countries with low birth rates include Monaco (6.5), Andorra (6.9), Japan (6.9), South Korea (7) and Italy (7.1).

A similar measure is the **fertility rate**, which measures the average number of children born per woman. This indicates the potential for population change in a country. Economists consider a fertility rate of two children per woman to be the minimum **replacement fertility rate** for a stable population (that is, the number of children that the average woman must have to replace the existing population). According to the United Nations *Population Fund*, in 2024 Niger had the highest birth rate at 6.6 births per woman. In joint second place were Chad, the Democratic Republic of the Congo and Somalia, all with 6 births per woman. In contrast, South Korea had the lowest birth rate at 0.9 per woman. Other countries with low birth rates include Singapore (1.1), China (1.2), Italy (1.3) and Finland (1.4).

Death rate

This measures the number of deaths per thousand of the population in a year. It is measured by dividing the total number of deaths in a country by the population size, expressed per thousand of the population. The lower a country's **death rate**, the greater its population growth will tend to be. According to *The CIA World Factbook*, in 2024 Ukraine, Lithuania and Serbia had the highest death rates (of 18.6, 15.2 and 14.9 respectively). In contrast, Qatar, the United Arab Emirates and Kuwait had the lowest death rates (of 1.4, 1.7 and 2.3 respectively). The death rate is dependent on factors that affect the quality of life (see Chapter 29), such as income levels, health technologies, nutrition and housing.

Net migration rate

The size of a population can also change due to the physical movement of people in and out of a country. **Immigration** occurs when people enter a country to live and work. **Emigration** occurs when people leave a country to live and work abroad. The **net migration rate** measures the difference between the number of people entering and leaving a country per thousand of the population in a year. It is calculated using the formula:

Net migration rate = immigration − emigration

If more people enter a country than leave in the year, there is said to be **net immigration**. If more people leave a country than enter the country, there is said to be **net emigration**. In 2024, Ukraine, South Sudan and Venezuela had the highest net migration rates (of 36.5, 19.1 and 13.2). The Cook Islands, American Samoa and the Federated States of Micronesia had the lowest net migration rates (i.e. net emigration rates) of −25.1, −24.8 and −21.0. For further information, see World Migration Report 2024 (International Organization for Migration).

Reasons for different rates of population growth

The world's population has continually grown (see Figure 31.1). However, there are differences in population growth rates in different countries (see Table 31.1).

Definitions

The **fertility rate** measures the average number of births per woman. It is used as a component to measure population growth.

The **replacement fertility rate** is the number of children that the average woman must have to maintain a stable population size.

The **death rate** measures the number of deaths per thousand of the population in a year.

The **net migration rate** measures the difference between immigration and emigration rates for a country, thus indicating the physical movement of people into and out of a country.

Study tip

The net migration rate measures the overall level of population change resulting from all migrants. It does not distinguish between worker migrants, refugees and unlawful (undocumented) migrants.

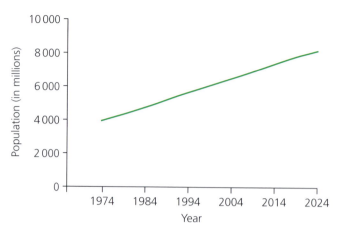

▲ **Figure 31.1** The world's population, 1974–2024

Source: Adapted from Worldometer, World population by year, From 1950 to current year: elaboration of data by United Nations, Department of Economic and Social Affairs, Population Division. World Population Prospects: The 2024 Revision. (Medium-fertility variant)

Table 31.1 The world's most and least populous countries, 2024

Most populous countries			Least populous countries		
Rank	Country	Population (millions)	Rank	Country	Population
1	India	1450.93	1	Holy See	496
2	China	1419.32	2	Niue	1819
3	USA	345.43	3	Tokelau	2506
4	Indonesia	283.49	4	Falkland Islands	3470
5	Pakistan	251.27	5	Montserrat	4389

Source: Countries in the world by population (2024), Worldometer website

▲ Japan has an ageing population in which around 30 per cent of the population are aged 65 and older
Source: Statista, 2022

There are several reasons for the different rates of population growth in different countries. These reasons involve differences in the factors that affect population growth (also explained above):

» **Birth rate** – more economically developed countries tend to have lower birth rates than less economically developed countries. This is partly due to education, access to contraception, the high costs of raising children, and women choosing to pursue careers and therefore opting to have fewer children and at a later stage in their lives.

» **Death rate** – due to better-quality education, healthcare, nutrition and sanitation, people in more economically developed countries tend to live longer. Famine, poverty, poor housing, high infant mortality rates and diseases tend to reduce life expectancy in less economically developed countries.

» **Net migration rate** – people migrate for different reasons, such as in search of better job opportunities, to take advantage of lower taxes, or to avoid civil unrest in their home country. For example, hundreds of thousands of Filipinos and Indonesians work as domestic helpers in Hong Kong, Singapore and Malaysia due to the higher salaries available. The net effect of immigration and emigration will clearly have a direct impact on rates of population growth in different countries.

> **Activity**
>
> Investigate the costs of raising a child up to the age of 18 in your country or a country of your choice. Try to be as accurate as possible by including and itemising the costs of food, clothing, education, healthcare, recreation, entertainment, holidays and so on. Compare your results with others in the class. Why might such findings be of interest to economists?

Effects of changes in the size and structure of populations

The optimum population

While there are reasons for different population sizes and rates of population growth in different countries, economists argue that there is an optimal (best or ideal) population for each country. An **optimum population** exists when the output of goods and services per capita (as measured by GDP per head) of the population is maximised (see Figure 31.2).

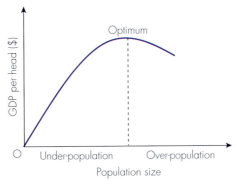

▲ **Figure 31.2** The optimum population

A country is under-populated if it does not have sufficient labour to make the best use of its resources. In this case, GDP per head of the population could be increased if there were more human resources. Fertility rates below the replacement level can lead to under-population, causing potential economic decline. In this case, to reach the optimum population, the government could introduce measures to increase the population size, such as encouraging immigration.

A country that is **over-populated** has a population that is too large given the available resources of the country. Fertility rates above the replacement level can lead to potential over-population, with negative economic consequences such as famine, housing shortages, energy shortages and diseases. This causes a fall in GDP per capita as there are insufficient resources to sustain the population. In this case, to reach the optimum population, the government could introduce measures either to reduce the population size or to boost investment and productivity in the economy.

▲ Over-population in Brazilian cities has contributed to creating vast informal settlements due to housing shortages

Countries with the highest and lowest population growth rates are shown in Table 31.2.

Table 31.2 Countries with the highest and lowest population growth rates, 2024

Highest population growth			Lowest population growth		
Rank	Country	Growth (%)	Rank	Country	Growth (%)
1	South Sudan	4.65	1	Cook Islands	−2.24
2	Niger	3.66	2	American Samoa	−1.54
3	Angola	3.33	3	Saint Pierre and Miquelon	−1.21
4	Benin	3.29	4	Puerto Rico	−1.2
5	Equatorial Guinea	3.23	5	Latvia	−1.14

Source: Population growth rate, 2024, *The World Factbook*, CIA gov website

Population distribution

Population distribution refers to the composition and structure of a country's population. The study of population distribution and trends in the composition of a population is called **demographics**. Such demographics include differences in the gender and age distribution.

Gender distribution

This refers to the number of males compared to the number of females in the population. For the vast majority of countries, the gender split is quite even. Data from *The CIA World Factbook* for Denmark, for example, show the following gender ratios in 2024:

» At birth: 1.07 male(s) per female.
» Under 15 years: 1.05 male(s) per female.
» 15–64 years: 1.03 male(s) per female.
» 65 years and over: 0.86 male(s) per female.
» Total population: 0.99 male(s) per female.

Age distribution

This refers to the number of people in different age groups in the population. Low-income countries tend to have a relatively larger proportion of their population in the younger age groups. For example, according *The CIA World Factbook*, as of 2020, around 56 per cent of the population in Ghana were under the age of 25, with only about 4.4 per cent of the population aged 65 and over in 2024. By contrast, higher-income countries tend to have an ageing population with a growing number of people in older age groups. For example, in 2023 only 12.1 per cent of people in Japan were aged 14 and below, while 29.5 per cent were aged 65 and above.

Dependency ratio

The **dependency ratio** is a comparison of the number of people who are not in the labour force with the number of people in active paid employment. For most economists, the dependent population typically includes all those aged between 0 and 14 (those below the school-leaving age) and those aged 65 and above (those above the retirement age). However, it also includes full-time students and the unemployed. The dependency ratio measures the dependent population as a proportion of the total active labour force (the **working population** comprises those aged between 15 and 65). It is therefore calculated using the formula:

Dependency ratio = Dependent population ÷ Working population

The higher the dependency ratio, the greater the tax burden on the working population to support those who are not economically active (not in paid employment). The dependency ratio can increase because of:

» higher birth rates, which mainly occur in less economically developed countries
» a higher compulsory school-leaving age, raising the number of people classified as part of the dependent population
» social changes such as workers entering the labour force at a later stage due to greater demand for higher education, or more people choosing early retirement (thus reducing the size of the working population).

Definitions

Population distribution refers to the composition and structure of a country's population.
Demographics is the study of population distribution and trends.

Study tip

Economics students are expected to be able to understand the effects of increases and decreases in population size and changes in the age and gender distribution of the population. However, students are **not** expected to interpret population pyramids.

Definitions

The **dependency ratio** is a comparison of the number of people who are not in the labour force with the number of people in active paid employment.
The **working population** refers to the active labour force aged 15–65, i.e. those who are willing and able to work. This consists of those in paid employment, the self-employed and the unemployed.

237

> **Activity**
>
> Investigate China's one-child policy (1979–2015); then answer these questions:
>
> **a** Why was the one-child policy introduced?
> **b** What were the exemptions to the policy?
> **c** What are the economic impacts of such a policy for future generations?

Practice question: structured question

Study the data below from *The CIA World Factbook*, showing the gender ratios in China in 2024, almost a decade after the one-child policy ended, and answer the questions that follow.

- At birth: 1.09 male(s) per female.
- Under 15 years: 1.14 male(s) per female.
- 15–64 years: 1.06 male(s) per female.
- 65 years and over: 0.86 male(s) per female.
- Total population: 1.04 male(s) per female.

    a Describe how China's one-child policy might have influenced the gender ratios in China.   [2]

    b Explain two economic implications for a country that has an uneven gender ratio.   [4]

Effects of population changes

Population growth

The world's population reached 1 billion people around 1804. This had doubled to 2 billion by 1927 and reached 5 billion in 1987. The world's population exceeded 8 billion people in November 2022 and will reach 9 billion by 2037 according to the United Nations *Population Division*. For economists, this phenomenal and unprecedented population growth offers both opportunities and challenges.

The economic consequences of population growth were first presented by the Reverend Thomas R. Malthus (1766–1834). He suggested that uncontrolled population growth would put pressure on the resources of the country, thus negatively impacting living standards. This is because, according to Malthus, population growth occurs at a geometric rate – that is, it grows at a common ratio of 2 (1, 2, 4, 8, 16, 32 and so on) whereas food production only grows at an arithmetic rate (1, 2, 3, 4, 5). If the theory was correct, this means that population growth would eventually exceed food output for the population.

This has not happened, for two main reasons:

» Slower population growth rates than expected, especially in more economically developed countries, due to social changes such as the high opportunity costs of raising children.
» A geometric progression in food production due to advances in food technologies, such as improved farm machinery, irrigation systems, genetics, pesticides and fertilisers.

Economists have found that concerns about the continuing depletion of Earth's finite resources and rising populations can be met by greater efficiencies in food production and the development of alternative renewable energy sources.

Population distribution

The changing size and structure of the population (such as age and gender) can also have effects on an economy. These consequences include impacts on the following:

» **Consumers** – the demand for goods and services changes with variations in population trends. For example, customers have different demands based on their age and gender. Elderly people in a country that has an ageing population might spend proportionately more of their money on healthcare and related products. By contrast, parents with young children might spend more of their income on housing, education, clothing, family vacations and toys. Firms will seek to exploit these changes in demand for different goods and services.

» **Firms** – the demand for and supply of labour will change following long-term changes in population trends. For example, rapid population growth should increase the future supply of labour. By contrast, the combination of low birth rates and net emigration will reduce the future supply of workers in a country. According to the World Health Organization, by 2050 the proportion of the world's population over 60 years will grow from 12 per cent to 22 per cent. By then many more countries are expected to have more than 30 per cent of their population aged at least 60. The ageing population of these nations, especially in high-income countries, will have profound impacts on the future supply of labour.

» **Government** – a growing population can bring benefits if it means the government is able to collect more tax revenues from a larger workforce. However, it can also mean added pressure for the government to provide more public services, welfare benefits and state pensions. As a result, many governments have introduced compulsory pension savings schemes and have raised the official retirement age in their country. For example, France increased the retirement age from 60 to 62 years in 2011, and it was raised again to 64 in 2023. There are further plans to increase the retirement age gradually to 68 years of age.

» **The economy** – continual population growth puts more pressure on an economy's scarce resources. This can lead to inflationary pressures or an increase in the demand for imports if the country cannot produce enough to meet the needs and wants of the population. For example, land in prime locations is scarce, so a larger population in these areas is likely to force land prices to soar. Inflation can cause problems for the economy (see Chapter 28) and cause economic growth to slow.

» **The natural environment** – an increase in the size of a population will also put strain on the environment. Non-renewable resources are depleted in the production process and so the increased level of production will also put strain on the natural environment. For example, pollution and traffic congestion are by-products of over-populated regions of the world.

> ### Activity
>
> Use the internet to investigate the effects of the changing size and structure of the population on a country of your choice. Consider the impact of these changes on households, firms and the government in the country.

Practice questions: structured questions

1 According to World Bank statistics, the population of Nigeria rose from around 45 million in 1960 to over 223 million by 2024, an increase of about 389 per cent. The graph below illustrates the growth in Nigeria's population over a 25-year period, ending in 2023.

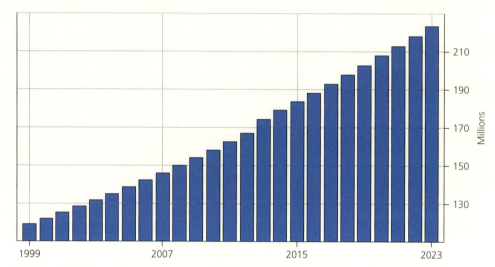

▲ **Figure 31.3** Nigeria's population, 1999–2023

Source: Nigeria population, World Bank, 2024, Trading Economics website

a Explain one possible cause of the increase in the size of Nigeria's population. [2]

b Explain two economic problems which could be associated with the increase in the size of Nigeria's population. [4]

c Discuss two measures the Nigerian government could use to overcome the problems of population growth in its country. [8]

2 The median age of the UK population was 35.4 years in 1985, but it had risen to 40.7 by 2022. It is projected that the median age will reach 42.2 by the year 2035. The percentage of people aged 65 and above also increased in the same time period and is expected to keep on increasing.

Source: National Population projections – Office for National Statistics gov website

a What is meant by an 'ageing population'? [2]

b Explain two causes of the increase in the percentage of people aged 65 and above in the UK. [4]

c Analyse the effects of an ageing population on government expenditure, government revenue and economic growth. [6]

❓ Chapter review questions

1 What are the three key factors that affect the rate of population growth?
2 How is the net migration rate calculated?
3 How do social changes impact on the population size and potential population growth?
4 What are the economic consequences of an ageing population?
5 What is the dependency ratio and why is it important?
6 What is the optimum population and why do governments strive to achieve this?
7 What are the economic consequences of rapid population growth for the economy and the natural environment?

Revision checklist

✔ Population refers to the total number of inhabitants in a particular country. Population growth refers to the rate of change in the size of a country's population.

✔ Changes in three key factors affect the rate of population growth: birth rate, death rate and net migration rate.

✔ Optimum population exists when the output of goods and services per head of the population is maximised. A country is under-populated if it does not have sufficient labour to make the best use of its resources. A country that is over-populated has too large a population given the available resources of the country.

✔ Demographics is the study of population distribution and trends.

✔ Population distribution refers to the composition and structure of a country's population.

✔ Population changes, such as an increase or decrease in population size or changes in the age and gender distribution, have effects on consumers, producers (firms), the government, the economy as a whole and the natural environment.

Differences in economic development between countries

Defining economic development

Economic development is an intangible concept that considers both quantitative and qualitative variables. Essentially, economic development refers to an increase in the standard of living within a country. Factors contributing to this include a reduction in poverty and income inequalities, and an increase in self-esteem, gender equality and political freedom.

Factors accounting for differences in economic development

Various factors account for differences in the economic development of countries. These factors include differences in income (GDP), productivity, population growth, the relative sizes of the primary, secondary and tertiary sectors, saving and investment, education, healthcare and natural resources.

Differences in income

The higher the national income (real GDP per capita) of a country, the greater economic development tends to be. There is a positive relationship between a country's economic growth and its economic development: the wealthier a country is, the higher the standard of living tends to be for the average person in the economy.

Less economically developed countries have a low national income per head of the population. This is partly due to their relatively low nominal GDP and partly due to their relatively high birth rate. Many of these countries suffer from high levels of extreme poverty. According to the United Nations, nearly half of the world's population currently lives in poverty.

Income, as measured by GDP per capita, is the most used single indicator of standards of living within a country (see Table 32.1).

Table 32.1 GDP per capita: selected countries, 2023

Country	GDP ($bn)	Population (million)	GDP per capita ($)
China	31,227	1,416	22,100
Indonesia	1,319	276	4,074
Sweden	676.4	10.59	64,200
Luxembourg	88.5	0.67	132,400

Source: Compiled from *The World Factbook*, Country summaries, 2024, CIA gov website

Practice question: structured question

Explain, with reference to Table 32.1, how national income as measured by GDP per capita can be used to measure economic development. [4]

However, higher real GDP per head does not always lead to a higher standard of living for the majority of people, due to inequalities in the distribution of income. We should therefore also consider the composition of GDP. For example, if a country spends significantly more money on national defence, then national income may grow, but development does not necessarily occur. Finally, economic growth can bring about negative consequences such as pollution, climate change and environmental damage. So, other factors must also be considered when measuring differences in the economic development between countries.

Differences in productivity

Economic development can vary between countries due to differences in productivity levels (see Chapter 32). For example, low-income countries are unable to gain access to the latest technologies and automated production systems. Such technologies help countries to be more efficient and productive, and so are likely to lead to economic development.

Different countries have different quantities and qualities of natural resources, which have a direct impact on productivity levels. Some countries have plentiful and productive resource endowments, such as Angola, with its natural oil and mineral reserves. For many less economically developed countries, the main exports consist of relatively cheap agricultural products, so this hinders their ability to develop economically.

Countries that are able to attract foreign direct investment (FDI) will also enjoy higher levels of productivity. FDI should lead to an increase in the quantity and quality of physical capital in the economy, thereby boosting its productive capacity and competitiveness in the long run. This should help to create jobs, further creating economic development.

Practice question: multiple choice

Which option is **least** likely to increase productivity in an economy? [1]

A advances in technology   **C** improved education and training
B greater specialisation of labour   **D** longer working hours

Differences in population growth

Rapid population growth (see Chapter 31) can limit any increase in real GDP, as it reduces the GDP per capita. In addition, high population growth can hinder economic development as it results in competing pressures on the Earth's scarce resources, such as agricultural land.

Some less economically developed countries, such as South Sudan, Niger, Benin and Equatorial Guinea, have large and/or very fast-growing populations. This tends to reduce their GDP per head, which limits their ability to develop economically. However, less economically developed countries, such as Bangladesh and Burkina Faso, do not have fast-growing populations (see Table 32.2).

Table 32.2 GDP per capita: selected less economically developed countries, 2022

	GDP ($bn)	Population (million)	Population growth rate (%)	GDP per head ($)
Niger	13.97	25.3	3.31	565
Rwanda	13.3	13.7	2.21	949
Bangladesh	460.2	169.4	1.03	1804
Ethiopia	126.8	125.4	2.66	844
Mali	18.8	23.1	3.06	733
Burkina Faso	18.9	22.5	2.34	737

Source: GDP by country, 2022, Worldometer website

Differences in size of primary, secondary and tertiary sectors

As an economy develops, there are likely to be changes in the employment patterns in the three production sectors.

» **Primary sector** output is concerned with the extraction of raw materials and other natural resources. Employment in this sector includes agricultural farming, fishing, mining and oil exploration. In less economically developed countries, primary sector activity tends to dominate in terms of output and employment.
» **Secondary sector** output involves manufacturing – that is, the use of natural resources to produce human-made resources such as machinery, vehicles, buildings and other capital goods. Examples of industries in this sector are car manufacturing, textile production, chemical engineering and textbook publishing. This is the predominant sector in most industrialising and developing countries.
» **Tertiary sector** output refers to the provision of services. Examples of professions in this sector are accountants, teachers, doctors, lawyers, financial advisers and retailers. The tertiary sector tends to be the most important in high-income economies.

As an economy develops, there tends to be a shift away from reliance on primary and secondary sector production towards tertiary output (see Table 32.3). In general, countries with a low level of GDP per capita are at the early stages of economic development, so most people work in the primary sector. As these countries advance, the majority of their GDP is generated from the secondary sector. Finally, in economically developed countries with high income per capita, the tertiary sector accounts for the largest share of employment and of the country's GDP.

Table 32.3 Comparison of employment by sector: selected countries, 2023

Country	Primary (%)	Secondary (%)	Tertiary (%)
Somalia	60.2	7.4	32.4
Kenya	34.5	17.8	47.7
China	7.9	40.5	51.6
India	15.4	23.0	61.6
United Arab Emirates	0.9	49.8	49.3
Luxembourg	0.3	12.8	86.9

Source: GDP – composition, by sector of origin, 2024, *The World Factbook*, CIA gov website

Differences in saving and investment

Savings (see Chapter 16) are required to give banks sufficient funds to lend to firms for investment purposes. However, most people in less economically developed countries are unable to have any savings as they barely have enough money to meet their basic needs. By contrast, the average person in more economically developed countries is able to save some money. Firms are able to borrow these funds, via financial lenders such as banks, to pay for their investments. More savings, and hence investments, can contribute directly to economic development.

In some countries, institutional changes to the banking, legal and political systems are needed in order for economic transactions to be carried out with relative ease. These changes are required to facilitate international trade, attract FDI and boost both consumer and business confidence.

Differences in education

The level of education in a country is an indicator of its economic development. Economists measure the mean (average) years of schooling and adult literacy rates in different countries for this purpose (see Table 32.4). In general, the greater the level of education in a country, the higher its standard of living tends to be.

Table 32.4 Education indicators: selected countries, 2024

	Education indicators	
	Mean years of schooling (years)	Adult literacy rate (% of population aged 15+)
United Kingdom	13.4	99
Norway	13.0	100
New Zealand	12.9	99
Ethiopia	3.2	44
Niger	2.1	30
Mozambique	3.2	49

Source: World Economics countries data, World Economics website

Case study: Finland's education system

Finland is often quoted as having the 'best' education system in the world, yet the country uses a rather unconventional approach to education. Finnish children do not have to start school until the age of 7. Children rarely take exams (they do not take a standardised test until the age of 16) and do not get regular homework until their teenage years. Science lessons are capped at 16 students to encourage greater productivity during class time. Teachers spend just 4 hours a day in the classroom, and 2 hours per week on their professional learning and development.

Of course, a relatively small population of 5.5 million people helps. For example, there are fewer students in Finland than in New York City, although they have the same approximate number of teachers.

Sources: 'How does Finland's top-ranking education system work?' by K Dickinson, 15 February 2019, World Economic Forum and 'Why are Finland's schools successful?' by L Hancock, September 2011, Innovation

> **Activity**
>
> Discuss how economists might measure which education system in the world is the 'best'.

Differences in healthcare

Healthcare is a key indicator of economic development. The better the healthcare in a country, the greater social and economic well-being tends to be. The quality of a country's healthcare can be measured in several ways, including the following:

» **Life expectancy at birth** – this measures the number of years an average person in the country is expected to live.
» **Annual expenditure on healthcare** – measured as a percentage of a country's GDP.
» **Child mortality rates** – that is, the number of deaths of children aged 5 and below, per thousand of the population (see Table 32.5).

Table 32.5 Healthcare indicators: selected countries, 2024

Economy	Healthcare indicators	
	Life expectancy at birth (years), both genders	Infant mortality rate (per 1000 live births)
Hong Kong	85.63	2.5
Japan	84.85	2
Switzerland	84.09	4
Singapore	83.86	2
Lesotho	57.8	56
Central African Republic	57.67	74
South Sudan	57.74	64
Chad	55.24	64
Nigeria	54.64	69
Macau	85.3	4.3

Sources: Life expectancy of the world population, data based on United Nations Population division estimates, 2024, Worldometer website; Mortality rate, infant (per 1,000 live births), UN Interagency Group for child mortality estimation, 2022, World Bank website

An increase in the quantity and quality of human capital through improved education and healthcare will boost the productivity of the labour force.

Practice question: multiple choice

Which of these is **not** a health indicator as a measure of economic development? [1]

A child mortality rates
B healthcare expenditure as a percentage of GDP
C life expectancy at birth
D population growth rate

Differences in natural resources

Natural resources (sometimes referred to as environmental resources) are natural assets that are used as factors of production. They are essential for supporting economic activities, sustaining life and maintaining ecosystems. Natural resources include:

» **Renewable resources** – these can be replenished naturally over time. Examples are sunlight, wind, water and biomass (e.g. wood, forest residues, plant material or animal manure that are used to generate energy).

» **Non-renewable resources** – these are finite and can be depleted. Examples are minerals, fossil fuels (oil, natural gas and coal) and metal ores.

▲ This is a copper mine – copper is an example of a non-renewable resource

Natural resources, such as minerals, forests and water, have a significant impact on the economic development of a country. Countries that are rich in environmental resources often experience economic growth as a result of exploiting and exporting these resources. However, overdependence on scarce resources can also lead to unequal development and environmental degradation, thus hindering sustainable growth and development. Conversely, countries with scarce resources might struggle to achieve growth. They might have to rely on alternative economic strategies such as technology and services in the tertiary sector. Thus, the availability and effective management of natural resources are both a cause and consequence of varying economic development levels between countries.

> **Activity**
>
> In pairs, research the roles of the World Bank and the International Monetary Fund (IMF) in promoting economic development. How does the World Bank differ from the IMF? What are the terms and conditions of the loans that they make to countries? Be prepared to present your findings to the class.

? Chapter review questions

1 What is meant by economic development?
2 How do differences in the national income of different countries affect their economic development?
3 What are the limitations of using only national income as an indicator of economic development?
4 What is productivity and how might this affect the level of economic development?
5 How does population growth impact on a country's economic development?
6 How do savings and investment contribute to economic development?
7 How do a country's mean years of schooling and adult literacy rate indicate its level of economic development?
8 What does a country's quality of healthcare indicate about its economic well-being?
9 What are natural resources? How can these resources cause differences in economic development between countries?

Revision checklist

✔ Economic development is an intangible concept that considers both quantitative and qualitative variables that indicate an increase in the standard of living within a country.

✔ The main factors that account for differences in the economic development of countries are differences in income (GDP), productivity, population growth, the relative size of the primary, secondary and tertiary sectors, saving and investment, education, healthcare and natural resources.

✔ Income is the most used single indicator of standard of living within a country. The wealthier a country is, the higher its standard of living tends to be.

✔ Differences in the productivity of factors of production can be explained by a country's ability to gain access to the latest technologies, differences in the quality and quantity of production resources, and the country's ability to attract FDI.

✔ Differences in population size and growth have a direct impact on real GDP per head. Economic development tends to be limited in countries with large and growing populations.

✔ As an economy develops, there tends to be a shift away from an overreliance on primary production, towards secondary sector production and then tertiary sector output.

✔ Savings are needed to enable banks to lend these funds to firms to finance their investment expenditure.

✔ In general, the greater the level of education in a country, the higher its standard of living tends to be.

✔ The better the healthcare in a country, the greater its social and economic well-being (and hence economic development) tends to be.

✔ Countries that are rich in environmental resources often experience economic growth as a result of exploiting and exporting these resources. Conversely, countries with scarce resources might struggle to achieve growth. They might have to rely on alternative economic strategies, like technology and services in the tertiary sector.

SECTION 6

International trade and globalisation

Chapters

33

Specialisation and free trade

This chapter will cover:

★ a definition of specialisation by country
★ the basis for specialisation of a country
★ the advantages and disadvantages of specialisation of a country
★ a definition of free trade
★ the advantages and disadvantages of free trade.

Defining specialisation by country

Specialisation occurs when individuals, firms, regions or countries concentrate on the production of a particular good or service. For example:

» **Individuals** – people might specialise, for example, as accountants, bankers, construction workers, hair stylists, dentists or engineers. Specialisation allows workers to become more skilled and efficient at their jobs, thus increasing the quantity and quality of the goods or services being provided.

▲ Hair stylists are specialists in their field

Activity

Discuss why primary school teachers are less specialised than secondary school teachers, who are less specialised than university lecturers.

» **Firms** – McDonald's, Burger King, KFC and Pizza Hut specialise in the output of fast food, whereas DHL, FedEx and TNT specialise in the provision of courier services. Further examples appear in Table 33.1.

Table 33.1 The world's three largest producers in selected industries, 2024

Industry	Rank		
	1st	**2nd**	**3rd**
Accountancy	Deloitte	PwC	Ernst & Young
Airline (freight)	FedEx Express	UPS Airlines	DHL Aviation
Airline (passenger)	American Airlines	United Airlines	Delta Air Lines
Car manufacture	Volkswagen	Toyota	General Motors
e-commerce	Amazon	Alibaba	eBay
Televisions	Samsung	LG	TCL
Mobile network operation	China Mobile	Reliance Jio Infocomm	China Telecom
Mobile phones	Samsung	Apple	Xiaomi
Personal computers	Lenovo	HP	Dell
Restaurant chain (sales)	McDonald's	Burger King	KFC
Social network sites	Facebook	YouTube	Instagram

Source: *The Economist Pocket World in Figures*

▲ Hollywood, Los Angeles, USA, is famous for its motion pictures industry

» **Regions** – Silicon Valley in northern California, USA, specialises in the provision of high-tech information communication technologies; London, Manhattan (New York City), Tokyo and Shanghai are financial districts; Paris and Milan are major cities for fashion and design.

» **Countries** – international specialisation (or **specialisation by country**) occurs when countries concentrate on the production of certain goods or services due to cost advantages (cheaper production methods) and their abundance of superior resources. Bangladesh and India are major producers and exporters of textiles; Scotland is famous for its whisky; Thailand and Vietnam specialise in the production of rice; and Caribbean countries such as Jamaica and Tobago specialise in tourism. Other examples are outlined in Table 33.2.

Table 33.2 The world's three largest producers of selected products, 2024

Product	Rank		
	1st	**2nd**	**3rd**
Aluminium	China	India	Russia
Coal	China	India	USA
Coffee	Brazil	Vietnam	Colombia
Copper	Chile	Peru	China
Cotton	China	India	Brazil
Fruit	China	India	Brazil
Meat	China	USA	Brazil
Oil	USA	Russia	Saudi Arabia
Rubber	Thailand	Indonesia	Vietnam
Sugar	Brazil	India	China
Tea	China	India	Sri Lanka
Vegetables	China	India	USA

Source: *The Economist Pocket World in Figures*

The basis for specialisation by country

The basis for specialisation of a country is the optimal (or best) allocation of the economy's scarce resources. Therefore, economists argue that countries should specialise in low-cost production. For example, while Sweden can produce its own tropical fruits, it is more economical for the country to import these and to specialise in timber (Sweden is a major world exporter of forest products).

Advantages and disadvantages of specialisation by country

Advantages of specialisation

The benefits of specialisation at a national level include the following:

>> **Efficiency gains** – specialisation makes better use of scarce resources. As a result, productivity increases, thereby increasing the country's GDP. Taiwan and South Korea, for example, have been able to raise their standards of living by specialising in the production of manufactured consumer electronic devices. Taiwan's Foxconn is the world's largest manufacturer of smartphones and tablet computers for companies such as Samsung and Apple.

>> **Labour productivity** – workers become more skilled in the jobs they do because they are able to concentrate on what they do best. Therefore, specialisation improves labour productivity (see Chapter 19) and enables better-quality products to be produced. Thus, specialisation can benefit firms, regions and the country as a whole.

>> **Increased productive capacity** – specialisation can help to shift the production possibility curve (PPC) of a country outwards due to its increased productive capacity, as shown in Figure 33.1. Thus, specialisation leads to increased national output.

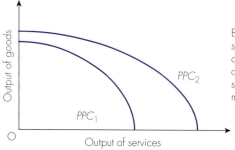

By specialising, the country's PPC will shift outwards. In this case, as the country chooses to specialise in the output of services, there is a larger shift along the x-axis as the economy moves from PPC_1 to PPC_2.

▲ **Figure 33.1** Specialisation and the PPC

>> **Economies of scale** – specialisation increases GDP and global trade. Therefore, firms are able to enjoy cost-saving benefits from large-scale operations, known as economies of scale (see Chapter 18). This can help to keep prices down and therefore control inflation (see Chapter 28).

>> **Improved competitiveness** – specialisation helps to enhance international trade and exchange. Competitive prices also improve the international competitiveness of a country, thereby boosting its economic growth. In this way, specialisation and trade are vital for improving a country's standard of living (see Chapter 29).

> ### Activity
>
> Investigate the economic reasons behind China's rising dominance in one of the following industries (or another one of your choice): coal mining, oil, steel, automobiles, commercial banking, insurance or telecommunications. Be prepared to share your findings with the rest of the class.

Disadvantages of specialisation

Despite the potential benefits of national specialisation, there are several drawbacks.

Definition
Overspecialisation occurs when an individual, firm, region or country concentrates too much on producing a very limited number of goods and services. This exposes the economic agent to a far higher degree of risk.

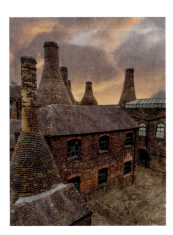

▲ Staffordshire, in the UK, used to have a thriving pottery industry (another example of overspecialisation) – now the area is full of derelict factories

>> **Overspecialisation** – this can cause regional and structural unemployment (see Chapter 27). For example, when specialised steel production in Sheffield, in the UK, decreased in the 1980s, there was high regional unemployment, and other key consequences for local people, including stress, depression and poverty.

Countries that overspecialise also suffer the most during an economic downturn as they do not have a variety of goods and services that they can rely on to survive. For example, Liberia is highly dependent on its agricultural output which accounted for around 70.3 per cent of its GDP in 2024. Adverse weather conditions could wipe out much of its agricultural production, thus severely harming the economy.

>> **Lack of variety for consumers** – specialisation often leads to standardised, mass-produced goods. An example is Foxconn, which manufactures the iPhone and iPad for Apple. These devices lack variety and only come in a very limited number of colours. Domestic customers may look at alternative imported products from foreign suppliers, thereby reducing the competitiveness of domestic firms that overspecialise.

>> **High labour turnover** – this occurs if lots of workers choose to leave their jobs in search of more challenging and less boring ones. Where a country has a labour turnover rate of 12.5 per cent, this means that one worker in every eight changes jobs each year. The higher the turnover rate, the more expensive it is for the economy as firms have to continually hire and train workers. Industries that suffer from high labour turnover tend to pay low wages to low-skilled workers. Examples include those working in call centres, retail, catering (including fast-food restaurants), supermarkets and hotels.

>> **Low labour mobility** – low-skilled and poorly paid workers tend to receive little training, so they may not develop the necessary skills to find alternative jobs. Again, this can lead to structural unemployment in the economy. Highly skilled and specialised workers, such as pilots, dentists, software developers,

financial advisers and attorneys can also find it extremely difficult to change to alternative professions and careers. A lack of labour market flexibility in an economy can reduce its overall efficiency and international competitiveness.

» **Higher labour costs** – firms that employ workers with highly specialised skills tend to face very high salary demands. For example, Forbes magazine estimates that in 2022 the earnings of the world's five highest-paid supermodels exceeded $166 million, with Kendall Jenner earning about $40 million. Cristiano Ronaldo, football's highest-paid player, was estimated to be earning around $260 million in 2024. However, high labour costs can have a negative impact on the profits of firms and potentially reduce their competitiveness.

Sources: Forbes list of the highest-paid models, Wikipedia website; 'Highest-paid football players in the world 2024: Who earns the most?' by Alex Harris, James Walters, 4 June 2024, Radio Times

International trade and free trade

International trade refers to the exchange of goods and services beyond national borders. It entails the sale of exports (goods and services sold to overseas buyers) and imports (foreign goods and services bought by domestic households, firms and government).

Free trade means that international trade can take place without any form of protection (barriers to international trade), such as quantitative limits or taxes being imposed on exports.

The advantages of free trade

The merits of international trade (that is, the reasons why countries trade with each other) apply to consumers, producers and the economy as a whole. These advantages include the following:

» **Access to resources** – international trade enables producers and consumers to gain access to goods and services that they cannot produce themselves. For example, the Maldives can purchase laptop computers, motor vehicles and Hollywood movies from the USA.

» **Lower prices** – free trade reduces the costs of trading. For example, it is cheaper for Germans to purchase foreign-produced smartphones made in China and Taiwan because of the high labour costs in Germany. Unfavourable weather conditions in Iceland mean it is better off importing tropical fruits from Jamaica. By contrast, trade protection (see Chapter 34) increases the costs of trading. For example, the imposition of trade barriers would mean that both domestic firms and consumers have to pay more for imported goods and services.

» **Economies of scale** – as firms are operating on a larger scale in global markets, international trade enables them to benefit from economies of scale (see Chapter 18). These cost savings can be passed on to consumers in the form of lower prices and/or kept by the producers in the form of higher profits.

» **Greater choice** – free trade enables consumers and firms to access a larger variety of goods and services from different producers around the world. For example, while Germans can choose from domestic motor vehicles such as Audi, BMW and Mercedes-Benz, they are also able to choose from foreign suppliers such as Lexus (Japan), Jaguar (India) and Cadillac (USA).

» **Increased market size** – international trade enables firms to earn higher revenues and profits. For example, US firms can sell products to a domestic market of 334 million people, whereas they can reach a market of more than 2.83 billion potential customers by selling their products to China and India.

» **Efficiency gains** – free trade forces domestic producers to focus on improving the quality of their output due to foreign competition. For example, competition from Japanese car makers and South Korean electronics firms has forced US producers such as General Motors and Apple to create better-quality products. By contrast, protectionist measures give domestic firms a false sense of security and limit their exposure to fair and genuine competition. This can make domestic firms inefficient.

» **Improved international relations** – the absence of trade barriers encourages international trade and cooperation between countries. By contrast, if a country imposes trade barriers (see Chapter 34), other nations are likely to retaliate by doing the same.

Activities

1 Look at some of the products you have at home, such as a television, smartphone, car and clothes. How many of these products have been imported? Why might this be?
2 Use the internet to investigate the types of goods and services that are exported and imported from one high-income country and one low-income country of your choice. Find out the main trading partners of these countries. As a starting point, you may want to use a search engine to find *The Economist*'s country briefs and/or the CIA's *The World Factbook*.

The disadvantages of free trade

Free trade, while offering numerous benefits, also comes with several disadvantages:

» **Job losses in certain industries** – domestic industries that cannot compete with international producers may suffer. There may be job losses and economic disruption in those sectors unless the domestic government intervenes to protect these industries (see Chapter 34).

» **Income inequality** – free trade can worsen income inequality. Highly skilled and high-income workers benefit from free trade more than unskilled workers. This can widen the gap between rich and poor.

» **Exploitation of labour** – free trade enables producers to move production to countries with lower labour standards and wage costs. This can lead to poor working conditions and the exploitation of workers.

» **Environmental degradation** – increased trade and exchange (including production and transportation associated with free trade) can lead to environmental harm. This could include the depletion of natural resources and higher carbon emissions.

▲ People queuing outside a job centre in Spain

Practice questions: structured questions

1 Bangladesh is one of the world's largest producers of rice and tropical fruit. In Brunei Darussalam, crude oil and natural gas account for a large percentage of the country's gross domestic product (GDP). This makes Brunei Darussalam one of the leading producers of oil in Southeast Asia.

   a Describe one problem for Brunei Darussalam in relying on oil exports.   [2]

   b Explain two reasons why countries such as Bangladesh and Brunei Darussalam trade with each other.   [4]

   c Analyse how Bangladesh's export of rice and tropical fruit helps its farmers to achieve economies of scale.   [6]

2 **a** Define 'specialisation'.   [2]

   b Explain why, during a recession, highly specialised firms are less likely to survive than diversified firms.   [4]

3 **a** Explain how the concept of specialisation can explain why nations trade with each other.   [4]

   b 'Specialisation in international trade always benefits nations.' Analyse this statement.   [6]

? Chapter review questions

1 What is meant by specialisation by country?
2 What are two examples of specialisation by country?
3 What are the advantages of specialisation by country?
4 What are the disadvantages of specialisation by country?
5 What is free trade?
6 What are the advantages of free trade?
7 What are the disadvantages of free trade?

Revision checklist

✔ Specialisation occurs when individuals, firms, regions or countries concentrate on the production of a particular good or service.
✔ International specialisation (or specialisation by country) occurs when countries concentrate on the production of certain goods or services due to cost advantages and superior resource allocation.
✔ Benefits of specialisation by country include efficiency gains, higher labour productivity, increased productive capacity, economies of scale and improved competitiveness.
✔ Disadvantages of specialisation by country include overspecialisation, lack of variety for consumers, high labour turnover, low labour mobility and higher labour costs.
✔ International trade is the exchange of goods and services beyond national borders.
✔ Free trade means that international trade takes place without protectionist measures (barriers to international trade).
✔ Advantages of free trade include access to resources (choice), lower prices, efficiency gains and improved international relations.
✔ Disadvantages of free trade include job losses in certain industries, widening income inequality, potential exploitation of labour and environmental degradation.

Globalisation and trade restrictions

Definition
Globalisation is the process by which the world's economies become increasingly interdependent and interconnected.

Defining globalisation

Globalisation is the process by which the world's economies become increasingly interdependent and interconnected due to greater international trade and cultural exchanges. Globalisation has increased the exchange of goods and services throughout the world. Globalised markets include fast food, financial markets, motor vehicles, consumer electronics, sports (such as football) and entertainment (such as Hollywood movies).

Globalisation has existed for a very long time but it has intensified in the twenty-first century. The increased use of social media and the continued expansion of multinational companies have contributed to the globalisation process.

Globalisation has resulted in positive and negative impacts:

» There is increased international trade, creating wealth and jobs throughout the world.
» There is freer movement of labour, capital, goods and services.
» By operating on a global scale, firms can enjoy greater economies of scale (lower costs per unit when operating on a larger scale).
» There is greater choice of goods and services for consumers around the world.
» There is greater cultural understanding and appreciation.
» However, globalisation has led to greater dependence on the global economy.
» It has also widened income and wealth gaps between the world's poorest countries and the world's richest nations (see Chapter 32).

Causes of changes in globalisation

The four main causes or drivers of changes in globalisation are outlined below:

» **Changes in trade restrictions** – trade restrictions can significantly impact globalisation by either facilitating or hindering the flow of goods, services, capital and labour across national borders. For example, when countries reduce trade restrictions (covered in the latter part of this chapter) such as tariffs and quotas, it becomes cheaper and easier for firms to export and import goods. This leads to an increase in global trade and economic interdependence. Lower trade barriers also make countries more attractive to foreign investors and **multinational companies** (MNCs). For example, the establishment and enlargement of the European Union (EU) has facilitated the free movement of goods, services, capital and labour among member states. This has reduced trade restrictions and improved economic growth, competitiveness and consumer choice across the EU.

» **Changes in transport costs** – transport costs can significantly influence the pace and extent of globalisation by affecting the efficiency, reach and cost of moving goods, services and people across national borders. Lower transport costs reduce the overall cost of trading goods internationally, making it cheaper for firms to export and import products. This facilitates greater economic integration and interdependence among countries. For example, the use of container shipping in the mid-twentieth century revolutionised global trade and exchange. Standardised containers made it easier and cheaper to load, unload and transport goods across long distances. This significantly lowered shipping costs and fostered globalisation.

» **Changes in communication costs** – lower communication costs facilitate better coordination and management of global business operations, enabling firms to operate seamlessly across international borders. For example, the rise of the internet and video telephony software (such as Zoom or Teams) has drastically reduced the cost and time required to communicate. Multinational companies can now manage their operations across different countries and time zones in real time, enhancing efficiency. Globalisation and international trade have also been enhanced by the growth of e-commerce. Digital platforms such as Amazon, eBay and Alibaba have leveraged low communication costs to create vast online marketplaces where buyers and sellers from around the world can interact and trade more efficiently.

» **Movement of multinational companies** (MNCs) – MNCs expand their operations by setting up operations in overseas markets. This increases global trade and investment flows, as goods, services, capital and technology move across international borders. For example, Coca-Cola operates in over 200 countries, producing and distributing its products globally. Its extensive production and distribution networks boost trade between these countries and facilitate the flow of capital and technology, further contributing to economic integration. Another example is Toyota, the world's largest car maker. It relies on a global supply chain: motor vehicle parts and components are sourced from different countries and the cars are assembled in various regions of the world. This integration helps to achieve economies of scale (see Chapter 18) and optimises efficiency. It also connects economies through improved trade relationships.

Effects of changes in globalisation

The impacts of changes in globalisation are outlined below:

» **International trade** – changes in globalisation have a significant impact on international trade by altering the volume and patterns of international trade as well as international relationships. Increased globalisation typically boosts international trade by reducing trade restrictions and enhancing information and communication technology (ICT). For example, China's integration into the World Trade Organization (WTO) in 2001 reduced trade barriers and spurred huge growth in international trade across the world, with China being a central hub in global manufacturing. Conversely, a trade war, marked by increased trade restrictions, leads to a decline in international trade.

» **Competition** – changes in globalisation have an impact on competition by opening international markets, fostering innovation and increasing competitive pressures. The growth in globalisation allows firms to enter new markets, increasing international competition. For example, the rise of e-commerce giants such as Amazon and Alibaba has disrupted traditional retail across the world. This has forced local firms to innovate and adapt to survive and remain competitive. Globalisation also encourages multinational companies to leverage economies of scale and advanced technologies, further intensifying international competition. For example, the expansion of Chinese manufacturers, such as Huawei in the telecommunications sector, has challenged established market leaders like Apple and Samsung. This has pushed them to further improve products and reduce costs.

» **The environment** – changes in globalisation have a significant impact on the environment by influencing resource consumption, pollution levels and ecological degradation. Increased globalisation leads to higher production and transportation activities, raising greenhouse gas emissions and contributing to climate change. Conversely, globalisation can also promote environmental awareness and the adoption of sustainable business practices. International agreements such as the Paris Agreement (see Chapter 22), which aims to collectively reduce carbon emissions and combat climate change, are facilitated by global cooperation. Additionally, multinational companies are increasingly adopting greener practices (such as the use of renewable energy) due to global consumer awareness of the need for environmental sustainability.

» **Migration** – changes in globalisation significantly impact labour migration by altering economic opportunities and labour market dynamics. Increased globalisation tends to promote labour migration as workers move to countries with better job opportunities and higher wages. For example, the EU's open borders for member states have facilitated the free movement of labour in pursuit of better employment opportunities. Conversely, reduced globalisation or restrictive immigration policies can hinder labour migration. For example, the Brexit decision (the UK's decision to

▲ Globalisation can have harmful impacts on the natural environment

leave the EU on 31 January 2020) led to tighter immigration controls in the UK, reducing the influx of EU workers and causing labour shortages in sectors such as agriculture and healthcare.

»» **Income distribution** – changes in globalisation impact income distribution by affecting job markets, wages and economic inequalities. Increased globalisation can create jobs and stimulate economic growth. However, this often disproportionately benefits skilled workers and larger firms, thereby widening income distribution. For example, in the USA, globalisation has boosted high-tech sectors and increased incomes for high-skilled workers. On the other hand, many manufacturing jobs have moved abroad due to lower labour costs. This has led to wage stagnation and job losses for less-skilled workers in the domestic economy. Conversely, reduced globalisation or protectionist measures (trade restrictions) can protect domestic jobs but may also limit economic opportunities and efficiency. For example, tariffs imposed by the USA on imports from China, intended to protect US jobs and industries, resulted in higher consumer prices and disrupted supply chains. This impacted lower-income households more severely.

»» **Economic development** – changes in globalisation significantly impact economic development by altering access to international markets, technology and investment. Increased globalisation boosts economic development by facilitating international trade, attracting foreign direct investment (FDI) and spreading improved technologies. Conversely, reduced globalisation or trade restriction policies can hinder economic development by limiting market access and investment flows. Essentially, globalisation can drive economic development by creating more opportunities for international trade, investment and technology transfer. Reduced globalisation tends to constrain economic growth and development.

Role of multinational companies

A **multinational company** (MNC) is an organisation that operates in two or more countries. Examples of some of the largest MNCs in the world are Apple, Saudi Aramco, Samsung and Toyota.

Various factors have made it easier for MNCs to operate on a global scale. These include lower transportation costs, advances in technology such as e-commerce, more efficient communication systems and trade liberation.

The costs and benefits of MNCs

MNCs also create advantages and disadvantages for their host and home countries.

Advantages

The following are some advantages of multinational companies for the host country and/or the home country:

»» Through job creation, MNCs are able to help improve standards of living (see Chapter 29) in the countries in which they operate. For example, Walmart, the world's largest private sector retailer, employs many people worldwide.
»» MNCs operate on a very large scale and are therefore able to exploit economies of scale (see Chapter 18). This means that MNCs can pass on cost savings to their customers in the form of lower prices.

▲ A Levi's store at AlphaOne shopping mall in Amritsar, India

»» By operating in overseas markets, MNCs are able to generate more profit by selling to a larger customer base. This benefits their home country too, as profits are repatriated.

»» An MNC is often able to avoid trade restrictions by producing its products in a foreign country. For example, Japan's Nissan is able to avoid import taxes in the European Union as it has manufacturing plants in Belgium and Spain. This contributes to job creation in the host country.

»» MNCs can access new markets by locating overseas. This may reduce transportation costs as they no longer have to export products to these markets. For example, German car manufacturers Audi, BMW and Mercedes-Benz all have factories in China – the world's largest market for private cars. This also brings benefits for the host country in terms of employment.

»» MNCs might choose to move or expand their operations in foreign countries to benefit from lower rates of corporation tax. This benefits both the MNC and the countries into which it chooses to expand. For example, corporation tax is far lower in the United Arab Emirates, Singapore and Bahrain than in Japan, Australia and Brazil.

Disadvantages

The following are some disadvantages of multinational companies for the host country and/or the home country:

»» MNCs have often been criticised for their unethical and cost-cutting practices, such as poor working conditions and low wages for workers in low-income countries.

»» Although MNCs might create jobs in their host countries, they can also force local firms that are less competitive to close down. Their huge market power and ability to exploit economies of scale (see Chapter 18) mean that local firms might struggle to compete. Moving and expanding overseas can also have a detrimental impact on domestic employment.

»» Many MNCs earn far higher sales revenue than the gross domestic product (GDP) of the host country. This means they are often in a powerful position to exploit foreign governments over decisions such as the location of the business and access to finance (government subsidies, grants, loans and tax concessions).

»» The overreliance on MNCs in low-income countries means that there are major consequences should an MNC choose to relocate its operations to another country. For example, in 2020 British bank Standard Chartered pulled out of Sierra Leone, Zimbabwe, Gambia, Angola and Cameroon. This resulted in huge job losses in these African economies.

> ### Activity
>
> Research the global operations of an MNC that operates in your country and assess the advantages and disadvantages to the firm and the host country. Make a judgement about whether the benefits to the host country outweigh the costs.

Practice question: structured question

Multinational companies (MNCs) are attracted to the United Arab Emirates (UAE) because of its low taxes, political stability and high GDP per capita. Examples of MNCs in the UAE are Microsoft, Marriott Group, DHL and Huawei Technologies, along with a number of international engineering, law and accountancy firms. An influx of MNCs to the area brings workers from many countries and this creates a demand for international goods, services and schools. There are many shopping malls filled with international brands. Dubai, one of the seven Emirates that make up the UAE, has gained a reputation as a destination for shopping. This has attracted many tourists to Dubai for shopping and leisure trips.

a Explain the characteristics of a multinational company (MNC). [4]
b Analyse the advantages and disadvantages for the UAE of MNCs locating their operations there. [6]

Types of trade restrictions

Despite the benefits of free international trade, there are also strategic and economic reasons for trade restrictions. **Trade restrictions** (or methods of **protection**) refer to the use of trade barriers to restrain foreign trade, thereby limiting overseas competition.

Methods of protection

The most common type of trade restriction is **tariffs**. The other types of trade restrictions, collectively known as **non-tariff barriers**, include import quotas, subsidies and embargoes. These are explained below.

Definitions
Trade restriction, or **protection**, refers to the use of trade barriers to restrict international trade, thereby limiting overseas competition.
A **tariff** is a tax on imports, which increases production costs for foreign firms.
An **import quota** is a quantitative limit on the sale of a foreign good.

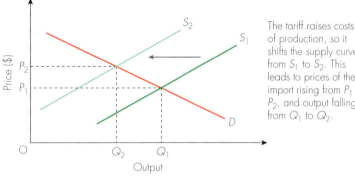

The tariff raises costs of production, so it shifts the supply curve from S_1 to S_2. This leads to prices of the import rising from P_1 to P_2, and output falling from Q_1 to Q_2.

▲ **Figure 34.1** The impact of tariffs

»» **Tariffs** – a tariff (or customs duty) is a tax on imports. For example, the USA places a 25 per cent tariff on all tyres imported from China. Tariffs increase the costs of production for importers. This raises the price of foreign goods in the domestic market and lowers the quantity of products imported (see Figure 34.1).

»» **Import quotas** – an import quota sets a quantitative limit on the sale of a foreign good in a country. For example, the Indonesian government imposes import quotas on fruits and vegetables from Thailand. The quota limits the quantity imported and thus raises the market price of foreign goods (see Figure 34.2).

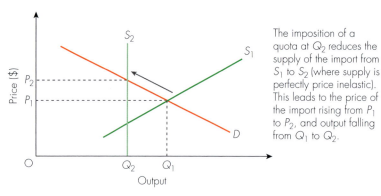

The imposition of a quota at Q_2 reduces the supply of the import from S_1 to S_2 (where supply is perfectly price inelastic). This leads to the price of the import rising from P_1 to P_2, and output falling from Q_1 to Q_2.

▲ **Figure 34.2** The impact of import quotas

» **Subsidies** – governments can provide subsidies (lump-sum payments or low-interest loans to domestic producers) to help domestic firms to compete against foreign imports. Subsidies lower the costs of production for home firms. This helps to protect local jobs. For example, the European Union subsidises its farmers to encourage agricultural output (see Figure 34.3).

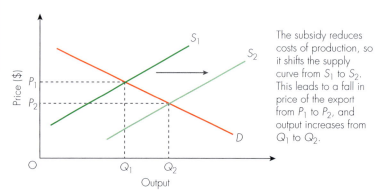

The subsidy reduces costs of production, so it shifts the supply curve from S_1 to S_2. This leads to a fall in price of the export from P_1 to P_2, and output increases from Q_1 to Q_2.

▲ **Figure 34.3** The impact of subsidies

» **Embargos** – an embargo is a ban on trade with a certain country, often due to a trade dispute or political conflict. An embargo rarely benefits local consumers, who suffer from a lack of choice and higher prices (due to the lack of supply). For example, Malaysia has imposed trade embargoes on the Philippines while the USA has trade embargoes with Cuba.

» **Rules and regulations** – countries often use bureaucratic rules and regulations as a form of protection. Examples are strict rules regarding food safety, environmental standards and product quality. These rules and regulations consume a lot of time and increase the costs for overseas firms, while also helping to protect domestic consumers.

Practice questions: structured questions

1 British mutton is sold throughout the world. Using an appropriate demand and supply diagram, explain the consequences on the price and quantity demanded of British mutton if an import tariff is imposed on British mutton. [4]

2 Different stakeholders are affected by the imposition of an import tariff.
Discuss the impacts of an import tariff on producers and consumers of British mutton. [8]

Advantages of restricting free trade

Protectionist measures may be introduced because they offer the following advantages:

▲ *The Battle at Lake Changjin* (2021) is China's highest-grossing home-grown film; trade protection enables the Chinese movie industry to develop

» Protectionist measures help to safeguard **infant industries** (or sunrise industries). These are new or unestablished businesses that need protecting from larger and more established foreign competitors. The Chinese government, for example, only allows 15 Hollywood movies to enter the country's cinemas each year, thus allowing the Chinese movie industry to develop.

» Trade protectionist measures, such as tariffs and quotas, help safeguard **declining industries** (or sunset industries) by limiting foreign competition. This provides these industries with temporary relief, allowing them to restructure, innovate and potentially regain competitiveness while preserving domestic jobs and economic stability within the affected sectors. For example, the US imposition of tariffs on imported steel and aluminium in 2018 aimed to protect the domestic steel and aluminium industries, which were struggling due to cheaper imports.

» Protection from free international trade can also help to safeguard **domestic jobs** (beyond sunrise and sunset industries). For example, according to the Economic Policy Institute, the USA lost more than 5 million manufacturing jobs between 1998 and 2020 due to its growing trade deficit (see Chapter 36) in manufactured goods with China, Japan, Mexico, the European Union and other countries. In extreme cases, fierce competition from foreign rivals can even force domestic firms out of business.

» In terms of strategic arguments, the government might use trade restrictions to safeguard the country from being too dependent on goods and services from other countries. For instance, if a war were to break out then protectionist measures give the country the ability and capacity to produce the goods and services that it needs, rather than having to rely on foreign countries. A country such as Canada or the UK might want to have more oil production in order to be less reliant on imports from oil-rich nations that are able to distort world oil prices and oil supplies.

» Trade restrictions prevent foreign countries from **dumping** their goods in the domestic economy. Dumping occurs when foreign firms sell their products in large quantities at prices deliberately below those charged by domestic firms, often even below the cost of production. This clearly gives the foreign firms an unfair price advantage, so trade restriction measures may be needed. For example, the USA accused Vietnam of dumping certain shrimps in 2012. Bangladesh and India have accused each other of dumping a range of goods, including fishing nets and textile products.

Sources: Anti-dumping measures on certain shrimp from Viet Nam, Dispute settlement DS429, 18 July 2016, World Trade Organization website; 'Anti-dumping threats to Bangladesh exports' by Khandoker Kawset, 27 April 2018, The Financial Express website

» Protection might also be required to overcome a current account **deficit on the balance of payments** (see Chapter 36). If a country spends more on imports than the revenue it earns from its exports, the country will experience problems, as it spends more than it earns. Protectionist measures to restrict imports would help to deal with this imbalance.

» Protection can be an important source of **government revenue**. For example, India imposes tariffs of $396 per 10 grams on the import of gold, thus helping to raise tax revenues for the government. (Source: Indian Trade Portal, 2024)

Figure 34.4 shows the increasing import duties collected by the British government from 2000 to 2024.

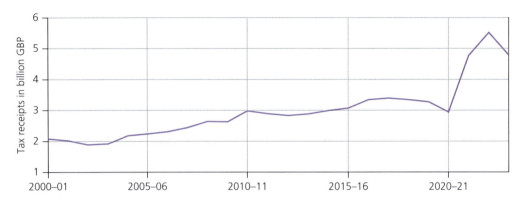

▲ **Figure 34.4** Customs duty tax receipts in the United Kingdom from 2000–01 to 2023–24 (in billion GBP)

» A country can restrict the import of **demerit goods** through trade protection to reduce the consumption of harmful products (see Chapter 13). For example, many countries impose high tariffs on tobacco and alcohol to discourage their production and consumption and to protect public health. India's significant import duties on foreign cigarettes since 2013 aim to reduce smoking rates and safeguard public health.

» Methods of trade restriction can be used to promote **environmental sustainability** by imposing tariffs or other controls on environmentally harmful goods. For example, the European Union's carbon border adjustment mechanism targets carbon-intensive imports to encourage greener production practices. Similarly, Brazil has imposed restrictions on logging to protect the Amazon rainforest, supporting global environmental sustainability efforts.

Practice question: structured question

China has accounted for a large percentage of the world's output of car tyres. Since 2009, it has been the world's largest producer, consumer and exporter of tyres. The China Association of Automobile Manufacturers reported that over 30.1 million new cars were sold in China in 2023, with an annual sales growth of 12 per cent expected over the following years.

Source: China 2023 vehicle sales rise 12%, 11 January 2024, Reuters website

According to the USA's Bureau of Labor Statistics, in June 2024 the average US employer had to pay about $44 per hour (salary and benefits) to hire a production-line worker whereas an employer in China could do the same for significantly less. The USA simply cannot compete on labour costs, thus prompting the need for protectionist measures.

a Explain, with reference to the above information, two reasons why countries use trade restrictions. [4]
b Discuss possible methods of trade protectionism that the USA could use. [8]

Disadvantages of restricting free trade

Despite the advantages of protectionism, there are potential drawbacks. These disadvantages (and therefore the negative consequences) of trade restrictions include the following:

» Government intervention **distorts market signals** and therefore can lead to a global misallocation of resources. For example, domestic consumers may not be able to purchase lower-priced imports which are of higher quality than those produced domestically. Protected firms and industries can become too reliant on the government and thus become inefficient.

» Protection can lead to **increased costs of production** due to the lack of competition and incentives to be innovative. Domestic producers may need to pay higher prices for vital imported raw materials and components. This could lead to imported inflation (see Chapter 28) and thus higher domestic prices.

» Other countries are likely to react by **retaliating** and imposing their own trade barriers. For example, in 2024, the USA increased tariffs on Chinese goods, including electric vehicles (EVs), solar panels and computer chips. In response, China imposed import tariffs of polyoxymethylene copolymer from the USA, which is used in electronics and cars. Such sanctions can hinder global economic growth and prosperity for both nations.

Source: 'China hits back at US and EU as trade wars deepen' by Peter Hoskins, 20 May 2024, BBC news website

Case study: The Banana Wars

The Banana Wars were a trade dispute between the European Union and Latin American countries that lasted for two decades, making it one of the longest trade disputes since the Second World War. Latin American banana exporters argued that an EU tariff imposed against them was unfair. It had been introduced to protect banana growers in former European colonies, which were exempt from the tariff.

A formal agreement ending the dispute was signed in late 2012 between the EU and ten Latin American countries. The EU agreed to reduce its tariffs on imported bananas from €176 ($230) per tonne to €114 ($148) over eight years.

Activity

Use the internet to investigate the following:

a What is the World Trade Organization (WTO)?
b What are the main functions of the WTO?
c How effective has the WTO been in encouraging free international trade?

? Chapter review questions

1 What is globalisation?
2 What are multinational companies?
3 What are the advantages and disadvantages of MNCs for their host and home countries?
4 How do tariff and non-tariff trade barriers differ?
5 What are the advantages of trade restrictions?
6 What are the disadvantages of trade restrictions?
7 What are the main causes of globalisation?
8 What are the main consequences of globalisation?

Revision checklist

✔ Globalisation is the process by which the world's economies become increasingly interdependent and interconnected.

✔ The causes of changes in globalisation include changes in trade restrictions, changes in transport costs, changes in communication costs and movement of multinational companies (MNCs).

✔ Changes in globalisation have an effect on international trade, competition, the environment, migration, income distribution and economic development.

✔ An MNC is an organisation that operates in two or more countries.

✔ Advantages of MNCs for the host and home countries include investment, jobs, a reduction in prices (through economies of scale), enhanced technology transfer and the boosting of local economies in host countries.

✔ Disadvantages of MNCs for host and home countries include unethical and cost-cutting practices, forcing domestic firms out of business and the potential to exploit foreign governments (especially those in low-income countries).

✔ Methods of protection (or trade restrictions) refers to the use of trade barriers to restrain foreign trade, thereby limiting overseas competition.

✔ Methods of protection include tariffs and non-tariff barriers (import quotas, subsidies and embargoes).

✔ Reasons for trade protection include to protect infant industries and safeguard domestic jobs, to protect sunset (declining) industries, to protect strategic industries, to prevent dumping, to generate tax revenue, to tackle a balance of payments deficit, to restrict the import of demerit goods and to promote environmental sustainability.

✔ Arguments against trade restrictions include market distortions and inefficiencies, higher production costs for domestic suppliers relying on imported supplies and possible retaliation from foreign countries.

✔ Trade restrictions can increase prices, reduce choices for consumers, harm exporters and potentially lead to trade disputes with trading partners.

Foreign exchange rates

This chapter will cover:

★ a definition of foreign exchange rates
★ the reasons for buying and selling foreign currencies
★ the determination of equilibrium foreign exchange rates
★ the causes of foreign exchange rate fluctuations
★ the consequences of foreign exchange rate fluctuations.

Defining foreign exchange rates

Definition

An **exchange rate** refers to the price of one currency measured in terms of other currencies.

An **exchange rate** refers to the price of one currency measured in terms of other currencies. For example, the exchange rate of the Malaysian ringgit (MYR) in terms of the Pakistani rupee (PKR) might be MYR1 = PKR60 (or PKR1 = MYR0.0167). This means that a Malaysian tourist spending PKR84,000 on hotel accommodation in Pakistan would need to exchange the equivalent of MYR1400 (84,000 ÷ 60).

Exchange rates tend to change over time, so if for example the Malaysian ringgit fell against the Pakistani rupee to MYR1 = PKR56, then the tourist would need to pay MYR1500 (84,000 ÷ 56) for staying at the hotel in Pakistan. In other words, the Malaysian tourist would pay the same price in Pakistani rupees (PKR84,000), but this now requires more Malaysian ringgits (MYR1500 instead of MYR1400).

Activities

1 Use a currency converter website to find out which country uses the following currencies:
   a afghani
   b dong
   c lek
   d won
   e kwacha
2 How many countries can you find that use these currencies?
   a peso
   b real
   c pound
   d franc
   e dollar

Practice questions: structured questions

1 Suppose the exchange rate between the Australian dollar (AUD) and the Chinese yuan renminbi (CNY) is AUD1 = CNY6.5. Calculate the price in renminbi for customers in China buying textbooks priced at AUD65 from Australia. [2]
2 Suppose that the exchange rate between the Canadian dollar (CAD) and the British pound (GBP) is CAD1 = GBP0.65 and the exchange rate between the Canadian dollar and the euro (EUR) is CAD1 = EUR0.75. Calculate the exchange rate of the British pound to the euro. [2]

Reasons for buying and selling foreign currencies

Here are some of the reasons why people might buy and sell foreign currency:

» **Trade in goods and services** – if a business wants to engage in international trade, it needs to buy and sell foreign currencies to facilitate cross-border transactions. For example, if a US firm selling goods to France will only accept US dollars then the French buyer, who uses euros, must exchange euros for dollars. Similarly, a Japanese firm importing raw materials from Australia might need to pay the Australian firm in Australian dollars. These currency exchanges are essential for maintaining the flow of international trade (see Chapter 33) and supporting global economic integration (see Chapter 34).

» **Speculation** – speculation involves buying and selling foreign currencies to profit from fluctuations in exchange rates. Traders and investors anticipate changes in currency values based on economic indicators, political events and market trends. For example, if foreign currency speculators believe the euro will strengthen against the dollar due to robust economic data from the EU, they will buy euros and sell dollars, ceteris paribus. If the euro appreciates, speculators will then sell the currency to earn a profit. For example, speculators predicted the pound sterling would weaken following Brexit due to the intensified economic uncertainties, so they sold the currency before it would depreciate in value. Speculation adds liquidity to the foreign exchange market, but can also increase exchange rate volatility and affect economic stability.

» **Government intervention in currency markets** – governments can intervene in currency markets to stabilise their national currency, control inflation and manage economic stability. Central banks (see Chapter 15) buy or sell foreign currencies to influence exchange rates. For example, a government might intervene in the currency markets to maintain stability of its currency against other currencies, thereby supporting export competitiveness and economic growth. A central bank might sell its currency to weaken it, in order to make the nation's goods and services more affordable abroad. Such intervention helps to protect domestic industries and ensure economic stability. However, intervention can lead to political and economic tensions with trading partners.

> ### Activity
> Prepare a presentation on why a government might want to have a lower exchange rate. Consider whether this is a sustainable economic policy.

» **Payment of profit, interest and dividends between countries** – to make such payments across borders, firms need to buy and sell foreign currencies. When multinational companies (MNCs) or investors earn profits, interest or dividends from foreign investments, they need to convert these earnings into their home currency. For example, an American MNC earning profits from a subsidiary in Germany would need to convert euros into US dollars to repatriate the earnings. Similarly, an investor from Japan receiving interest payments on US investments would need to convert those payments from dollars to yen.

» **Workers' remittances** – the remittances of workers in overseas locations involve these migrant workers transferring money to their home countries. Migrant workers earn wages in the host country's currency then convert this to their home currency when they send money home to support their families. For example, Filipino workers in Hong Kong, Singapore and the United Arab Emirates send billions of dollars annually back to the Philippines. These remittances, converted from Hong Kong dollars, Singaporean dollars and the UAE dirham to the Philippine peso, help to boost household incomes and contribute to economic growth and development in the Philippines. Similarly, Indian workers in the Gulf countries remit substantial sums of money back to India, converting currencies like the Qatari riyal and Bahraini dinar to the Indian rupee. Such remittances are vital for the home country's economy, improving living standards and driving consumer spending.

» **Investment in capital goods between countries** – when a firm in one country purchases machinery, equipment or technology from a foreign manufacturer, it needs to pay in the seller's currency. This process involves converting the buyer's local currency into the seller's currency. For example, if a German car manufacturer buys robotics technology from Japan, it must convert euros into yen to complete the purchase. Similarly, if a US tech company invests in advanced semiconductor manufacturing equipment from South Korea, it needs to exchange US dollars for the South Korean won. These transactions are crucial for business investments and technological advancements, thereby highlighting the need for foreign currency exchange.

Determination of foreign exchange rates in the foreign exchange market

The equilibrium foreign exchange rate is determined by the supply and demand for currencies in the **foreign exchange market**. In theory, the demand for exports of goods and services increases if exports become cheaper. Likewise, the demand for imports falls if the price of imports rises. Since different countries use different currencies, exchange rates are fundamental in facilitating international trade (see Chapter 33).

Consider the following as an example. Table 35.1 shows that the price of a 128GB iPad is HKD6000 (Hong Kong dollars). Study the impact that fluctuations in the exchange rate of the pound sterling have on the price of the iPad for British tourists in Hong Kong.

> **Definition**
>
> A **foreign exchange market** is the marketplace where different currencies can be bought and sold.

Table 35.1 The price of an iPad at different exchange rates (GBP : HKD)

Exchange rate (GBP : HKD)	HKD price ($)	GBP price (£)
£1 = $10.5	6,000	571.43
£1 = $11.5	6,000	521.74
£1 = $12.5	6,000	480.00
£1 = $13.5	6,000	444.44

Hence, as the exchange rate of the pound sterling increases from $10.5 to $13.5, the price of the iPad falls from £571.43 to £444.44 for the British tourist in Hong Kong. This means that as the value of a country's currency rises, its demand for imports tends to increase. Hong Kong's exports to the UK should therefore increase.

Looking at this from the perspective of Hong Kong, the fall in its exchange rate (from $10.5 = £1 to $13.5 = £1) means that imports will become more expensive. For instance, suppose that a Hong Kong supermarket imports supplies from the UK. An order valued at £50,000 used to cost the Hong Kong firm HK$525,000 (i.e. £50,000 × $10.5), but will now cost $675,000 (i.e. £50,000 × $13.5). This means that as the value of a country's currency falls, its demand for imports tends to fall. The UK's exports to Hong Kong should therefore fall.

However, the demand for some imports is price inelastic (see Chapter 10) because they are not readily available in the domestic economy yet are essential for production (such as oil and other vital raw materials). Therefore, domestic firms have to spend more on these essential imports when the exchange rate falls in value. For example, if the Mexican peso (MXN) falls against the Canadian dollar (CAD) from 12.5:1 to 14:1, then Mexican firms buying Canadian oil at a price of CAD100 per barrel pay a higher price of MXN1400 per barrel instead of the previous price of MXN1250 per barrel. This means Mexican firms may need to reduce their price by around 12 per cent to remain competitive, despite their higher costs of production resulting from the fall in the value of the Mexican peso.

In the same way that changes in the exchange rate can affect the demand for exports and imports, they can also affect the amount of tourism revenue, the profitability of businesses and therefore the rates of unemployment and economic growth.

▲ Demand for oil is price inelastic, so it is not very responsive to exchange rate fluctuations

Floating exchange rate system

In the **floating exchange rate system**, the value of a currency is determined by the market forces of demand for the currency and supply of the currency. For example, overseas tourists buy (demand) the foreign currency by selling their domestic currency. Countries that adopt this system allow market forces to determine the value of their currency. Examples are Belgium, Chile, Japan, Luxembourg, Malaysia, New Zealand, Spain, Sweden and the United Kingdom.

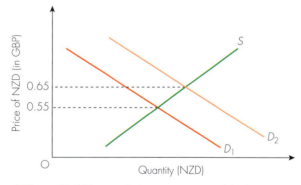

▲ **Figure 35.1** Changes in interest rates and the impact on exchange rates

If banks in New Zealand offer investors higher interest rates than those in the UK, this can cause investors to take advantage by buying the New Zealand dollar (NZD). This will increase the demand for the NZD, thus shifting its demand from D_1 to D_2 in Figure 35.1. This raises the price (or exchange rate) of the NZD from £0.55 to £0.65. By contrast, a fall in interest rates is likely to drive investors away as they search for investments that generate a better financial return.

In a floating exchange rate system, there is an **appreciation** in the exchange rate if the exchange rate is rising against other currencies. By contrast, there is a **depreciation** of the exchange rate if its value falls against other currencies.

Causes of foreign exchange rate fluctuations

Any factor that influences the demand for a currency or its supply will have an impact on the exchange rate. These factors include the following:

» **Changes in demand for exports** – an increase in the demand for exports, perhaps due to improved quality or successful advertising, will increase the demand for the country's currency. Therefore, this increases the exchange rate.

» **Changes in demand for imports** – an increase in the demand for imports, perhaps due to an increase in the competitiveness of foreign firms, will raise the value of the foreign currency in order to facilitate the purchase of foreign goods and services.

» **Changes in interest rates** – higher interest rates offer better returns on investments, increasing demand for the currency and appreciating its value, ceteris paribus. Conversely, lower interest rates reduce investment attractiveness, reducing the demand for the currency and causing it to depreciate.

» **Prices and inflation** – an increase in the price of goods and services caused by domestic inflation will tend to decrease the demand for exports. This will therefore cause the exchange rate to fall in value.

» **Foreign direct investment (FDI)** – globalisation and the expansion of MNCs mean that investment in overseas production plants requires the use of foreign currencies. For example, Nissan's car manufacturing plant in India requires the Japanese car maker to buy Indian rupees to pay for the materials, recruitment of labour and other production costs. Thus, inward FDI (such as the entry of an MNC) will boost the demand for a currency. By contrast, outward FDI (such as the departure of an MNC) will increase the supply of a currency.

▲ A Nissan car plant in Chennai, India

» **Speculation** – foreign exchange traders and investment companies move money around the world to take advantage of higher interest rates (see Chapter 24) and variations in exchange rates to earn a profit. As huge sums of money (known as 'hot money') are involved, speculation can cause exchange rate fluctuations, at least in the short run. Speculators might also lack confidence in certain economies and therefore withdraw their investments, thereby depreciating the currency (see the Landsbanki and Kaupthing case study).

» **Government intervention** – all the above factors can affect the exchange rate under a freely floating exchange rate system. In addition, government intervention in the foreign exchange market can affect the exchange rate. For example, if greater demand for US goods causes an appreciation of the dollar, the US Federal Reserve can sell its dollar reserves (thereby increasing supply of the dollar). This would lead to a fall in the value of its currency.

> ### Case study: The collapse of Landsbanki and Kaupthing
>
> The global financial crisis of 2008 saw the collapse of Iceland's major banks, including Landsbanki (founded in 1886) and Kaupthing (founded in 1930). Investors across Europe feared the Icelandic banks would default on their debts, and this caused a selling frenzy. This in turn led to a rapid fall in the value of the krona (Iceland's currency).

> ### Activity
>
> The value of a currency will change if the demand for and/or supply of the currency changes. Explain, with the use of demand and supply diagrams, the effects of the following events from the perspective of the USA.
>
> a   The USA buys more imports from Brazil.
> b   Millions of US tourists visit France.
> c   There is an increase in US exports to Russia.
> d   The Federal Reserve (the USA's central bank) raises the rate of interest.
> e   Speculators feel that the US dollar will rise in value against other major currencies.

Consequences of exchange rate fluctuations

Exchange rate fluctuations affect different stakeholders in different ways, depending on whether the consequences are seen from the perspective of consumers or producers (both importers and exporters).

The following is an analysis of a strong US dollar due to a currency appreciation. The opposite results would apply in the case of a currency depreciation.

» **Customers** have greater purchasing power when the exchange rate increases. For example, if the exchange rate changes from $1 = 45 Mauritian rupee to $1 = 50 Mauritian rupee, then Americans will require fewer dollars to buy goods and services from Mauritius. Thus, US firms and individuals are likely to buy more Mauritian goods and services.

» **Exporters** face more difficult trading conditions when the exchange rate increases. This is because their goods and services will become more expensive for foreign customers. For example, if the exchange rate changes from $1.5 = €1 to $1.3 = €1, then customers from the European Union will need to spend more money to buy US goods and services. Therefore, demand for US exports from the EU is likely to drop.

Study tip

The effects of foreign exchange rate fluctuations on a country's export and import prices and spending on imports and exports depend on the value of the price elasticity of demand for its imports and exports. A currency depreciation will have the desired effects of reducing demand for imports and increasing demand for exports only if the demand for imports and exports is price elastic.

»» **Importers** in the USA potentially gain from a strong dollar because this makes it cheaper for US firms to import raw materials, components and finished goods from abroad. For example, if the US dollar appreciates from $1.5 = €1 to $1.3 = €1, US importers only need to spend $1300 on each €1000 order of goods and services from Europe, instead of $1500. While this is bad for domestic US firms trying to compete with imports in the USA, it can help to reduce cost-push inflation (see Chapter 28).

Exchange rate fluctuations also have consequences for macroeconomic objectives. An increase in the exchange rate will have the following consequences for the balance of payments, employment, inflation and economic growth:

»» **Balance of payments** – if a currency appreciation has a larger impact on exports than imports (that is, there is a fall in the value of net exports), then the current account of the balance of payments will worsen (see Chapter 36). This is because a strong currency will make it more difficult for exporters to sell their goods and services in overseas markets.
»» **Employment** – a fall in net exports and deteriorating profits will, in the long run, cause job losses in export-oriented industries. This will therefore cause unemployment in the economy.
»» **Inflation** – lower levels of spending in the economy, caused by higher unemployment, will tend to reduce the rate of inflation. In addition, if the country relies heavily on certain imports, such as oil or food supplies, then the higher exchange rate will help to reduce the general price level even further.
»» **Economic growth** – in the long run, as a result of the higher exchange rate, economic growth is likely to fall due to the combination of lower export sales and higher unemployment.

Practice question: structured question

In December 2023, Argentina's government announced that it would weaken the value of its currency by more than 50 per cent against the US dollar, deliberately keeping its exchange rate artificially low. The relatively low value of the peso compared to the dollar has contributed to economic challenges in the Argentine economy.

a Define 'exchange rate'.   [2]
b Explain two advantages of a weak peso for the Argentinian economy.   [4]

Coping with a strong exchange rate

Firms can deal with a higher or strong exchange rate in a number of ways (the opposite applies in the case of a weaker or depreciating exchange rate):

»» Cutting export prices to maintain their price competitiveness against foreign rivals, although this means the domestic firms will have to accept lower profit margins.
»» Seeking alternative overseas suppliers of cheaper raw materials and components.
»» Improving productivity (efficiency) to keep average labour costs under control.
»» Focusing on supplying more price inelastic products because customers will then become less sensitive to exchange rate fluctuations.
»» Focusing on non-price factors that are important to overseas customers, such as brand awareness, environmental sustainability and corporate social responsibility.
»» Relocating production processes overseas, where costs of production are relatively low and where operations are less exposed to exchange rate fluctuations.

Study tip

It is possible for some firms to gain from a stronger currency while others lose out. Review the main points in this chapter to make your own judgement on this.

Practice questions: structured questions

1 Explain, with the aid of a numerical example, what is meant by an 'appreciation' in the value of a currency. [2]

2 Analyse the likely effects of a country's currency appreciation on its exports and imports. [6]

? Chapter review questions

1 What is an exchange rate?
2 What is the likely impact on a country's exchange rate following an increase in the demand for its exports?
3 What is the likely impact on a country's exchange rate following a decision of its government to cut interest rates?
4 What is a floating exchange rate system?
5 What are the causes of exchange rate fluctuations?
6 What are the consequences of exchange rate fluctuations for importers, exporters and consumers?
7 How are equilibrium foreign exchange rates determined?

Revision checklist

✔ An exchange rate refers to the price of one currency measured in terms of other currencies.

✔ A foreign exchange market is the marketplace where different currencies can be bought and sold.

✔ The reasons for buying and selling foreign currencies include trade in goods and services, speculation, government intervention in currency markets, payment of profit, interest and dividends between countries, workers' remittances and investment in capital goods between countries.

✔ The equilibrium foreign exchange rate is determined by the supply and demand for currencies in the foreign exchange market.

✔ In a floating exchange rate system, the currency is allowed to fluctuate against other currencies according to market forces, without any government intervention.

✔ An appreciation of the currency occurs when there is an increase in its value in a floating exchange rate system. A depreciation of the currency occurs when there is a fall in its value in a floating exchange rate system.

✔ Causes of exchange rate fluctuations include changes in the demand for imports and exports, changes in interest rates, price levels (inflation), the degree of foreign direct investment, speculation in the foreign exchange market and the degree of government intervention.

✔ Different stakeholders are affected by changes in the exchange rate in different ways. Exporters tend to lose out from a higher currency value. Consumers and importers tend to gain, in the short term, as their purchasing power of foreign goods and services increases.

✔ Changes in the exchange rate have a direct impact on a country's balance of payments, employment levels, inflation rate and economic growth.

36

Current account of the balance of payments

This chapter will cover:

★ the structure of the current account of the balance of payments
★ the causes of current account deficit and surplus
★ the consequences of current account deficit and surplus
★ the policies to achieve balance of payments stability.

Defining the current account of the balance of payments

The **balance of payments** is a financial record of a country's transactions with the rest of the world over a given time period, usually one year. This primarily includes the country's trade in goods and services with other countries.

In theory, the balance of payments must always balance over time. This is because a country, like an individual, can only spend (on imports, for example) what it earns (from export earnings, for example).

The largest component of the balance of payments is the **current account**. This is a record of the value of all exports and imports of goods and services between a country and the rest of the world, plus net income transfers from abroad, over a given time period. The current account is structured in four parts: trade in goods, trade in services, primary income and secondary income.

Trade in goods

This part of the current account is a record of the exports and imports of physical goods, hence it is also known as the **visible balance**. It is the trade in raw materials, semi-manufactured products and manufactured goods. **Visible exports** are goods which are sold to foreign customers, with money flowing into the domestic economy. For example, the export of Toyota cars results in an inward flow of money to Japan's visible balance. **Visible imports** are goods bought by domestic customers from foreign sellers, such as Japanese residents buying German cars. This results in money flowing out of the Japanese economy.

▲ Toyota cars are an example of visible exports for Japan

Trade in services

This is a record of the export and import of services (intangible products). Examples include the trade in services such as banking, insurance, consultancy, shipping and tourism. It is sometimes called the **invisible balance**. For example, tourism expenditure of Americans in France would represent export earnings (or an **invisible export**) for the French economy. By contrast, French customers who fly on American Airlines represent an **invisible import** for France.

Primary income

Also known as **investment income**, this is a record of a country's net income earned from investments abroad. Examples are:

» profits earned by subsidiary companies based in overseas countries
» interest received from loans and deposits in overseas banks
» dividends earned from financial investments in overseas companies
» foreign direct investments (FDI) of firms in overseas business ventures.

Secondary income

The final section of the current account records **net income transfers**, per time period. It shows income transfers between residents and non-residents. Transfers arise from financial gifts between residents of different countries, such as:

» donations to charities abroad
» foreign aid
» subsidies or grants paid to companies based in overseas locations
» payments of pensions to retired people now based in overseas countries
» scholarships paid to students based in overseas universities
» money sent home by people working abroad (that is, workers' overseas remittances).

Therefore, the current account is calculated as follows:

Current account = Balance of trade + Primary income + Secondary income

Table 36.1 shows the current account balance of the countries with the highest and lowest balances in 2023, according to the World Bank.

Table 36.1 The current account balance: selected countries, 2023

Top five countries			Bottom five countries		
Rank	Country	$bn	Rank	Country	$bn
1	Germany	262.72	1	USA	−905.38
2	China	252.99	2	UK	−110.39
3	Japan	150.69	3	Turkiye	−44.96
4	Netherlands	112.95	4	India	−32.34
5	Singapore	99.13	5	Brazil	−30.83

Source: Current account balance (BoP, US$), 2023, World Bank Group website

> **Activity**
>
> Investigate the main exports and imports for your country, or a country of your choice. Does your chosen country currently have a positive or negative trade balance?

> **Activity**
>
> Copy the following table and classify each transaction by using a tick in the correct column, from the perspective of the Indian economy.
>
> | Transaction | | Visible | | Invisible | |
> | --- | --- | --- | --- | --- | --- |
> | | | Export | Import | Export | Import |
> | a | A German company purchases Indian-produced chemical products | | | | |
> | b | American tourists fly to India on Air India | | | | |
> | c | Indian supermarkets purchase French wine and cheese | | | | |
> | d | The Indian government maintains foreign embassies overseas | | | | |
> | e | German tourists buy theatre tickets to see the latest Bollywood movie in Mumbai | | | | |
> | f | The Indian government pays interest on its borrowing (debts) | | | | |
> | g | An Indian firm buys a fleet of lorries (trucks) from Japan | | | | |
> | h | Global sales of books by Bhavik Sarkhedi, a best-selling Indian author | | | | |

Practice question: structured question

Study the data below and answer the questions that follow.

Trade balance for Country B ($bn), 2024

Exports	85
Goods	57
Services	28
Imports	_____
Goods	88
Services	15
Visible balance	_____
Invisible balance	_____
Trade balance	_____

a Define 'invisible balance'. [2]
b Calculate the missing figures in the data above. [4]

Current account deficits and surpluses

Definitions

A **current account deficit** occurs when a country spends more money than it earns, i.e. imports exceed exports.

A **current account surplus** exists if a country exports more than it imports.

A country has a **current account deficit** if its import expenditure is greater than its export earnings over a given time period (usually one year). Hence, the current account has a negative balance. By contrast, a **current account surplus** exists if the country exports more than it imports. This means the country will have a positive balance on its current account of the balance of payments.

Causes of current account deficits

A deficit on the current account can occur due to a combination of two factors:

» **Lower demand for exports** – this could be caused by a decline in manufacturing competitiveness, perhaps due to higher labour costs in the domestic economy. Another factor is declining incomes in foreign markets, perhaps due to an economic recession. This means households and firms have less money available to spend on another country's exports. A third cause of lower demand for exports is a higher exchange rate (see Chapter 35). This makes exports more expensive for foreign buyers, so reduces the volume and value of exports.

» **Higher demand for imports** – domestic buyers will tend to buy more imports if they are cheaper or of better quality. For example, a higher exchange rate means the domestic currency can buy more foreign currency, so this makes it cheaper to buy imports. Alternatively, domestic inflation means that imports are relatively cheaper, so more domestic residents and firms will tend to buy foreign goods and services.

Practice question: structured question

Examine the graph, which shows the balance of trade for Greece, and answer the questions that follow.

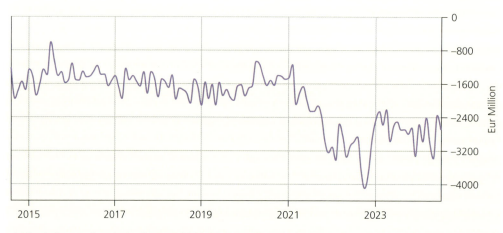

▲ The balance of trade for Greece, 2014–2024

Source: Greece Balance of trade, National Statistical Service of Greece, 2024, Trading Economics website

a Define 'balance of trade'. [2]

b Explain two possible causes of the trend in Greece's balance of trade. [4]

Consequences of current account deficits

Like an individual, a country cannot spend more (on imported goods, services and capital) than it earns (from the export of goods, services and capital). The severity of the consequences of a deficit depends on its size and duration. Nevertheless, a current account deficit is generally considered to be unfavourable for the economy for several reasons:

» **Impact on GDP of reduced demand in the economy** – a trade deficit means the economy is spending more money on imports than it is receiving from the export of goods and services. This can cause total demand in the economy to fall (a fall in the country's GDP), thus triggering a recession (see Chapter 26). For example, the USA's trade deficit with China has contributed to much of America's recent economic problems. The fall in GDP is also likely to reduce any likelihood of demand-pull inflation in the economy (see Chapter 28).

» **Unemployment** – as labour has a derived demand (see Chapter 17), a fall in overall demand in the economy is likely to cause cyclical unemployment (see Chapter 27). Workers may also have to take a pay cut in order to correct the deficit. For example, the UK has experienced a decline in manufacturing jobs as there has been a fall in the demand for British exports of coal, steel, textiles and motor vehicles.

» **Lower standards of living** – if the current account deficit is caused by a negative balance on net incomes (primary and secondary income flows), this means capital outflows exceed capital inflows for the country. An economy with less income is likely to suffer from lower standards of living. In addition, to cut the current account deficit, households and firms may need to reduce their spending.

» **Increased borrowing** – just as an individual cannot spend more than he or she earns in the long run, countries need to borrow money or attract foreign investment in order to rectify their current account deficits. In addition, there is an opportunity cost of debt repayment as the government cannot use this money for other areas of public sector expenditure or to stimulate economic growth.

» **Lower exchange rate, leading to inflation** – a fall in demand for exports and/or a rise in the demand for imports (causing the current account deficit) reduces the exchange rate. While a lower exchange rate can mean exports become more price competitive, it also means that essential imports (such as oil and foodstuffs) will become more expensive. This can lead to imported inflation (see Chapter 28). The consequences of fluctuating exchange rates are covered in more detail in Chapter 35.

In general, large and persistent current account deficits are a sign that the country is internationally uncompetitive. These deficits tend to have a negative impact on GDP, economic growth, employment and standards of living.

Causes of current account surplus

A surplus on the current account can occur due to a combination of two factors:

» **Higher demand for exports** – this can be caused by an improvement in manufacturing competitiveness, perhaps due to higher labour productivity in the domestic economy. Another factor is higher incomes in overseas markets, meaning foreign households and firms have more money to spend on the

Study tip

A deficit on the current account that is manageable is not necessarily a bad thing. For example, the deficit might be the result of strong economic growth, with residents purchasing more foreign goods and services. This allows the country's residents to enjoy a higher standard of living as they are able to benefit from access to a range of good-quality imports.

country's exports. A third cause of higher demand for exports is a lower exchange rate (see Chapter 35). This makes exports less expensive for foreign buyers, so tends to increase the demand for exports.

» **Reduced demand for imports** – domestic buyers will tend to buy fewer imports if they are more expensive or of lower quality than those provided by domestic firms. For example, a lower exchange rate means the domestic currency can buy less foreign currency, so this makes it more expensive to buy imports. Another reason is that inflation in overseas countries causes imports to be more expensive, so individuals and firms buy more home-produced goods and services.

Practice question: structured question

Despite China being the USA's largest customer, the USA has a persistent trade deficit with China (see Table 36.2). US imports from China include consumer electronics, clothing, toys, sports equipment, furniture, footwear and machinery (such as power generators).

Table 36.2 Trade between the USA and China, selected years

	2023 ($m)	2016 ($m)	2010 ($m)
US exports to China	147,777.8	115,602.1	91,911.1
US imports from China	426,885.0	426,618.1	364,952.6

Source: Trading Economics website (adapted from the US Census)

a Calculate the trade balance for the USA with China in 2010, 2016 and 2023. [2]

b Explain how it is possible that the USA has a persistent trade deficit with China even though the USA has reported record export sales to China. [4]

Consequences of current account surplus

The consequences of a country having a persistent current account surplus include the following:

» **Employment and GDP** – a sustained current account surplus can be desirable as higher export sales help to create jobs and improve the country's GDP. However, a negative consequence of this is that job losses are created in other countries. For example, the USA's large and persistent current account deficit with China is likely to have caused large-scale job losses in the USA's manufacturing sector.

» **Standards of living** – a favourable current account balance means the country receives a higher income because domestic firms have a competitive advantage in the products they export. This tends to lead to a higher standard of living (see Chapter 29).

» **Inflationary pressures** – higher demand for exports can lead to demand-pull inflation (see Chapter 28). Therefore, the current account surplus can diminish the international competitiveness of the country over time as the price of exports rises due to inflation.

» **Higher exchange rate** – the higher demand for exports can cause the currency to appreciate in value (see Chapter 35). Subsequently, foreign buyers will find it more expensive to import goods into their countries.

▲ Oil-exporting countries such as Saudi Arabia, Kuwait, Qatar and the United Arab Emirates have consistently enjoyed current account surpluses, thus boosting their GDP and standards of living

Practice question: structured question

The graph shows the current account balance for Kuwait (expressed in Kuwaiti dinar). The graph shows that Kuwait has generally experienced a current account surplus for the period 2014–2024. Kuwait has significant oil reserves and has the capacity to produce 2–3 millions of barrels of oil per day.

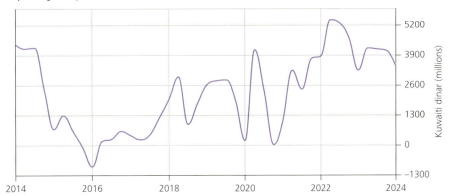

▲ Current account balance for Kuwait, 2014–2024

Source: Kuwait current account balance. Used with the permission of The Central Bank of Kuwait

a Define 'current account surplus'. [2]
b Explain two consequences of Kuwait's continual current account surplus. [4]

Policies to achieve balance of payments stability

There are four main policies that can be used to improve a country's current account balance – fiscal and monetary policies (which tackle demand-side issues), supply-side policies and trade protection measures. These macroeconomic policies are covered in more detail in Chapters 23–25 and 34 respectively.

▸▸ **Fiscal policy** – these measures use a combination of higher taxes and reduced government spending to decrease the amount of money available to spend on imports. In theory, this helps to reduce the current account deficit.

» **Monetary policy** – higher interest rates make new and existing loans more expensive for households and firms. This reduces their demand for imports. Alternatively, the central monetary authority of a country (see Chapter 15) might decide to devalue the exchange rate to improve the country's competitiveness. This also has the effect of reducing the price of exports and making imports more expensive.

» **Supply-side policies** – these policies strive to raise the productive capacity of the economy. Examples are:
– investment in education and healthcare services to improve the economy's human capital, productivity and international competitiveness
– investment in infrastructure to support businesses and industries, especially those engaged in export markets
– measures to encourage export-driven business start-ups and industries, such as government subsidies and tax incentives.

» **Trade protectionist measures** – trade restriction measures reduce the competitiveness of imports, thereby making domestic consumption more attractive. For example, tariffs (import taxes) raise the price of imports, while quotas (see Chapter 34) limit the volume of imports available.

Practice question: structured question

'A current account deficit on the balance of payments is undesirable during a recession but is not really a problem during periods of economic growth.'

a Define 'current account deficit'. [2]
b Explain the validity of the above statement. [4]

Practice questions: multiple choice

1 What is **not** part of the current account? [1]
  A debt (borrowing)
  B primary income
  C trade in goods
  D trade in services
2 Which option is secondary income? [1]
  A earnings from foreign direct investments
  B interest earned from deposits held in overseas banks
  C overseas donations for domestic charities
  D profits earned by multinational companies based in foreign countries

? Chapter review questions

1 What is the balance of payments?
2 What is the difference between the visible trade balance and the invisible trade balance?
3 What is the balance of trade?
4 How does primary income differ from secondary income?
5 How does a current account deficit differ from a current account surplus?
6 What are the two main causes of a current account deficit?
7 How might a government deal with a current account deficit?
8 Why might a current account surplus be detrimental to a country?

Revision checklist

✔ The balance of payments is a financial record of a country's transactions with the rest of the world, per time period. In theory, the balance of payments must balance over time.

✔ The current account is the largest component of the balance of payments.

✔ The current account is structured in four parts: trade in goods, trade in services, primary income and secondary income.

✔ The trade in goods records the balance of exports and imports of physical goods.

✔ The trade in services is a record of the exports and imports of services (intangible products).

✔ The balance of trade is the sum of the trade in goods plus the trade in services – that is, visible balance + invisible balance.

✔ Primary income (also known as investment income) is a record of a country's net income earned from investments abroad.

✔ Secondary income is the final section of the current account, which records net income transfers between residents and non-residents of a country.

✔ The two key causes of current account deficits are lower demand for exports and higher demand for imports.

✔ Consequences of current account deficits include reduced demand in the economy, unemployment, lower standards of living, increased borrowing and a lower exchange rate.

✔ The two key causes of current account surpluses are higher demand for exports and lower demand for imports.

✔ Consequences of current account surpluses include more employment, improved standards of living, inflationary pressures and a higher exchange rate.

✔ There are four main macroeconomic policies that can be used to improve the current account: fiscal policy, monetary policy, supply-side policies and trade protection measures.

Glossary

Absolute poverty exists when there is extreme outright poverty, i.e. income equal to or less than $2.15 per day.

Appreciation of a currency occurs when there is an increase in its value relative to another currency operating in a floating exchange rate system.

Average fixed cost refers to a firm's fixed cost per unit of output.

Average total cost is the cost per unit of output, i.e. the total cost of making one product.

Average variable cost refers to the variable cost per unit of output.

Balance of payments is a financial record of a country's transactions with the rest of the world for a given time period, usually one year.

Barriers to entry are the obstacles that prevent firms from entering a market. Examples are the existence of intellectual property rights, large advertising budgets of existing firms and legal constraints to prevent wasteful competition.

Bartering is the act of swapping items in exchange for other items through a process of bargaining and negotiation, due to the absence of money in the economy.

Base year refers to the starting year when calculating a price index.

Basic economic problem is concerned with how best to allocate scarce resources in order to satisfy people's unlimited needs and wants.

Birth rate measures the number of live births per thousand of the population in a year.

Borrowing occurs when an individual, firm or the government takes out a loan, paying it back to the financial lender over a period of time, with interest payments.

Budget deficit exists when the government spends more than its sources of revenue per time period. The deficit contributes to the national debt of the country.

Budget surplus exists when the government collects more revenue than it spends, per time period. Any surplus can be used to pay off parts of the national debt.

Business cycle (or **trade cycle**) describes the fluctuations in the economic activity of a country over time, creating a long-term trend of economic growth in the economy.

Capital expenditure is money spent on fixed assets (items owned by an individual or firm which last more than 12 months), such as computers, cars, furniture, buildings and equipment.

Capital-intensive industries is where the use and cost of capital is more prominent than that of any other factor of production, e.g. car manufacturing.

Central bank of a country is the monetary authority that oversees and manages the economy's money supply and banking system.

Commercial bank is a retail bank that provides financial services to its customers, e.g. savings, bank loans and mortgages.

Complements are products that are jointly demanded, e.g. tennis balls and tennis racquets.

Conglomerate merger occurs when two or more firms from unrelated areas of business integrate to create a new firm.

Consumer Price Index (CPI) is a weighted index of consumer prices in the economy over time. It is used to measure the cost of living for an average household in the economy.

Consumption expenditure is the value of all private household consumption within a country.

Contraction in demand means a fall in the quantity demanded for a product following an increase in its price.

Contraction in supply means a fall in the quantity supplied of a product following a fall in its price.

Cost-push inflation is a cause of inflation, triggered by higher costs of production which forces up prices.

Costs of production refer to a firm's expenditure in the process of producing goods and/or providing services.

Current account is the largest component of the balance of payments. It records the value of all exports and imports of goods and services between a country and its trading partners, plus net income transfers from abroad.

Current account deficit occurs when a country spends more money than it earns, i.e. imports exceed exports.

Current account surplus exists if a country exports more than it imports.

Current expenditure is money spent on goods and services consumed within the current year. Unlike capital expenditure, it is often recurrent, such as the spending on food, clothing, entertainment and haircuts.

Cyclical unemployment is unemployment caused by a lack of demand, which causes a fall in national income. It is a severe type of unemployment as it can affect every industry in the economy.

Death rate measures the number of deaths per thousand of the population in a year.

Deflation is the sustained fall in the general price level in an economy over time, i.e. the inflation rate is negative.

Demand refers to the quantity of a good or service that consumers are both willing and able to buy at various prices, over a given period of time.

Demand for labour is the number of workers that firms are willing and able to hire at a given wage rate.

Demand-pull inflation is a cause of inflation. It is triggered by higher levels of total demand in the economy, which drive up the general price level.

Demerger occurs when two previously merged firms decide to break up and become two separate firms.

Demerit goods are goods or services which when consumed cause negative spillover effects to a third party in an economy.

Demographics is the study of population distribution and trends.

Dependency ratio is a comparison of the number of people who are not in the labour force with the number of people in active paid employment.

Depreciation of a currency occurs when there is a fall in its value relative to another currency operating in a floating exchange rate system.

Derived demand means that labour (or any other factor of production) is not demanded for itself but for the goods and services it is used to produce.

Diseconomies of scale occur when average costs of production increase as the size of a firm increases.

Disposable income is the amount of income a person has available to spend on goods and services after compulsory deductions such as income tax.

Division of labour occurs when a production process is split between different workers, who become experts in a part of the process.

Economic agents are households (private individuals in society), firms that operate in the private sector of an economy and the government (the public sector of an economy).

Economic development is an intangible concept that considers both quantitative and qualitative variables in raising the standard of living within a country.

Economic goods are those which are limited in supply.

Economic growth is the annual increase in the level of national output, i.e. the annual percentage change in gross domestic product.

Economies of scale are the cost-saving benefits of large-scale operations, which reduce average costs of production.

Embargo is a ban on trade with a certain country.

Employment refers to the use of factors of production in the economy, such as labour.

Environmental sustainability is the management of an economy's resources to meet current needs without jeopardising the needs of future generations.

Equilibrium price is the price at which the demand curve for a product intersects the supply curve for the product. The market is therefore cleared of any excess demand or supply.

Excess demand refers to a situation where the market price is below the equilibrium price, thus creating a shortage in the market.

Excess supply refers to a situation where the market price is above the equilibrium price, thus creating a surplus in the market.

Exchange rate refers to the price of one currency measured in terms of other currencies.

Extension in demand means an increase in the quantity demanded for a product following a fall in its price.

Extension in supply means an increase in the quantity supplied of a product following an increase in its price.

External benefits are the positive side-effects of production or consumption experienced by third parties for which no money is paid by the beneficiary.

External costs are the negative side-effects of production or consumption incurred by third parties, for which no compensation is paid to these third parties.

External economies of scale are economies of scale that arise from factors outside of the firm, e.g. the location of the firm, proximity to transport and the availability of skilled workers.

Factors of production are the resources required to produce a good or service, namely land, labour, capital and enterprise.

Fertility rate measures the average number of births per woman. It is used as a component to measure population growth.

Fiscal policy is the use of taxes and government spending to affect macroeconomic aims such as economic growth and employment.

Fixed costs are costs that a firm has to pay irrespective of how much it produces or sells.

Floating exchange rate system means that the currency is allowed to fluctuate against other currencies according to market forces, without any government intervention.

Foreign exchange market is the marketplace where different currencies can be bought and sold.

Free goods are goods which are unlimited in supply. Hence, there is no opportunity cost in terms of their output.

Free riders benefit from public goods without paying for them.

Free trade means that international trade takes place without protectionist measures (barriers to international trade).

Frictional unemployment is transitional unemployment which occurs when people change jobs or are in between jobs.

Full employment means that everyone in a country who is willing and able to work has a job.

GDP per head measures the average value of annual GDP per capita (person).

Geographical mobility refers to the extent to which labour is willing and able to move to different locations for employment purposes.

Globalisation is the process by which the world's economies become increasingly interdependent and interconnected.

Goods are physical items such as tables, cars, toothpaste and pencils.

Government budget refers to a government's financial plans in terms of planned revenues (mainly tax revenues) and expenditure (such as healthcare, education and welfare payments).

Gross domestic product measures the monetary value of goods and services produced within a country for a given period of time, usually one year.

Horizontal merger occurs when two or more firms in the same economic sector of industry integrate.

Human Development Index (HDI) is the United Nations' composite indicator of living standards in a country. It comprises three dimensions of human development: education, healthcare and income.

Hyperinflation refers to very high rates of inflation that are out of control, causing average prices in the economy to rise very rapidly.

Imported inflation is a cause of inflation. It is triggered by higher import prices, which force up costs of production and thus cause domestic inflation.

Import quota is a quantitative limit on the sale of a foreign good.

Inflation is the sustained rise in the general level of prices of goods and services in an economy over time, as measured by a Consumer Price Index (CPI).

Innovation is the commercialisation of new ideas and products. It is a vital source of productivity.

Interdependence means that the three sectors of industry depend on each other and cannot operate independently to produce goods and services.

Internal economies of scale are economies of scale that arise from the internal organisation of the business, e.g. financial, bulk-buying and technical economies of scale.

International trade refers to the exchange of goods and services beyond national borders.

Investment expenditure is the sum of capital spending by all businesses within a country.

Labour force survey uses the ILO's standardised household-based survey to collect work-related statistics.

Labour-intensive industries is where the cost of labour is proportionally higher than the cost of other factors of production, e.g. accountancy, real estate services and tourism.

Law of demand states that quantity demanded falls as price rises, while the quantity demanded rises at lower prices.

Law of supply states that there is a positive relationship between price and the quantity supplied of a product.

Market refers to any place where buyers and sellers engage in trade. Examples of markets include retail outlets, supermarkets and stock markets.

Market demand is the sum of all individual demand for a particular product at given prices.

Market disequilibrium occurs when the quantity demanded of a product is unequal to the quantity supplied of the product, i.e. there are shortages or surpluses in the market.

Market economy relies on the market forces of demand and supply (in the private sector) to allocate resources with minimal government intervention.

Market equilibrium occurs when the quantity demanded of a product is equal to the quantity supplied of the product, i.e. there are no shortages or surpluses.

Market failure occurs when the market forces of demand and supply are unsuccessful in allocating resources efficiently and cause external costs or external benefits.

Market structure refers to the key characteristics of a particular market (or industry), such as the number and size of firms in the market, the degree and intensity of price and non-price competition, and the nature of barriers to entry.

Market system refers to the method of allocating scarce resources through the market forces of demand and supply.

Maximum price occurs when the government sets a price below the market equilibrium price in order to encourage consumption.

Merger occurs when two or more firms join together to form one firm.

Merit goods are goods or services which when consumed create positive spillover effects in an economy.

Minimum price occurs when the government sets a price above the market equilibrium price in order to encourage output of a certain good or service.

Mixed economic system is a combination of government-controlled resource allocation and a market economic system.

Monetary policy refers to the use of interest rates, exchange rates and the money supply to control macroeconomic objectives and to affect the level of economic activity.

Money is any commodity that can be used as a medium of exchange for the purchase of goods and services, e.g. banknotes and coins.

Money supply refers to the amount of money in the economy at a particular point in time, e.g. coins, banknotes, bank deposits and central bank reserves.

Monopoly is a market structure where there is only one supplier of a good or service, with the power to affect market supply and prices.

Multinational company is an organisation that operates in two or more countries.

Nationalisation is the purchase of private sector assets or businesses by the government.

National minimum wage is the lowest legal amount any firm can pay its workers and is set by the government.

Natural resources are natural assets (comprising renewable and non-renewable resources) that are used as factors of production.

Needs are goods and services that are essential for survival.

Net exports refers to the monetary value of the difference between a nation's export earnings and its import expenditure.

Net migration rate measures the difference between immigration and emigration rates for a country, thus indicating the physical movement of people into and out of a country.

Occupational mobility refers to the extent to which labour is able to move between jobs.

Opportunity cost is the cost of the next best opportunity forgone when making a decision.

Optimum population exists when the output of goods and services per head of the population is maximised.

Overspecialisation occurs when an individual, firm, region or country concentrates too much on producing a very limited number of goods and services. This exposes the economic agent to a far higher degree of risk.

Perfectly price elastic demand means that consumers are indefinitely responsive to a change in the price.

Perfectly price inelastic demand means that the quantity demanded of a product is independent of its price.

Population refers to the total number of inhabitants of a particular country.

Population distribution refers to the composition and structure of a country's population.

Population growth refers to the rate of change in the size of a country's population.

Poverty is a condition that exists when people lack adequate income and wealth to sustain a basic standard of living.

PPC diagram is a graphical representation of the maximum combination of the amounts of two products that can be produced in an economy, per period of time.

Price discrimination occurs when firms charge different customers different prices for essentially the same product due to differences in PED.

Price elastic demand describes demand for a product that is relatively responsive to changes in price, usually due to substitutes being readily available.

Price elasticity of demand (PED) measures the extent to which the quantity demanded for a product changes due to a change in its price.

Price elasticity of supply (PES) measures the degree of responsiveness of the quantity supplied of a product following a change in its price. Supply is said to be price elastic if producers can quite easily increase supply without a time delay if there is an increase in the price of the product. Supply is price inelastic if firms find it difficult to change production in a given time period due to a change in the market price.

Price inelastic demand describes demand for a product that is relatively unresponsive to changes in price, mainly because of the lack of substitutes for the product.

Price makers are firms that set their own prices. They have the market power to do so, and they do not have to base their price on the equilibrium price determined by the forces of demand and supply.

Price mechanism refers to the system of relying on the market forces of demand and supply to allocate resources.

Price takers are firms that set their price according to the market price, rather than determining their own prices.

Private benefits are the positive aspects of production and consumption enjoyed by a firm, individual or government.

Private costs of production and consumption are the actual costs for a firm, individual or government.

Private sector refers to the economic activity of private individuals and firms. The private sector's main aim is to earn profit for its owners.

Privatisation is the transfer of the ownership of assets from the public sector to the private sector.

Production refers to the total output of goods and services in the production process.

Production possibility curve (PPC) represents the maximum combination of goods and services which can be produced in an economy, i.e. the productive capacity of the economy.

Productivity is a measure of efficiency found by calculating the amount of output per unit of a factor input, e.g. output per worker or output per machine hour.

Profit is the difference between a firm's total revenues (TR) and its total costs (TC). It is calculated using the formula TR − TC.

Public goods are goods and services that are non-excludable and non-rivalrous, and which are a cause of market failure as there is a lack of a profit motive to produce them.

Public sector refers to economic activity directly involving the government, such as the provision of state education and healthcare services. The public sector's main aim is to provide a service.

Real GDP refers to the value of national income (GDP) adjusted for inflation to reflect the true value of goods and services produced in a given year.

Recession occurs in the business cycle when there is a fall in GDP for two consecutive quarters.

Redistribution of income refers to the macroeconomic aim of achieving greater equality in the distribution of income in an economy.

Relative poverty is a comparative measure of poverty, referring to those who have a lower standard of living in comparison to the average member of society.

Replacement fertility rate is the number of children that the average woman must have to maintain a stable population size.

Sales revenue (or **total revenue**) is the sum of money received from the sale of a good or service. It is calculated by the formula P × Q.

Saving occurs when a person puts away part of their current income for future spending.

Seasonal unemployment is unemployment that arises when jobs are seasonal.

Services are non-physical items such as haircuts, bus journeys, telephone calls and internet access.

Shortage occurs when demand exceeds supply because the price is lower than the market equilibrium.

Social benefits are the true (or full) benefits of consumption or production, i.e. the sum of private benefits and external benefits.

Social costs are the true (or full) costs of consumption or production to society as a whole, i.e. the sum of private costs and external costs.

Specialisation by country occurs when nations concentrate on the production of certain goods or services due to cost advantages, perhaps due to their abundance of resources.

Specialisation of labour refers to workers being experts in a particular profession.

Standard of living refers to the social and economic well-being of individuals in a country at a particular point in time.

Stocks (or **inventories**) are the raw materials, components and finished goods (ready for sale) used in the production process.

Structural unemployment occurs when the demand for products produced in a particular industry continually falls, often due to foreign competition.

Subsidy is a form of government financial assistance to help cut production costs of domestic firms, enabling them to compete against foreign producers.

Substitutes are goods or services that can be used instead of each other, e.g. tea or coffee.

Supply refers to the quantity of goods and services that firms are **able** and **willing** to provide at various prices over a given period of time.

Supply of labour refers to everyone in an economy who is of working age and is both willing and able to work at different wage rates.

Supply-side policies are long-term measures to increase the productive capacity of the economy, leading to an outward shift of the production possibility curve.

Surplus is created when supply exceeds demand because the price is higher than the market equilibrium price.

Takeover occurs when a firm is taken over by another firm. A takeover may be hostile, or the two firms might have agreed to the takeover.

Tariff is a tax on imports, which increases production costs for foreign firms.

Tax is a government levy on income or expenditure.

Tax avoidance is the legal act of minimising payment of taxes, such as by avoiding spending on items with a large sales tax.

Tax evasion is the illegal act of not paying the correct amount of tax, perhaps due to a firm under-declaring its corporate profits.

Total cost is the sum of all fixed and variable costs of production.

Total revenue (or **sales revenue**) is the sum of money received from the sale of a good or service. It is calculated by the formula P × Q.

Trade restriction, or **protection**, refers to the use of trade barriers to restrict international trade, thereby limiting overseas competition.

Trade union is an organisation which aims to protect the interests of its worker members, i.e. the terms and conditions of employment, including their pay.

Unemployment occurs when people of working age are both willing and able to work but cannot find employment.

Unemployment rate is a measure of the percentage of a country's workforce that is out of employment.

Unitary elastic demand occurs when the percentage change in the quantity demanded is proportional to the change in the price, so there is no change in the sales revenue.

Variable costs are those that change as the level of output changes. The higher the level of production, the greater the total variable costs will be.

Vertical merger occurs when integration takes place between two firms from different economic sectors of industry.

Wage-price spiral occurs when trade unions and workers negotiate higher wages to keep income in line with inflation but this simply causes more inflation as firms raise prices to maintain their profit margins.

Wants are goods and services that are not necessary for survival but are demanded by economic agents to fulfil their desires.

Working population refers to the active labour force aged 15–65, i.e. those who are willing and able to work. This consists of those in paid employment, the self-employed and the unemployed.

Index

Note: **bold** page numbers indicate where definitions of key terms are to be found.

E